2/02

"I Remain Alive"

"I Remain Alive"

THE SIOUX LITERARY RENAISSANCE

Ruth J. Heflin

SYRACUSE UNIVERSITY PRESS

Copyright © 2000 by Syracuse University Press
Syracuse, New York 13244-5160
All Rights Reserved

First Edition 2000

00 01 02 03 04 05   6 5 4 3 2 1

Illustration 2 was reproduced from *Land of the Spotted Eagle,* by Luther Standing Bear, by permission of the University of Nebraska Press. Copyright 1933 by Luther Standing Bear. Renewal copyright 1960 by May Jones.

Library of Congress Cataloging-in-Publication Data
Heflin, Ruth J.
"I remain alive" : the Sioux literary renaissance / by Ruth J.
Heflin. — 1st ed.
p.   cm.
Includes bibliographical references.
ISBN 0-8156-2805-6 (cloth : alk. paper)
1. American literature—Indian authors—History and criticism.
2. Dakota literature—History and criticism.   3. Dakota Indians in
literature.   I. Title.
PS153.I52H44   1999
810.9'89752—dc21   99-20302

Manufactured in the United States of America

CONTENTS

ILLUSTRATIONS   *vii*

PREFACE   *ix*

1. INTRODUCTION
Redefining a Type Through Example   *1*

2. THE BRAVE THING TO DO
Charles Eastman's Warpath to the
Creation of a New Literary Form   *41*

3. "AS LONG AS YOU THINK I CAN'T,
I WILL SHOW THAT I CAN"
Luther Standing Bear's Quest for Honor   *79*

4. WEAVING A MAGIC DESIGN
Gertrude Bonnin Creates a New Literary
Tradition as Zitkala-Sa   *105*

5. LITERARY KINSHIPS
Ella Deloria as Interstitial Author   *139*

6. BLACK ELK PASSES ON THE POWER OF THE EARTH
Melding Religions, Purposes, and Literary Traditions
in *Black Elk Speaks*   *161*

APPENDIX A

Indian Publishing Chronology, 1890–1955   *195*

APPENDIX B

The Five Writers   *203*

WORKS CITED   *205*

INDEX   *215*

ILLUSTRATIONS

Charles Alexander Eastman (Ohiyesa)   40

Luther Standing Bear   78

Zitkala-Sa (Gertrude Bonnin)   104

Ella C. Deloria   138

Black Elk   160

Ruth J. Heflin earned her Ph.D. at Oklahoma State University in 1997. Her dissertation, "Examples for the World: Four Sioux Writers and the Sioux Literary Renaissance," laid the groundwork for this book, *"I Remain Alive": The Sioux Literary Renaissance.*

Currently, Dr. Heflin is an assistant professor at Kansas City Kansas Community College, where she teaches American Indian Literature and African American Literature. She is also in the process of developing an Asian American literature course and an intercultural studies program, which will recognize student efforts and interests in studying a variety of cultures.

PREFACE

When scholars discuss individuals who have crossed into or adopted aspects of other cultures in addition to their primary cultures, they often use words such as liminal (on the threshold), transitional (between stages of change), and nebulous (hazy, vague, indistinct, or confused) to describe the individual's experiences with both cultures. Such words convey and often emphasize the negative aspects of intercultural experiences, often implying that one culture will ultimately surmount the other. Yet, as with the five American Indian authors discussed herein, many intercultural people lead more *interstitial* lives, wherein their interculturalness allows them access to more than one culture upon which they can draw to lead highly successful professional and personal lives. Much can be learned about the intricacies of intercultural living by examining the positive and the negative aspects, both of being an interactive part of two or more cultures, as well as of being caught, with few available choices, between two or more cultures.

I like to envision interstitial cultural existence something like having an interstitial floor, which is becoming an architectural norm in the construction of many buildings, especially ones devoted to maintaining the ability to quickly and easily adapt to the needs of its tenants. Often half as high as a normal floor, an interstitial floor allows easier access to both the floor below and the floor above, providing room to move in, take out, or rearrange any materials, such as plumbing or even high-tech computer equipment, without having to work in the limited spaces normally provided in ceilings, walls, and floors. Like this "sandwich" floor, individuals living between cultures are not necessarily caught in a winless void, wherein they are denied positive interaction with either culture—neither being wholly Indian nor wholly non Indian. To push the metaphor further, just as the sandwich filling creates connections to both slices of bread, it also makes each slice of bread both distinct *and* part of a larger whole. Such intercultural people can then draw on, add to, or modify aspects of each culture to suit their individual needs, creating their individual flavor out of the substances of their lives.

Dr. Charles A. Eastman (*Ohiyesa*), Luther Standing Bear (*Ota K'te*), Gertrude Bonnin (*Zitkala-Sa*), Ella Cara Deloria (*Anpetu Waste*), and Nicholas Black Elk (*Hehaka Sapa*) all used aspects of Sioux literary traditions, in combination with their various understandings of Euro-American literary traditions, to create twenty book-length texts (see Appendix A). Except for *Black Elk Speaks*, their writings have largely been dismissed by scholars, with the writers labeled transitional, because, historically, American Indians were thought to be in transition from their traditional lifestyles to adopting more "progressive" Euro-American ways of living and believing. Scrutiny reveals much of the scholarship has focused on biographical concerns, rather than literary ones, even though literary scholars are beginning to note the intricacies of Indian writings in general. Examination of several of these writers' texts reveals the levels, degrees, and subtleties with which these five Sioux writers wrote. Comparisons, though unnecessary to some scholars and unwarranted to others, with modernists of the same period, also reveal many similarities.

This study explores the positive and negative aspects of scholarly intercultural approaches to these writings, posing reasons why they should be considered and analyzed with the same care any other modernist work receives. Special attention is paid to analyzing aspects of several of the works, employing, especially, knowledge of the Sioux literary tradition to illuminate interstitial choices made by each writer. Throughout, theories and questions are posed about each writer's contributions to what I call the Sioux Literary Renaissance—the outpouring of writings by Sioux writers from the time of the Wounded knee massacre to shortly after World War II.

•   •   •

This study was made possible by creative suggestions that started with Dr. L. G. Moses, who introduced me to Eastman and Standing Bear's works, which I combined with my interests—spurred by Bonnin's *American Indian Stories,* which my husband purchased for me, and by my long-standing respect for *Black Elk Speaks*—in the uses of folklore in literature.

Dr. Eric Anderson then helped me shape my ideas as the book progressed, proving to be a very valuable reader and commentator on the issues explored herein.

Dr. Clyde Holler guided me in expanding the work and encouraged me through the publication process.

Kirtland Card from the University of Nebraska Press provided me with information and sales figures on several of the books by these writers. Linda Van Hamme, Director of Research at Akta Lakota Museum at St. Joseph's Indian School, also willingly supplied me with some of the few available materials written by other modern Indians about these writers and their works. The Mid-American All-Indian Center in Wichita, Kansas, graciously allowed me the use of their library, for which I am grateful. I am also grateful to Alan L. Hoskins for my own photograph and to Jeff Cochran and Mike Kimbrough for reproducing the illustrations.

Thanks also to Dr. George Keiser and Dr. Linda Austin for reminding me that those who persevere succeed.

Of course, most important to my scholarly efforts have been my husband, Dr. James P. Cooper, and my son, Harley Cooper. They provide the healthy balance I need to stay sane and productive. Their love and support is the balm and the fire I need to persevere.

"I Remain Alive"

1

INTRODUCTION

Redefining a Type Through Example

According to Deborah Sue Welch, "the conscience pangs of White America peaked in 1881 with the publication of Helen Hunt Jackson's *A Century of Dishonor* denouncing U.S. Indian policy" (1985, 76). Yet, if the public felt guilty over government policy and the subsequent mistreatment of Indians on reservations, they had not overcome the stereotypical views of Indians as savages, worthless heathens, and seemed to devour every word about conflict between Indians and the government, with the press keeping a persistent eye on militant, and even not so militant, activities on the reservations. Indians were news makers. Not only did military leaders such as Custer write articles for eager newspapers and magazines, but newspaper correspondents also followed military troops whenever possible (Brady 1992, 346; Moses 1996, 19-20), and harassed Indian agents for news, inflating situations beyond their real scope to appease a bloodthirsty reading audience (McGillycuddy 1990, 202). By the time three thousand troops amassed on Pine Ridge Reservation in 1890 to quell the Ghost Dance craze, as newspapers had labeled it, the general non-Indian reading public was undoubtedly preparing itself for gory details (Mooney 1975, 850).

Why should we have expected anything else? Most Euro-Americans'

1. In reference to Americans who descend from any Western culture, primarily those known as European descendants, I will primarily use the term Euro-American. I choose to

had frequently treated Indians as less than human since contact. Perhaps subconsciously, though, Euro-Americans had always known otherwise, given the fact that they had tried to ease their consciences by making an attempt at being fair with treaties for land rights and by sending missionaries to help and enlighten. But the only Indians most Euro-Americans knew were fictional, like those in *The Last of the Mohicans,* or on display, such as at a Wild West show or in a live exhibit at a museum, wearing loincloths and war paints, as if that were always how all Indians dressed. Captivity narratives, which often provided gruesome details to justify non-Indian views of Indian "savagery," were also popular. All these stereotypical images worked their way into the fabric of everyday life for the general American public. As Western movies became popular, images of Indians became so stilted, besides being inaccurate, that almost all Indians were fashioned as Plains Indians.[2]

·   ·   ·

In contrast, most transitional-period Indians, especially the five Sioux[3] writers of this study—Charles Eastman (Ohiyesa), Luther Standing Bear

---

use the term primarily to highlight cultural influences. I will also use the word non-Indian to refer to anyone other than American Indians, where appropriate. Other terms commonly used, such as whites, Anglos, and Caucasians, will not be used here because of their inaccuracies, as well as because the terms white and Caucasian refer to race, not culture. Admittedly, just like the term American Indian, Euro-American glosses over the variety of cultures contained within its bounds. However, when I quote a source that has used one of the other terms, I will repeat that source's term instead of inserting my own to preserve the tone and context of the quotation.

2. Although movies have been examined for their racist depictions of Indians, cartoons have largely been overlooked. Even the Algonquian Indians in Disney's *Peter Pan* (1953) dress like Plains Indians and sing that interestingly racial song, "Why Is the Red Man Red?" Friz Freleng's cartoon short *Sweet Sioux* (1937) is racist to many, but does provide some interesting parodies of common Euro-American perceptions of Indians by inserting recognizable Euro-American symbols and characters into Indian life, such as when the war party circling settlers' wagons becomes a carousel. The question, of course, is, What is being parodied? Euro-American racist attitudes, Hollywood's stereotypical depictions of Indians, or Indians themselves?

3. The word Sioux has been translated variously as "a French corruption of the Algon-

(Ota K'te), Gertrude Bonnin (Zitkala-Sa), Ella Cara Deloria (Anpetu Waste), and Nicholas Black Elk (Hehaka Sapa)—saw themselves and the lives they led as examples of being American Indians in modern America, even though Deborah Welch asserts such a hope was an ideal only of the youthful and naïve. These writers were not just "visible example[s] of what . . . Indian[s] could accomplish if given the opportunity for advanced education" (D. Welch 1985, 14), but also were written and heard examples of Indians as real human beings who found value in their cultures. And I do mean *cultures*, plural, because there are subtle variances between their three Sioux cultures—Lakota, Dakota, and Nakota. I also want to call attention to the fact that three of these writers, Eastman, Bonnin, and Standing Bear, were also part Euro-American, which undoubtedly influenced them from early on in their lives. Even Black Elk, the full-blooded Sioux who remained with his band of Oglala Sioux most of his life,

---

quian *nadowesiib* 'little adders'" (M. Powers 1986, 23) and as "a French word [that] means 'cutthroat'" (Standing Bear 1988a, 2). As Raymond DeMallie points out, the designation for Sioux of all dialects and bands was the sign for cutthroat in common Plains Indian sign language (1984, 318 n. 20). All agree that the word was used as a derogatory reference by enemies of the Sioux to describe the nation, with the French, Europeans with the earliest contact with the tribe, accepting the term without question.

Edward Lazarus, Marla Powers, and William Powers are the only historians I have found who offer a Siouan word—Oceti Sakowin, meaning Seven Fireplaces, Seven Fire Circles, or Seven Council Fires (M. Powers 1986, 24; W. Powers 1977, 11), for the seven major tribes who spoke the three dialects—Nakota, Dakota, and Lakota, although all three scholars still refer most often to the nation as Sioux.

According to Lame Deer, an Oglala Lakota, the Sioux also have called themselves the Ikce Wicasa, or the Nature Humans (1991, 175). Joyzell Godfrey, a contemporary Yankton Sioux, says it is most simple to call the Sioux Nation the Oyate, meaning the People (1995, 18), although Kelly Morgan calls them the Oyate Tatanka, the Buffalo People (3). Although many Sioux prefer to call themselves Lakota (probably because their numbers are greater), not all the writers in this volume are Lakota. Charles Eastman is Santee Dakota. Gertrude Bonnin and Ella Deloria are Yanktan Nakota. Black Elk is Oglala Lakota, and Standing Bear is probably Brule Lakota. In fairness to the three non-Lakotas, I attempt here to introduce into more general use the terms Oyate and Oceti Sakowin, instead of relying heavily on the term Sioux. Where possible, I will refer to each writer's individual primary culture, such as Oglala Lakota or Santee Dakota.

adopted elements of Euro-American culture, especially Catholicism, into his life.

Perhaps it is coincidence that Sioux writers began publishing so much material about their culture soon after the Wounded Knee massacre. Although the Sioux were one of the last Indian nations to be fought in the Indian wars and to be forced into reservation life, they were one of the first, and perhaps most vocal, groups of Native American voices to address Indian issues to non-Indian audiences in print. Even though "civilized" tribes, such as the Cherokees, had their own publishing media, many of which were printed in both Native American languages and English, they were largely addressed to intratribal audiences. In contrast, Sioux writers such as Eastman, Bonnin, Standing Bear, and Black Elk primarily sought out larger, non-Indian audiences, particularly Euro-American children with whom they hoped to influence the future, for their stories.

Why did the Sioux possess some of the strongest as well as the most prolific literary voices of this era? Were they, the Oyate, writing out of political motives, attempting to influence current and future generations of both Indians and non-Indians by impressing them with the values of traditional Indian cultures? Did they write with the hope of preserving the Oceti Sakowin cultures as the anthropologists were doing? Did any of them act out of literary ambition? Or did their writings come out of a firm belief that their stories are important to the sum of human knowledge because personal narratives of various sorts were and are important to the shaping of Indian cultures? And why, given all the writing and publishing Indians did during the first half of the twentieth century, do most literary scholars assert that the Native American literary renaissance (Lincoln 1983, 8) did not begin until the late 1960s—less than five years before the second military confrontation with Indians at Wounded Knee?

The American Indian literary renaissance may have started with N. Scott Momaday's *House Made of Dawn* in 1968, but the Sioux Literary Renaissance began almost immediately after their subjection to permanent reservation living.[4]

---

4. See Kenneth Lincoln's *Native American Renaissance*. Of course, my literary distinction comes from an acceptance of nonfiction, especially nontraditional nonfiction, as literature.

How can I assert there was such a phenomenon as the Sioux Literary Renaissance? As Kenneth Lincoln defines it in his seminal book, *Native American Renaissance,* "without question a renaissance or 'rebirth' springs from roots deep in the compost of cultural history, a recurrent past" (1983, 41). Lincoln also points out that Indian literature has such a richly fertile (and recurrrent) past. Although most Indian literature before 1900 was orally based,[5] "once these oral works were translated into English and printed in books, America began to recognize, belatedly, the long presence of Native American literatures" (1983, 42-43).

Lincoln, however, focuses on *Black Elk Speaks* as the text most responsible for combining oral and written literary traditions. As Lincoln states it, "Black Elk dreamed and lived a tribal 'life-story' that Neihardt transcribed with poetic license and fixed in history. The oral 'sending' of words came through a new voice, a printed text" (82).

Yet Sioux writers had written extensively before *Black Elk Speaks* was ever published, bridging and combining the traditions long before Black Elk and Neihardt. Beginning with articles by Charles Eastman that were first published in 1893 through Black Elk's last cooperative work, *The Sacred Pipe,* in 1953, and into continuing publications by Ella Deloria, Sioux writers published extensively, producing twenty-seven books and three plays about their or other Indian cultures. Considering the fact that publishing by all Indian tribes, including the Sioux, about all manner of subjects produced about seventy-five books from 1890 to 1955, it is clear that the Sioux, or Oceti Sakowin, produced, as a tribe, the most written materials—including articles published in popular magazines such as *Atlantic Monthly* and *Harper's Monthly*—in particular producing the most information as a group about their nation's culture. In fact, more Oyate writers *initiated* the production of their books, as opposed to a Euro-American amanuensis prompting the text's creation, than did writers from any other Indian na-

5. Lincoln cites nonoral, as well as oral forms of Indian literature, mainly pictographs and "ritual codes embedded in artifacts" such as birchbark rolls, wampum belts, winter counts, totem poles, sandpaintings, and designs on pottery and woven goods (1983, 42-43). Hertha Wong cites these as belonging to both pre-Columbian picture writing and pictograph ledger and art books, which are two of three "distinct historical periods of Native American autobiography" and literature in the United States (1992b, 157-58).

tion. No other contemporaneous tribe was so represented in print. It is little wonder, with this proliferation of information, nearly a third of which was produced by the Sioux, that the image of Sioux life became, for modern America, the quintessential image of Native American life.

These writers and the images created by their stories—autobiographical, anthropological, and fictional—helped shape the future of America: its identity; its developing appreciation for nature and for alternative religions and medical practices; its awareness of history (both written and oral) as a moving force in the present; and its sense of being a polycultural country. Eastman, Standing Bear, Bonnin, Deloria, and Black Elk all shared a common purpose: to educate and preserve. These five writers are more than just transitional Sioux writers; they are transitional historians, guides, and Indian writers, with an even more important impact on the artistic milieu of their time and ours. As such transitional influences, as the primary writers of the Sioux Literary Renaissance, and as active participants in modernist literary development, they deserve to be studied in detail.

Why have these early Indian writers been ignored as literary modernists? How can I justify my claim that a Sioux *Literary* Renaissance occurred? Scholars must first appreciate Indian writings as literature and understand the cultural and personal forces that created these writers and helped forge their texts.

Although may critics, such as Louis Owens, see Euro-American and Indian cultures as having "completely alien set[s] of assumptions and values" (1992, 14), Eastman, Standing Bear, Bonnin, Deloria, and Black Elk find bridges of interstitial commonality that support their individual approaches to dealing with modern American life. This interstitiality, or "intersections," as Amritjit Singh, Joseph Skerrett, and Robert Hogan call them, allow us to recognize "the plural self, shaped by the ongoing dialogue between the ethnic individual and mainstream culture" (1996, 13). Yet, scholars such as Owens also blend all five hundred or so Indian cultures together, assuming that all Indians read texts the same way (1992, 14). Such a belief in pan-Indianism was a goal for Eastman and Bonnin, but, like Owens, they tended to see other Indians through a particular tribal point of view. Although Owens, who is of Choctaw-Cherokee-Irish descent, has three different cultural perspectives from which to draw his views, Eastman and Bonnin envisioned a common Indian culture through a decidedly Siouan lens (D. Welch 1985, 111).

Cultural influences are significant in all four writers' lives and their writings. Four of the five were born into traditional Sioux living. Bonnin was removed from its influences at eight, a few years earlier in age than both Eastman and Standing Bear, who were both teenagers when they left their tribal bands for boarding schools. Deloria was born into a family directed by her Episcopalian minister father, yet grew up surrounded by remnants of traditional Lakota culture—her grandmother refused to live in a cabin (Morgan 1974, 83). Black Elk left his tribe briefly as a young man, returning to stay a couple of years later after performing in America and Europe with a Wild West show. All five writers maintained aspects of their Sioux identities, and all five writers used traditional Sioux literary techniques, blended, of course, with Euro-American considerations of craft and tradition, in their writings.

Standing Bear, the one with the least Euro-American schooling (excluding Black Elk, who had the benefit of a Euro-American literarily trained amanuensis), is the most rudimentary writer of the five. Because of his lack of Western literary training, Standing Bear's writing shows Siouan influences more blatantly than those of the others. But even Black Elk's collaborator, John Neihardt, does not prevent such Sioux literary traditions and techniques as kill talks, multiple-voiced corroboration, or repetition from surfacing in *Black Elk Speaks,* even though he takes liberties with other parts of the text.

Eastman, Bonnin, and Deloria also successfully combined Euro-American and Sioux literary techniques, using one literary tradition to modify another, just as other literary modernists reached back into previous literary traditions, such as folktales and mythologies of other cultures, to amplify or alter reader expectations. The art of literature, like the art of dance, attempted to reach back to "primordial . . . rituals in an attempt to recover something they thought lost to the modern world" (Mester 1997, 3). As Kenneth Lincoln points out, two special "aboriginal" issues of *Poetry* magazine featured interpretations of American Indian works by such noted writers as Carl Sandburg, Lew Sarett, and Amy Lowell (1991, xvii). The transitional Sioux writers also anticipate more contemporary Indian writers, such as N. Scott Momaday and James Welch, by choosing to incorporate into their works, both in their autobiographies and in their recounting of tales, such elements of Indian oral traditions as breathing life and personality into inanimate objects and animals. Eastman, Bonnin, and Deloria wrote fiction, using Sioux literary touches such as invoking ceremonial elements and "piling meaning upon meaning, until accretion finally results in a story" (Allen 1992, 79).

Perhaps these Sioux writers have been overlooked as modernist scholars because their ties to traditions and the past were not as distant as most modernist writers' ties were, so that what high modernists had to reacquire, mythical ties to the past such as Eliot's legend of the Fisher King, the Sioux never lost. As Paula Gunn Allen points out, "American Indians are tribal people who define themselves and are defined by ritual understandings, that is, by spiritual or sacred ceremonial shapings," which in turn shapes their approaches to writing (1992, 79). To struggle with literary texts and ideals in forming new literary concepts was laudable to the modernists, so the relative ease with which many modern Indians, such as Eastman and Bonnin, slipped into combining cultural values into literary texts (even though they might have personally struggled with incorporating Euro-American values into their lives) could have been one prejudice against them.

Yet, as Monroe Spears points out, literary modernism required "the self-conscious awareness of a break with the past" (1970, 7). Such a break manifests two feelings—emancipation, or a sense of freedom, and disinheritance, "a loss of tradition, belief and meaning" (1970, 7). Does the fact that Indians were *forced* to remove themselves from their cultural traditions mean they struggled less with the assertion of new values in their lives?

Paul de Man insists that "modernity exists in the form of a desire to wipe out whatever came earlier, in the hope of reaching at last a point that could be called a true present, a point of origin that marks a new departure" (1983, 148). Yet, he warns, "as soon as modernism becomes conscious of its own strategies . . . it discovers itself to be a generative power that not only engenders history, but is part of a generative scheme that extends far back into the past" (1983, 150). Early Indian writers created and established forms that were a departure from traditional Indian literary concepts, es-

tablishing a point of origin that *does* extend "far back into the past." Most
obviously, then, Indian writers were ignored by Euro-American writers and
scholars because the Indian pasts, their literary traditions, were different,
perhaps alien. But, as Henry Louis Gates Jr. reminds us, "Europeans and
Americans neither invented literature and its theory nor have a monopoly
on its development" (1988, xiv). Yet, as Kevin Dettmar and Stephen Watts
argue, there was a deliberate turn away from the democratic ideals of
equality—of reaching the "little" man—in literature because "marketing
forces exerted so strong a force over artists in all media . . . during the first
four decades of this century," with the high modernists marketing their
effluent most devoutly (1996, 4-5).

In this self-marketing fervor, racial and gendered bigotry were significant. Europeans and Euro-Americans felt constricted, ironically, by attempting to constrict the movements of nonwhites. Some men, seemingly
bullied back by the "new woman," felt the need to reaffirm their mas-
culinity. Jayne Marek cautions us, however, not "to attach the metaphor of
'sex war' to the modernist sense of cultural turbulence" because it "skews
the reading of modernist works by presupposing a serious, even deadly,
contest between the sexes" (1995, 195).

Like other modern scholars, Spears believes the individual's development somehow repeats, in a fairly close parallel, the development of the
larger culture, moving, as it were, from primitive to sophisticate (1970, 10),
a belief based on social evolutionist theories. Modernist theories, much
like the Spencerian philosophies of cultural evolution so widely accepted
by the turn of the century, assumed a hierarchy of values, with the primitive being the lowest and the sophisticate being the highest. Indian writers
such as Eastman, Standing Bear, Bonnin, and Deloria were able to think of
themselves as the best the Sioux nation, indeed even all of American Indians, could offer to modern America. They seemed to enact the literary
modernist theory that one moves from primitivism to sophistication as one
breaks away from the confines of historical and cultural pasts.

In the process, as Kenneth Lincoln points out, Indians and non-Indians alike began a campaign to preserve what they saw as a vanishing
culture—traditional American Indian lifestyles, values, and literature. Lincoln argues that, in the midst of preserving Indian poetry, chants, songs,

and other works, traditional American Indian cultures influenced the flow-ering of literary modernism:

> Sorely, to be sure, the West needed a revised myth to supersede New World carte blanche. . . . So in a curious turnabout, the mythographers reached into the presence of the past and reinvented the Indian at the heart of this continent's humanity. The resurrected noble savage, re-duced by a factor of sixteen since 1492, would rise above the ruins of anarchic Manifest Destiny on literary wings. (1991, xvii)

Native American cultures, according to Lincoln, still widely influence the general American culture today, especially literarily (1991, xxv), just as Euro-American literary traditions have influenced most, if not all, of the individual tribal literary traditions.

Although Linda Wagner-Martin argues that most definitions of mod-ernism are too exclusionary (1990, 1), she believes that "perhaps more sig-nificantly than its themes, modernism's craft came to be its focal point. . . . Modern writing meant structural and linguistic experimentation" (1990, 3). All five Sioux writers experimented within their texts. Eastman's auto-biography, *Indian Boyhood,* is subtly nonlinear, not unlike Faulkner's blatantly nonlinear *Absalom, Absalom,* and several of Eastman's works ap-pear objectively anthropological, with authorial intrusion used as parody. Standing Bear combines points of view—"objective" anthropological with subjective autobiographical. Bonnin mixes autobiography, fiction, and leg-end into one text, not unlike Eliot's epic poem *The Waste Land.* Delo-ria filters other storytellers' tales through her Euro-American/Oyate-influenced creativity, like Mary Webb's *Precious Bane. Black Elk Speaks* uses many voices, not unlike Woolf's *Mrs. Dalloway,* and combines forms and mythical structures, not unlike Joyce's *Finnegans Wake.* Such blending, jux-taposing, and intersecting of textual forms and reader expectations are readers' clues to the combining of the two literary traditions—Sioux and Euro-American—these writers use to create literary montages, one textual characteristic highlighted during the literary modernist movement (Ellman and Feidelson 1965, viii).

Admittedly, not all the works by these Oyate writers merit the literary distinctions of Western sophistication that the other mentioned modernist works do, simply because their writers did not have, *or did not value,* those literary distinctions, or—more probably—because they knew that such "sophisticated" works had limited audiences who could appreciate them. Their primary goals for contributing to "the blind worship of . . . books, of the written word," a worship that has allowed "the written word [to become] established as a criterion of the superior man—a symbol of emotional fineness" (Standing Bear 1978, 249) were to correct misinformed ideas about Indians, to influence non-Indian sympathies so that they would "look upon the Indian world as a human world" (Standing Bear 1978, 251), and to be the "spark [that] lights a fagot of thought with which to bring back to life the fires of Indian faith" (Standing Bear 1978, 246).

Although they often just wrote about themselves as Indians, these five writers wrote twenty-two books among them, all of them, including Bonnin's coauthored report *Oklahoma's Poor Rich Indians: An Orgy of Graft and Exploitation of the Five Civilized Tribes—Legalized Robbery,* use combinations of traditional Sioux and Euro-American literary elements. No other transitional Indian nation produced writers who wrote so extensively for the general American reading audience, let alone wrote so many works that use both Native American and Western literary techniques. Was this not, then, a Sioux Literary Renaissance?

Together with their contemporaries, these five writers not only helped redefine what being Indian meant at the turn of the twentieth century, but also helped begin and strengthen the still evolving concept of what being an Indian writer means. Simultaneously, they preserved images of both traditional and modern Indianism for future generations and created new ones for themselves, for other Indians, for all non-Indians—for the world. They were, as Vizenor states, "the first generation to hear stories of the past, bear the horrors of the moment, and write to the future" (1994, 51)

Some Historical and Cultural Background

Kenneth Lincoln, Paula Gunn Allen, and other American Indian literary scholars, assert that, to best understand texts written by Indians, readers should learn as much about each Indian tribal culture writers draw on as possible (1983, 9; 1992, 75). To better illuminate the cultural contexts from which Eastman, Standing Bear, Bonnin, Deloria, and Black Elk emerged as writers, I will provide a brief Oyate history.

The Sioux—or the Seven Fire Circles, the Oceti Sakowin, or simply the People, the Oyate—did not always live on the plains. The Oyate, especially the Lakota and the Nakota, were forced to migrate onto the plains from the Great Lakes region in the 1700s when their enemies, the Crees and Chippewas, began obtaining guns from the British and French (M. Powers 1986, 25), when diseases carried by traders began ravaging their neighbors (Anderson 1984, 22), and when animal resources declined in the woodlands because of disease and overhunting by trappers (Anderson 1984, 27). The Oyate adapted well and quickly to plains life, perhaps more easily and quickly than non-Indian settlers—who tried to tame the land, not cooperate with it—did a century later. The Lakota and Nakota transformed from living as a semisedentary, horticultural people to a nomadic hunter-gatherer one, highly dependent on the horse, which thrived and multiplied on the plains for more than a century (M. Powers 1986, 25; W. Powers 1977, 18-19), while the Dakota remained near the Great Lakes region. Eventually, the Oceti Sakowin, as a whole, were subdued by an even larger group of enemies who wanted their lands—the "American" people. Ironically, settlers often included many international immigrants who became American simply through homesteading. Indians would not officially become Americans until 1924.

The fact that the Oyate thrived in a new environment[6] is a testament to their versatility and adaptability, hence their survivability. The Sioux, like most American Indians, seem to have always tried to cope with living as themselves among "others." It was natural, in vying for hunting grounds,

---

6. Most of the Indian nations migrated over the centuries a great deal. The Navajos and Apaches came from western Canada five hundred years before Columbus. The Cheyenne and Crow were pushed ahead of the Sioux in their movement toward the west. Most of the tribes have explanations, usually in myth or enacted in traditional ceremonies, for why they lived where they were last found. A few remember back to a time before they came to live in certain places. The Cheyenne and Oyate, for instance, still remember in some of their tales and rituals, when they were sedentary and grew corn (Cox and Jacobs 1991, 109-10, 131).

to attack and counterattack enemy camps and to raid for goods such as horses. To support their military endeavors, to strengthen their spirituality, and to ensure their safety (as well as to allow greater possibilities for inter-clan marriages), the Lakota and Nakota also held periodic celebrations, known as the annual Dakota rendezvous, where dispersed communities, including those of their allies, came together for several days of trading and ceremonies (Swagerty 1978, 361). The three largest dialectical segments of the Sioux Nation, the Lakota, Dakota, and Nakota, because of infre-quent contact with one another, developed several distinct ceremonies and social mores, while retaining a sense of belonging to the Nation of the Seven Fire Circles.

Historically, the Sioux have had a tremendous impact on the Ameri-can imagination. Early on, dime novels, and later movies and cartoons, as well as notorious Sioux victories over the United States military, helped make the image of the plains warrior the quintessential Indian image in America and abroad. Although other native tribes also experienced suc-cesses against many of their non-Indian enemies, the facts that the Sioux controlled a large territory in cooperation with their various allies, were the largest, last Indian nation to be conquered, and were the most com-mon Indian represented in Wild West shows (Moses 1996, xiii) helped emblazon images of their culture—the tepee, the eagle feather warbonnet, and Ghost Dance shirts, to name a few—into American mind-sets for what we think of when we hear the word "Indian."

Undoubtedly, images offered in books, even those by our five writers, also had a great influence. Three of Charles Eastman's early books, *Indian Boyhood* (originally published in 1902), *Red Hunters and the Animal People* (1904), and *Old Indian Days* (originally published in 1907) projected images of Indians that were so attractive that Euro-Americans sought to instill in their children similar values and knowledge of nature lore. Such images and values enticed Euro-Americans out-of-doors to enjoy the burgeoning national parks and summer camps "for relaxation and inspiration . . . turn[ing] to the Heritage of the American Indian to learn moral and prac-tical lessons" (Miller 1978, 66). Although Eastman's first three books pre-cede the establishment of the Boy Scouts in England in 1908, Eastman's book *Indian Scout Talks: A Guide for Boy Scouts and Camp Fire Girls* (originally

published in 1914; now titled *Indian Scout Craft and Lore,* 1974) speaks directly
to children interested in the Boy Scouts and Camp Fire Girls—groups Eastman helped found in the United States (Miller 1978, 66).

Creating a strong influential set of values for children to follow is so
important to the Oyate that Eastman, Standing Bear, and Bonnin make a
pointed effort to address Euro-American children in many of their writings. All five writers attempt to depict their own or fictional childhoods—
the only time Eastman, Standing Bear, Bonnin, and Black Elk lived in the
traditional Sioux manner—as a time for developing spiritually, intellec-
tually, skillfully, morally, and socially. Eastman, Bonnin, and Standing
Bear, through autobiography, fiction, and anthropological reporting, go
into the practical details of everyday Oyate life. In the process, they make
Indian ways of living attractive and noble.

Although the three men seem to be primarily concerned with passing
on their personal knowledge, Bonnin and Deloria wrote from different
purposes, purposes taken up by Eastman and Standing Bear in their later
writings, and from a different perspective. Although both women also
wanted to promote Euro-American understanding of Indian ways of living,
Bonnin especially desired to continue to be Indian in all aspects of her life,
especially her spirituality. Many of the women's writings were responses to
misconceived beliefs by non-Indians about Indians. Bonnin, known under
her self-created Lakota pen name of Zitkala-Sa, was one of the first, if not
the first Indian, to argue for being allowed to live as both Indian and
American. She was probably one of the first people to argue for an understanding and appreciation for "other" cultures, not unlike her contemporary John Collier and his cultural pluralism movement (D. Welch 1985,
194). All five writers addressed Indian concerns, including spirituality, but
Bonnin was the first to push directly for Indian rights—especially the right
to remain culturally Indian—with Standing Bear following suit some years
later in calling his people "back to the blanket."

Most of the autobiographical stories these writers relate occurred before 1900. Eastman, the oldest, recalls the Great Sioux Uprising in Minnesota in 1863, when he was five and when his father was arrested as one of
the many warriors responsible for the massacre. The men all recall the

Battle of Little Big Horn, which occurred the same year Bonnin was born on the Yankton Reservation—1876.

All three men and Deloria discuss the Ghost Dance religion, with decidedly different points of view about the "craze" and the subsequent Wounded Knee massacre in 1890, when Deloria was two years old. Eastman served as the official government physician for Pine Ridge Reservation and aided in treating the survivors and burying the dead. Standing Bear was a teacher on the neighboring Rosebud Reservation. As it did to Eastman, the incident shook Standing Bear's faith in the white man's ways and in his newly adopted Christian religious convictions, but, unlike Eastman, Standing Bear describes himself (and two of his Carlisle graduate friends) as ready to fight for his people[7] (1975, 225), while also attempting to talk the dancers out of Ghost Dancing (1975, 219-20). In contrast, Eastman had tried persuading the Pine Ridge Indian agent not to mass military forces against the Ghost Dancers, because he thought it was a passing fad—a last-ditch effort to return to traditional ways for a despondent people (1977, 97-98). Black Elk was a Ghost Dance participant and later one of its leaders, claiming to have envisioned the ghost shirts himself,[8] and believing the message of Ghost Dancing part of his great vision (Neihardt 1979, 237-47), and joining the massacre survivors who holed up in the O-ona-gazhee stronghold in the Badlands (Neihardt 1979, 267-69).

As is typical of memories, thus of autobiography, all three men remember a different individual as being responsible for persuading the postmassacre "hostiles" to turn themselves in: Eastman remembers a "black robe" (1977, 114); Standing Bear believes it was his father and nine other chiefs who were later given medals by the government (1975, 228-30); and Black Elk remembers a lone Indian, Afraid-of-His-Horses, persuading Red Cloud to surrender (Neihardt 1979, 269).

Black Elk and Deloria, the only two full-blooded Sioux of the five

---

7. It should be noted that the Lakota of South Dakota were not Eastman's "people," because he grew up Dakota in Minnesota.

8. Several people claimed to have been given visions directing them to make ghost shirts, a phenomenon that will be discussed further in the chapter on Black Elk.

writers, were the only two of the five who maintained close ties with their original bands of Oglala and Yankton Sioux, although the other three writers did return periodically to their ancestral bands. Perhaps in part because of their mixed blood, thus influenced by their Euro-American sides, Eastman, Bonnin, and Standing Bear sought educations away from their respective reservations, learning English fluently, as did Deloria. Even after relating information to two amanuenses, Neihardt and Brown, for the two books that bear his name, Black Elk clung to his native Lakota language throughout his life, even as he served in various positions for the Catholic Church. Deloria, though highly educated in Western-styled schools like Eastman and Bonnin, spent much of her life on the reservations, using her family ties to acquire materials for her anthropological and linguistic studies.

Neither Black Elk nor Deloria had anything to do with Capt. Richard H. Pratt's Carlisle Indian School. Standing Bear prides himself, in *My People the Sioux* (originally published in 1928), on being the first Sioux boy to enter the school grounds when the old military barracks that served as its campus were first opened for use as a school (1975, 133). Bonnin taught at Carlisle from 1898 to 1899, after becoming known as an outstanding orator, and directed the same school band Standing Bear had played in more than a decade earlier. Through traveling with the band, as well as through her own assertiveness in contacting literary societies (D. Welch 1985, 17), she sometimes met influential people who aided her publishing and speaking careers. Because of her strong stance in valuing Indian culture and choosing to remain a "pagan," Bonnin was the only one of our writers who knew him to fall out of favor with the very influential Captain Pratt. Eastman served as an outing agent[9] for the school in 1899-1900, nearly twenty years after Standing Bear attended. Eastman and Standing Bear's support of Pratt's endeavors at Carlisle is surprising, given Pratt's

---

9. An outing agent found farms or businesses that would "host" Indian students during the summer months by providing them with work, guidance, room, and board. But, as Susan Bernardin points out, the domestic training students received "was not intended to grant Indian students the privileges associated with middle-class culture, but rather was intended to relegate them to the status of domesticated 'slaves' of the nation" (1997, 219).

notorious motto "Kill the Indian, save the man" (Warrior 1995, 6), unless seen in the contexts of their lives and modern American culture.

The first half of the twentieth century was difficult for most Indians, for both those who willingly (if begrudgingly) acculturated and those who resisted the acculturation being forced on them. Most Americans, including Indians, looked nostalgically upon the "old" ways of Indian life, firmly entrenched in the belief that such ways of living were either already gone or soon would be. One pan-Indian group, the Society of American Indians, of which Eastman was a founding member and Bonnin a later member, sought to modernize Indians as quickly as possible (D. Welch 1985, 85).

For most Americans, even many of those who sympathized with Indian causes, Indians, like people and things from most ancient cultures at this time, were a curiosity, as was exemplified in Ishi, the last Yahi Yana Indian. In 1911, when starvation drove him out of hiding in the hills, he walked into Oroville, California, seeking help. His remarkable survival led him to become a living exhibit at the University of California's Museum of Anthropology in San Francisco until his death in 1916 (*Indians of California* 1994, 145-48). He was, sadly, not the first Indian used as live zoological attraction. Earlier, in 1897, Robert Perry enticed six Eskimos to New York City with him as polar "fauna" specimens. Five died from pneumonia within months, leaving seven-year-old Minik alone. He died of influenza in 1918 in New Hampshire, where he was working as a lumberjack (*People of the Ice and Snow* 1994, 143).

Wild West shows also exhibited Indians and fragments of their lifestyles well into the twentieth century. Although Sitting Bull was the most well known Sioux to perform with a Wild West show, both Black Elk and Standing Bear were also paid performers who traveled around the United States and Europe with the shows. As L. G. Moses points out, Indians

> gave the Wild West show its most distinctive features. Although Indians played supportive roles in the victory tableau of pioneer virtue triumphing over savagery, they themselves had nevertheless survived the contest. They may have been defeated; but they were never destroyed. Instead, they were portrayed as worthy adversaries, for how else could the showmen-entrepreneurs like Cody validate their prowess in battle? (1996, 8)

Yet these images of cunning and savage fighters fed into the stereotypes about Indians that already existed, which were easily found in newspaper, magazine, and dime novel accounts of "the Indian wars." Although "Indian actors, playing themselves, would provide an aura of immediacy otherwise missing from proscenium or printed page" (Moses 1996, 20), the general public continued to limit their beliefs about Indians to stereotypical images of "bucks" and "squaws." Indian reformers protested the images, lamenting the fact that appearances of Indians as sideshow entertainment overshadowed the "achievements of American Indian education" (Moses 1996, 145).

Like the reformers, such limiting, rather two-dimensional, images propagated by show Indians, however, are not the primary images that our Oyate writers wanted readers to remember about Indian cultures and their importance in their quickly changing world. Their complex intercultural texts contain stories about themselves and about their tribal and nontribal experiences, revealing five very complex, intercultural, interstitial human beings who try very hard, and not always very successfully, to do what is right for their families, their tribes, the Sioux nation, and even their country, but primarily themselves.

How does one stay true to oneself when straddling two (or more) different cultures? Although this is not an unusual question, one asked by many different ethnic groups trying to "fit in" to American life, it is an important one because most critics tend to focus on the tensions created within these writers as they deal with being both Indian and American. Most critics tend to overdramatize the conflicts these writers faced as something all Indians (or people of any "other" culture) face, instead of analyzing the individual writers' responses to these dilemmas to see them as people, not just types. It is difficult for late-twentieth-century scholars to understand Eastman's rather calm assessment of the Wounded Knee massacre in *From the Deep Woods to Civilization,* for instance. Not only was Eastman a physician, trained to assist the wounded, not to get involved in the conflict, but also he was a Santee Dakota Sioux, not an Oglala Lakota Sioux like most of the wounded and killed. He was not as emotionally tied to the wounded as Standing Bear was. He had also predicted conflict if soldiers tried to stop the Ghost Dance, so he was not surprised.

Although many critics of autobiographical writing, such as Michel Foucault and James Olney, argue over what the "self" is, what "truth" is, and how individuals create stories about themselves, few place such discussions in historical, cultural, or individual contexts, let alone within operative literary traditions. Like David Murray, Arnold Krupat, Gretchen Bataille, and Kathleen Sands, many scholars of American Indican literature fall into a pattern of pan-Indianism, viewing literature as though all Indians were receptive to all forms of Indian writing, while all non-Indian readers are a nuisance Indian writers must accommodate. Or scholars overemphasize the role of amanuenses (Brumble 1988, 16), neglecting to acknowledge that no text makes it into print without the aid and supervision of an editor unless it is "vanity publishing." Why have scholars, other than textual editors, not fretted over how much influence editors and "collectors," as H. David Brumble III calls people who compile texts, have had over Euro-American texts? Why is it such a remarkable thing that Indians and other ethnic groups have learned to write, and write well, in English and, often, in their native languages? Unfortunately, the egotism still exists that sophisticated use of language, especially in written form, requires some sort of superhuman ability—an ability privileged to Western-based writers, and nothing short of miraculous in non-Western-based writers.

Oversimplification plagues American Indian studies in that it does not allow scholars to connect the weblike structures and cultural supports of most texts. In studying the transitional Sioux writers, we would be neglecting a part of the influences on their texts if we did not examine the context from which they were created as thoroughly as possible. This contextualization means moving *beyond* merely examining the relationships and differences of the two cultures, Sioux and Euro-American, merely to note how one culture changes the "authenticity" of the other, *to* acknowledging that both cultures influenced all five writers—from within their own experiences, as well as from without through editors and collaborators. By examining how those two cultures work together to create the particular works, we can examine concepts such as the Sioux literary tradition, historical moments, the writers' personal struggles, and their contributions to the Sioux Literary Renaissance, if we can be so bold as to call it a rebirth.

Undoubtedly, these Oyate writers lived and wrote in a rapidly chang-

ing world. Changes would even touch Black Elk, who stopped living in a
tepee and started living in a cabin, on the Pine Ridge Reservation.
Neihardt's car transported Black Elk to Harney Peak in the Black Hills
from his home in Manderson, South Dakota, in a day, a trip that normally
would have taken several days by horseback.

The beginning of the twentieth century, for instance, saw a growing
concern for equality—for all people, regardless of gender, race, or ethnicity.
The push was strengthening (it had, after all, been going on for some
time) to eliminate, in America, the white male-dominated hierarchy. Even
though Jim Crow laws continued to reign in the South, all African Americans legally gained the full right to vote by 1929. Women, likewise, gained
suffrage in 1920; and Indians (those who had not yet gained citizenship
through homesteading or serving in the military during World War I)
gained their rights as citizens in 1924, although as Standing Bear emphatically points out, little changed for Indians (1978, 229 and 245). He and
Bonnin continued pushing for full rights and due compensation for Indians for years to follow.

Eastman and Bonnin, then, wrote first in times still largely dominated
by legal hierarchies and open prejudices. Little had really changed by the
time Deloria, Standing Bear, and Black Elk wrote, but American law at
least seemed to be bending in favor of the oppressed. The emphasis, in
literature, law, and society, was focused on the individual. Justifications,
even by Eastman, Standing Bear, and Bonnin, for the Dawes Act—the elimination of reservations for allotments of land to individual Indians—
abounded. Most thought it was as individuals that Indians could best assimilate into mainstream American culture. Indian rights supporters argued that for Indians to remain in "small, subject groups, isolated in
remote areas under the arbitrary rule of a bureaucracy, could only lead to
weakness and ultimate degredation" (E. Eastman 1978, 22). Many politi-
cians merely saw the opportunity to take yet more land from the Indians
because whatever land remained after each Indian received her or his allotment was given to the government.

By being forced repeatedly to give up large sections of land, the Great
Sioux Nation Reservation was reduced significantly. In this way, the Sioux
lost the Black Hills. The oldest mountain range on the continent, the Hills

had been "adopted" by 1776 from other tribes by the Sioux themselves (M. Powers 1986, 50). To the Lakota, the Black Hills were and are the center of the world, with their legends and myths about the tribe's creation adapting after their migration into the area to reflect their new homeland (just as all other peoples have done in this highly migratory world).

For the Sioux and most other Indian nations, the world's center shifted in the late nineteenth and early twentieth centuries decidedly in favor of the power of the United States government over that of the tribe. The government even went so far as to mandate Sioux religion—forbidding not only ceremonies such as the Ghost Dance, the Sun Dance, and Rabbit Dancing, but also rituals such as giveaways, and the centuries-old tradition performed for the especially beloved deceased as a means of devotion, Ghost Keeping. Thus, "transitional" change for the Sioux was rapid and forceful, cutting to the very core of their culture. Most people, including several prominent Indians, such as Eastman and Bonnin, thought such changes would only benefit Indians and make them more American.

But the country, and the developing world at large, was amid a tornado of change—technologically, socially, and personally. Automobiles and radios, altering personal standards and increasing the range and effectiveness of propaganda, connected the individual with the outside world at ever spreading distances. The automobile, hawked by automakers, tire manufacturers, and oil corporations as the modern vehicle for exploration, opened up land travel to the public and renewed the old promises of frontier excitement. As Phil Patton asserts, the "vision of the car offered a hopeful and reassuring response to Turner's notion that the frontier, the dominant force in American life, was now closed" (41). From the creation of national parks and parkways, Americans were enticed to "See America First," with the cars' names reflecting the renewed fervor of exploration— "De Soto, Cadillac, Hudson" (Patton 233). With this fervor, the desire to encroach still further on Indian lands increased.

Electricity illuminated most major cities making nightlife even more inviting. Sewer and running water connections appeared in most urban homes by 1900, improving hygiene and sanitation, thus the general public's health. By 1901, the life expectancy for white males in the United States lengthened to forty-eight years, for while females, fifty-one, as the U.S.

population passed 76 million. Better diets for most Americans in the preceding century pushed the age of menarche from seventeen to fourteen (Trager 642), increasing the potential for a population boom—a boom that does not come until post-World War II film propaganda begins convincing women to leave the workforce and return to focusing on motherhood. What slowed the population boom at the turn of the twentieth century was the increasing use of contraceptives as coalitions of women campaigned for the right to know about and to use birth control, allowing women to take more control over their lives. Another large factor in staying the population explosion was that women were needed to fill jobs men had vacated to fight in the Spanish-American and both world wars.

In contrast to the growing health and prosperity of the general American public, Indian populations continued to suffer from poverty and minimal health care. Counting only Indians in the lower forty-eight states, the 1899 Indian population "was estimated at 267,905. . . . Reported deaths during 1899 exceeded births by 1,016" (Berthrong 1988, 263). Life expectancy "of reservation-based men was just over forty-four years, with reservation-based women enjoying, on average, a life-expectancy of just under forty-seven years," even in the early 1990s (Krupat 1996, 30-31). Specifically, Sioux populations had declined "from 38,000 at white contact to 25,000 in 1805" (Anderson 1984, 22 and 27). While Krupat reminds us that not all Indians live in poverty (1996, 31), the contrast of the conditions of the general Indian population with the general non-Indian population is staggering.

The people of the first half of the twentieth century, ever in need of leaders, were looking for legends to admire. Elizabeth Bacon Custer tried, with abundant success, for the rest of her life to make "General" George Armstrong Custer, her husband, into a national hero/martyr. Yet, at the same time, people in major eastern cities flocked to see Sitting Bull, heralded as Custer's killer, in person, lining up for the opportunity to shake his hand (Standing Bear 1975, 185-87). Both Custer's and Sitting Bull's promoters gained attention and money on the coattails of their "heroes."[10]

10. In fact, Elizabeth Bacon Custer is not unlike Elaine Goodale Eastman, Charles Eastman's wife, who helps her husband promote himself almost as much as Elizabeth Custer

These larger-than-life heroes were part of the quest by modern Americans (and Europeans) for identifiable touchstones on which to stabilize their increasingly chaotic lives. The aftermath of the Spanish-American War; threat of World War I; the devastating and seemingly wholesale slaughter in trench warfare of Britain's most wealthy and promising youths—the original "Lost Generation" (French 1975, 2); the diminishing stature of Great Britain, whose colonial empire kept shrinking; the rapid economic growth of the United States, which seemed to be the promising offspring taking the place of parent England, despite two worldwide economic depressions in both the late nineteenth and the early twentieth centuries; the threat of yet another worldwide economic depression—all complicated personal and social lives, besides the seemingly rapid changes in living conditions brought on by technology. Most, if not all, of these changes would eventually touch even the Indians secluded on reservations—reservations that served as prisoner-of-war camps and, sometimes, despite government intrusions, as havens for cultural stabilization.

One sort of touchstone sought by the American public was historically based, an attempt to retain contact with the past, especially through the procuring of antiquities. "Tut mania," which quickly followed the 1923 discovery of Pharaoh Tutankhamen's elaborately gilded tomb in Egypt, swept Europe and America, with jewelry makers and clothing designers quickly incorporating, rather haphazardly, Egyptian symbols into their wares. Similarly, South and Central American pre-Columbian artifacts were sought, mainly by Europeans, but also by Americans, with mixed desires. Some collectors did appreciate the beauty of the pieces they paid for, but the antiquity, thus the monetary value, of the artifacts was often the primary motivation for purchase.

On a much less noticeable level, an "Indian mania" also existed, primarily in European countries, such as Germany and Spain. Many such artifacts—from Anasazi pottery to Ghost Shirts—ended up in European museums that could afford to pay more for them rather than in American

---

promotes hers. See also Julia B. McGillycuddy's biography of her husband, *Blood on the Moon: Valentine McGillycuddy and the Sioux*, in which she, too, attempts to create a legend out of her spouse.

museums, which were often restricted by congressional funding. Early on (in the 1870s), Smithsonian archaeologists such as William Henry Holmes "sought precious archaeological booty" as though sifting through ruins in the Southwest was a "treasure hunt." In Holmes's words, he and his fellow "'vandals'" invaded ancient Indian "'homes and sacked their cities'" (Hinsley 1981, 101-2). Later, after funding cutbacks, the Smithsonian restricted its excavations and, instead, paid numerous ethnologists to study and record Indian languages and customs before they could be lost forever (Hinsley 1981, 276), while the Field Museum in Chicago "set out in 1894 to obtain the best collections that money could buy" (Hinsley 1981, 270).

Even Indians collected Indian relics. According to Deborah Sue Welch, Marie L. B. Baldwin, "one of only two Indian women lawyers in the nation" in 1916 (1985, 121), "was a noted collector of Chippewa relics . . . not as pieces of an on-going Indian tradition, but as artifacts of a rapidly vanishing culture" (1985, 126). Eastman, too, helped museums, using his knowledge of "old-time Indian etiquette, as well as . . . all the wit and humor at [his] command" to obtain tribal histories, traditions, stories, and artifacts on commission (1977, 171-72). Unabashedly, he admits to obtaining, through the traditional Indian etiquette of gift exchanging, "some object of historic or ceremonial interest, which etiquette would not permit to be 'sold,' and which a white man would probably not have been allowed to see at all" (1977, 166-67). Similary, as anthropological interests took hold, Deloria began collecting stories from elders for Frank Boas and Ruth Benedict (Murray 1974, 13).

Such casual acquiring of ancient symbols was not restricted to the Egyptians or Indians. Many writers and scholars also became intensely interested in European roots. William Butler Yeats, for instance, had tried to educate Westerners about Celtic traditions and myths in much of his work, both dramatic and poetic. Critics such as Jesse L. Weston, who wrote the influential *From Ritual to Romance* (originally published in 1920), analyzed myths and legends in an effort to illuminate contemporary religious belief (or lack of it) and other social indicators, such as literature. Many writers, some of whom would come to be known as the "high modernists," took such interests in ancient myths and legends further, applying new psychoanalytical theories about the subconscious to Western interests in our predecessors' cultures, believing, for instance, that there is in us all a *spiritus mundi*," or a universal unconscious memory, as Carl Jung put it, that links us, regardless of individual race or ethnic background. But in some extreme cases, belief in such a unifying element will allow and even justify prejudices against, subjection of, and extermination of "others." Many modern thinkers clung to the belief that our past is always in our present, defining who we are and will be—something the Sioux also believed.

To make American Indians a part of the onflowing cultural nebula, some, such as the Mormons, theorized Indians were the lost Israelite tribe mentioned in the Bible. Most people still fervently believe Indians came from elsewhere, such as over an ice age land bridge from eastern Asia. Many modern Americans refused to believe that contemporary Indians were the progeny of "more sophisticated" pre-Columbian civilizations such as the Mound Builders or the Anasazi." Many non-Indians refused to believe Indians were people, pointing to "savages" such as Geronimo, Sitting Bull, and Crazy Horse—whose military exploits were made famous by sensation-seeking journalists—for justification.

And what was modern life like for the Sioux, the Oyate? The eastern Sioux, the Dakotas, were already on reservations while the western Teton Sioux, the Lakotas, still roamed the plains. Although the Dakotas tried to become more like Euro-American farmers," war for the Lakotas, until Custer found gold in the Black Hills, was primarily composed of short skir-

11. W. B. Yeats refers to the spiritus mundi, akin to Jung's idea of the collective unconscious, in his poem "Easter 1916."

12. According to David Reed Miller, in a speech Eastman made in January 1907, Eastman denied that Indians ever made arrowheads of flint and that "Mound Builders had ever existed, maintaining that mounds were really battlefields, formed by the accumulation of dirt and sand over time" (1978, 64). Miller attributes Eastman's assertions to his increasing anti-intellectualism.

13. The Dakotas were already a horticultural people, but social roles changed after reservation life began. In Euro-American farming, the men do most of the farming labor, while women tend the houses and small gardens.

This gender-based practice was a switch for the Dakotas, whose women were traditionally the horticulturalists—plants having been their agricultural mainstay—while the men hunted for the meat.

mishes with few casualties[14] performed to retaliate, to warn encroaching
enemies, or to steal horses. Social customs dictated silence and aversions
as forms of respect for elders and people of the opposite sex. Storytelling
and play, for children as well as adults, were the primary forms of education and entertainment. Feasting and giveaways marked significant occasions, such as births, naming ceremonies, first menses, first kill in the hunt
or battle, so that any kind of fortune was shared within the tribal band—
the *tiyospaye*. The annual Sun Dance marked the peak of the year for large
gatherings of bands, wherein participants sometimes gave flesh offerings to
Wakan Tanka, the Great Mystery, who was worshiped daily in such mundane acts as giving thanks for a successful kill by acknowledging the animal's spirit and everyone's ties to the web of life with offerings and songs.
By the time reservation living was quickly on its way to becoming the
enforced norm, the Sioux were looking for avenues, such as the Ghost
Dance, to halt the insurgence of Euro-American culture into their daily
lives.

As the increasing numbers of European immigrants and eastern Euro-
Americans pressed them closer together, creating more frequent contact,
many of the plagues that disseminated other tribes began devastating the
Oyate bands in great numbers, with the earliest recording of such disease
in 1818 on the Teton ideographic calendar (Lazarus 1991, 12). Even though
there were minor victories over the American military and settler encroachment, such as Red Cloud's successful, if only temporary, closing of
the Bozeman Trail, after the discovery of the Black Hill's gold the tide of
prosperity for the Sioux shifted. Although the Sioux were initially successful cattle ranchers, the General Allotment Act of 1887 (also known as the
Dawes Act), which ended up giving much of the best Sioux lands to Euro-
American homesteaders, threw the Lakota into a tailspin toward poverty
(D. Welch 1985, 82). In such an increasingly constricted, restricted, and
impoverished way of life, the Ghost Dance, with its promises of a return to

14. According to Lazarus, "the Sioux had always considered eight or ten casualties a
calamitous loss, and their entire history had never witnessed, or even contemplated, the loss
of a whole camp" (1991, 23).

traditional times and the elimination of all whites from their land, had its greatest appeal.

The subsequent massacre at Wounded Knee was the culmination of the violent confrontations between a still ethnocentric and paranoid Euro-American culture and a clearly overwhelmed and equally frightened Lakota culture. It was because, as Standing Bear says, "they did not try to understand us and did not consider the fact that though we were different from them, still we were living our destiny according to the plan of the Supreme Dictator of mankind. Being narrow in both mind and spirit, they could see no possible good in us" (1978, 227). Indeed, "who gave the white man the right to *guide* and *supervise* the Indian?" (1978, 246).

But even Indians often were susceptible to ideas of superiority. Black Elk gave up his healing practices because a priest's powers, thus his God, were apparently stronger than Black Elk's when the priest was able to oust him and his sacred tools from a healing ceremony (DeMallie 1984, 14). The founders of the Society of American Indians mostly, if not all, mixed bloods, believed "they were the best examples of the heights possible for Indian peoples" (D. Welch 1985, 86), so hoped to convince other Indians, according to their organizational goals, "'that any condition of living, habit of thought or racial characteristic that unfits the Indian for modern environment is detrimental and conducive only of individual and racial incompetence'" (D. Welch 1985, 85).

The increase in interracial marriages thinned the Sioux strength as well as its blood counts, and promoted factionalism within the tribe, although, as Marla Powers indicates, "the terms 'full blood' and 'mixed blood' are cultural rather than biological designations" usually, and "are based not on blood quantum but rather on the group a person identifies with socially and culturally" (1986, 144). Often, though, Sioux with some Euro-American blood were more attracted to American culture at large, and were more often accepting of the belief that traditional ways were of the past, not future, of the Sioux nation. Even full-blooded Lakota found themselves besieged by Christian ideals on their reservations. By removing children to off-reservation schools and away from their parents' influences, usually well-meaning Euro-Americans accomplished what a century of warefare had not—partial, if not complete, acculturation of Sioux children to Euro-American lifestyles and beliefs.

Into this rapidly changing world, our Oyate writers were born. Each handled being born into the influences of two distinct cultures in decidedly individual ways—reflected primarily through their writings.

Some Literary Concerns

Charles A. Eastman, Luther Standing Bear, Gertrude Bonnin, Ella Cara Deloria, and Nicholas Black Elk combined Sioux and Euro-American literary traditions out of necessity to reach the audiences they sought to affect. Each writer did so with varying degrees of success—success measured not only by literary standards, but also by social effectiveness and a lasting effect on both cultures. Ironically, *Black Elk Speaks,* a highly collaborative text between a Euro-American and a full-blooded Sioux, is most memorable, and, arguably, has maintained the longest and broadest impact on the American psyche. In fact, of all the books written by these writers, *Black Elk Speaks* has far outsold all the others, selling nearly 130,000 copies since its first publication, compared with Bonnin's *Old Indian Legends* at nearly 39,000, Standing Bear's *My People the Sioux* at nearly 32,000, and Eastman's *The Soul of the Indian* at nearly 28,000, according to information provided to me by the University of Nebraska Press in November 1996. *Black Elk Speaks* has decidedly colored our perspectives not only of Sioux Indians in particular, but also of American Indians in general. Yet, as we become increasingly aware of and appreciative of American Indian cultures and their writings, we search back further for earlier influences and try to come to terms with the perspectives about Indians, especially as writers, that many of us, including Indians, hold.

Must a person have inside knowledge pertaining to writers' backgrounds to study their written works with any sort of comprehension? A highly debated issue, this idea prevails throughout most American scholarly attempts at examining works written by "others," with the dominant "us" perspective still being that of Euro-Americans, because the vast majority of scholars, still, are Euro-American. Difference (with a capital D), as Arnold Krupat calls it, derives from a scholar's "commitment to a defini-

tion of [literature] deriving from his own culture, his own historical moment." He cautions, drawing on work by Fredric Jameson, that when we
choose to differentiate "the whole density of our own culture" from what
we designate as other or difference, we ironically eliminate our access to
an understanding of the Other and their possible relation to ourselves
(1983, 3).

For instance, it is a Western assumption that autobiography relates,
exclusively, the life of one individual. Most Western readers, according to
H. David Brumble, expect autobiographies "to explain just how it was that
[the writers] came to be as they are, just who they are, and how they stand
in relation to the forces that shaped them" (1988, 5). Through this expected
exposure, autobiographers should reveal their feelings, thoughts, and actions as completely and honestly as possible. Such baring of the soul is
thought to produce an accurate picture of the individual, something
readers can rely on to be true in the sense that it fits comfortably into their
realm of believability.

Most literary critics have come upon a dilemma in trying to fit the
above concept of autobiography to American Indian autobiographies. The
seeming interference of interpreters, stenographers, ghost writers, and editors forces the question of authenticity.[15] Are these Black Elk's words, for
instance, or John Neihardt's?[16] If they are Neihardt's words, does that
mean the ideas, the sentiments, the symbols and figurative language are
his, too? Because Black Elk adopted Neihardt as his nephew, does that
mean the book was written by two Sioux?

A much larger question, however, comes about because of perceived
cultural differences, often regarded by many scholars as viable barriers
between Euro-American and Native American worlds. Many believe these

15. See David Murray's "From Speech to Text," where he argues that "appeals to objectivity and authenticity, then, function as an expression of cultural bad conscience before the
inescapable authority of the white text" (1988, 30).

16. DeMallie argues quite effectively for the authenticity of *Black Elk Speaks* as
Neihardt's faithful translation of Black Elk's message, asserting that "Black Elk recognized in
Neihardt a kindred mystic, and he decided to transfer to him the sacred knowledge of the
other world that he had learned in the visions of his youth" (1991, xx). See further details on
this discussion in the chapter on Black Elk.

barriers must be overcome before an Indian can produce a written text, as though Indians could not understand the concept of writing or had never even used other nonoral forms of communication before Euro-Americans brought the concept of writing to them.[17] To even produce a written text means, for many scholars, that the Indian writer has already acquired some Western culture, because writing in script form—as opposed to pictograph—was not used by most Indians until whites came to America (Brumble 1988, 16-17; Murray 1991, 67). If these writers have been at least partly assimilated, are they producing "authentic" Indian texts or hybrid Western ones? And, if indeed they have become part of the dominant culture, how has this affected their perceptions of themselves and how will their subsequent writings affect Western readers' perceptions, since, presumably, an Indian must be at least bicultural (or have access to ways of crossing cultural barriers) to communicate with non-Indians?

By the early twentieth century, most readers saw many Native American autobiographers as success stories—individual Indians who overcame their so-called savage and primitive backgrounds to rise to a level, if not equal to, at least a little closer to their own, more highly evolved, Euro-American status. Evolutionary status, also known as social evolutionism, was popularized at the turn of the twentieth century by Herbert Spencer. It affected African Americans, who were moving en masse to urban areas from the beleaguered South in search of jobs and prosperity. Because so many people held the view that Euro-Americans, or so-called whites, were more evolved, thus more culturally superior to all other races, they encouraged "others" to want to attain this imaginary status. Many African American writers would go on to write stories about blacks attempting to "pass" as white, so that ideas of cultural supremacy aided racist views tremendously. And in America one is still supposed to be wholly Euro-American to be considered white; any fraction of other race in a person, especially that of an eighth or larger, usually makes that individual a member of the other race.

17. Arnold Krupat asserts that the "'graph' part" of autobiography stands, for him, for alphabetic writing, even though he admits "personal exploits might be presented pictographically" (1994, 3; emphasis mine).

Such racism had people of color turning on their own kind. So much so that many Indian writers, such as Charles Eastman—who looked very Indian, but was only partly so by blood—even considered themselves superior to other Indians in their ability to meet the challenges of Western culture. As H. David Brumble put it, Eastman "could compete because he was a member of perhaps the best family of the best tribe of the 'highest type of pagan and uncivilized man'" (1988, 158). In other words, Eastman seems to have seen himself, especially at the time he wrote *Indian Boyhood*, as the closest thing to a Euro-American his tribe had produced. In fact, the biographical note that introduces his book *The Indian To-Day: The Past and Future of the First American* states that at the time of publication Eastman "is generally recognized as the foremost man of his race to-day" (Eastman 1915, ix).

Other scholars focus the discussion on the differences between Indian ways of telling stories (often assumed to have had only *oral traditions*, despite pictographs ranging from sand and tepee paintings to elaborately carved rock art and totem poles)[18] and Western ways of telling stories, which presumes, with some exceptions, of course, that writing has risen above and beyond mere oral storytelling to attain that elite status of *literature*.[19] Traditional Euro-American views of autobiography, however, see the autobiographical act as an individual writing out his or her individual story. This philosophy stems from the Euro-American, or possibly just the Western, view that the individual is supreme, valuing independence above cooperation or other social values.

A few scholars, such as Paula Gunn Allen and Mary Stout, have come to realize that, contrary to what many assert, autobiography is as common in Indian narrative traditions as any other form of tale-telling. Brumble, in fact, breaks Indian narratives, including those that could be classified as

18. Col. Garrick Mallery, a Bureau of American Ethnology scientist, "collected vast amounts of data on sign language, pictographs, and other forms of early Indian writing that would otherwise have disappeared unrecorded" (Hinsley 1981, 169).

19. Even though English literary scholars still study Old English poetry and its oral tradition as a significant part of the English literary tradition, Native American literature rarely receives the same consideration. In fact, many literary scholars fail to acknowledge Native American influences on the American literary tradition.

autobiographical, into six types, asserting that each type is uniquely part of Indian culture. Brumble identifies these Indian narratives as:

1. the coup tales,

2. the less formal and usually more detailed tales of warfare and hunting,

3. the self-examination,

4. the self-vindications,

5. the educational narratives, and

6. the tales of the acquisition of powers (1981, 22-23).

Although Brumble acknowledges educational narratives as only those that give examples to listeners on how to behave or not behave, all six types could easily fit into this same category, because all six provide examples to the community about the consequences of both action and inaction by the speaker himself or herself, and vicariously by his or her listeners.

Hertha Dawn Wong broadens the range of narratives, particularly autobiographies, to include pictographs, which were commonly created and generally read by Plains Indians, who used them "to convey everyday messages—announcements, rosters, personal letters, business and trade transactions, and geographical directions and charts—as well as tribal histories (known as winter counts) and autobiographical narratives" (1992, 57). Her chapter discussing pictographs as narratives demonstrates one aspect of a pan-Indian literary tradition.

Similarly, Arnold Krupat claims there are two major Indian autobiographical forms, "the *coup* story on the Plains foremost; [and] accounts of dreams or mystic experiences" (1992, 216), although he argues that both forms, especially as oral tales, are essentially revelations of the synecdochic self, purposely revealing the teller's part in the whole community. Because Indian oral tales were told in public and often performed before or with members of the tribe, Krupat sees the tales as having a "collective effect" (1992, 216-17), so that the individual's experiences became part of the whole tribe's experience and lore.

Although Paula Gunn Allen stipulates that American Indian literature has only two categories, the ceremonial and the popular (1992, 72), she argues that

the purpose of traditional American Indian literature is never simply pure
self-expression . . . tribes do not celebrate the individual's ability to feel
emotion, for they assume that all people are able to do so . . . the tribes
seek—through song, ceremony, legend, sacred stories (myths), and tales—
to embody, articulate and share reality, to bring the isolated, private self
into harmony and balance with this reality, to verbalize the sense of the
majesty and reverent mystery of all things, and to actualize, in language,
those truths that give to humanity its greatest signifiance and dignity.
(1992, 55)

In fact, argues Allen, ceremonial literature redirects and reintegrates the
energy of private emotion into "a cosmic framework" (1992, 55).

By trying so hard to categorize Indian tales, their purpose, and their
manner of delivery, most scholars overlook an important correlation between autobiography, whether seen from a Western point of view or from
an Indian one, and between traditional Indian storytelling (which is not
unlike other traditions of storytelling in many other cultures).

Indians shared their stories with others, not just for entertainment, but
also for education and information. Most scholars and lay storytellers
agree that the primary purpose of an oral tradition is to pass on collective
knowledge. But most scholars fail to see this quality in autobiography,
instead choosing to focus on self-writing as the revelation of the individual, not the sharing of individual experiences with a larger community for
a possible greater good or deeper understanding of life in general, even
though most other literary forms have been traditionally discussed in the
terms of how the particular work illustrates universal, or at least common
among humanity, concepts.

Arguably, some autobiographers reveal their personal lives for exhibitionism, such as to flaunt who they know and to highlight aggrandized
feats. But such exhibitionism is as much of an attempt to produce verifica-
tion of the individual's self-worth (or lack of it) as is any Indian's coup
tale, war tale, or what Brumble calls self-examination or self-vindication
tales (1988, 42).

Many scholars point to the fact that Indian autobiographers, especially those in collaboration with a white amanuensis (or interrogator, depending on your view), often reveal information about subjects considered taboo by many Indians, such as talking about or speaking the names of the dead (Murray 1991, 70; Brumble 1988, 10). But one of the most titillating elements about Western autobiography has been the revelation of the unspeakable or unpardonable acts, the writings of which have always been seen as daring or, as in the case of Christian conversion stories and Indian self-examination tales, seen as proof of sin or wrongdoing to make redemption even more important in the author's life, or to make clear why particular tribal medicine failed to work to prevent tragedy (Brumble 1988, 42).

Some scholars point toward autobiographies which purport—usually unbelievably, once the text has been read—that the individual writing the story is unique, thus his story is worth hearing.[20] This Western ideal, aggrandizing the individual's importance, parallels the importance of the hero, like a messiah or a fairy godmother, whose very strength of individual character provides an example to the world, thus possibly saving it from its own weaknesses.

Yet, Krupat's native mystic experience tales also reveal strikingly individual experiences that verify for the teller his or her abilities to perform medicine. As Brumble puts it, the *telling* about [a] quest for powers is a culturally sanctioned means of setting forth [one's] credentials." Establishing that the individual conducting the ceremony is deserving of such recognition and responsibility is important to many traditional Indian cultures because the fate of the people involved relies on the individual's ability to perform the ritual correctly. For Brumble, shaman stories are the only Indian tales that closely resemble Western autobiographies (1988, 45), even though "such narratives were designed to call forth [feelings of awe and empathy] in those societies where courage, endurance, and self-sacrifice were essential attributes in warriors and leaders" (1988, 44).

So, though many scholars try to understand Indian autobiography by difference, they tend to overlook their similarities, sanctioning everything

---

20. See Jean-Jacques Rousseau's *The Confessions* (1770), considered the first nonreligious autobiography, in which he modestly states, "I am made unlike any one I have ever met."

that is part of the Indian experience, which they ironically assume is uniform, as totally alien to that of the Euro-American experience.[21] Some scholars waver back and forth in their convictions about the extent of difference (to the point of seeing Indians as alien) in Indian and non-Indian cultures. Arnold Krupat in "Identity and Difference in the Criticism of Native American Literature" (1983) argues vehemently against seeing the two cultures as radically different, yet argues in "Monologue and Dialogue in Native American Autobiography" that Indians must suppress their "native" community-oriented storytelling techniques to write a "text as given by the dominant Euramerican culture" (1989, 134). He goes further to assume in "Native American Autobiography and the Synecdochic Self" that oral storytelling "always assumes a present listener, as opposed to writing, where the audience is absent to the author, the author absent to the audience" (1992, 217)—ignoring that one writes for an imagined audience and that what many readers enjoy about reading works, from the popular story to the critical essay, is forming a mental picture of the author. Hence, he assumes the mere physical presence of an audience (as in traditional Indian storytelling) creates more community-oriented tales, whereas the absence of a physical audience in writing eliminates the idea of sharing with a community (thus the stories supposedly become more Westernly self-centered).

Although autobiographies are, perhaps, even more popular today than they were at the beginning of the century, some scholars, such as A. LaVonne Brown Ruoff, assert that the popularity of Indian personal narratives, and other writings, of this period "was the result of the great interest in the lives of the 'vanishing Americans'" (1990, 53). David Murray agrees, pointing out that "the marketability of Indians—their fascination—lay both in the sensationalism of accounts of inscrutable savagery *and* in the idea of nobility (albeit simple) doomed to destruction" (1988, 32). Brumble, tying the idea of the seemingly imminent disappearance of Indians to Spencerian ideas of social evolution's effects on Americans, asserts that most

---

21. There are exceptions, however. Albert E. Stone discusses how autobiographical collaboration, especially between two people of different cultures, can create "the most trustworthy—and often the most moving and culturally revealing—accounts" (1982, 154).

Americans felt "the tribes must vanish as social institutions, for it was the tribe that kept individual Indians from achieving all . . . [they could] as individuals, away from their tribes" (1988, 153). These kinds of negative attitudes toward their native lifestyles prompted Indian writers, such as Charles Eastman, Luther Standing Bear, Gertrude Bonnin, Ella Deloria, and Black Elk, to communicate the stories of their lives to the larger Euro-American public. How else could they hope to stop such racism or at least to create what many saw as a final monument to the culture from which they came and which seemed to be undoubtedly vanishing? Or, as Standing Bear pointed out, "America can be revived, rejuvenated, by recognizing a native school of tought. The Indian can save America" (1978, 255).

The Sioux as Examples to the World

In analyzing five writers' works from the same Indian nation, I will examine how racial elitism and white Americans' insistence that American Indians fully assimilate into Western ways of thinking and living affected the writers' perceptions of their lives, such as Zitkala-Sa's rebellion against acculturation, Deloria's dependence on sparse scholarly funding, Standing Bear and Eastman's initial acceptance and later rejection of acculturation, and Black Elk's sense of guilt for not having shared his vision with Euro-Americans earlier. I will also examine how cultural pressures from both sides ultimately affected the writers and their choices of textual forms and contents, going beyond the typical studies of Indian literature of the transitional period, which tend to focus solely on autobiography, to examine literary qualities, both Sioux and Euro-American, of the autobiographical, anthropological, and fictional works. All five transitional Indians lived at a time when more Euro-Americans began to see Indians as human beings, potential citizens, as Elaine Goodale Eastman and others like her saw them, and more Indians began seeing value in adopting aspects of Euro-American culture. One of the obvious values these five Sioux adopted was a belief in the potential power of the written word.

The chapter on Charles Alexander Eastman examines his influences on other Indian writers and his choices in combining Sioux and Euro-American literary traditions in his books. If there is a theme to Eastman's life, it is that his approach to living is modeled on being the Dakota brave he trained to be, with his warpath, on which his father sent him, being one of accommodation and survival in another culture. Instead of being submissive in his acceptance of Euro-American culture, he adopts useful aspects of it with a vengeance, embracing his "Christ ideal" as an operant form of Christianity that is complementary to his Dakota ideals. By combining comparative elements, such as Christian imagery and legendary Sioux figures, Eastman becomes one of the first Indian writers to successfully create a literary modernist text. Several of his stories are examined in the light of modernist contexts, revealing his sophisticated use of collage and parody.

The chapter on Luther Standing Bear discusses his need to establish his authority as a Lakota chief and as a Lakota authority. Because his writings are less sophisticated in their literary qualities, they reflect more clearly operant Sioux literary traditions, although they still combine Sioux and Euro-American literary elements. Like Eastman, Standing Bear feels compelled to live up to his Sioux role, in his case, that of chief. Through indirection and asserted credibility, two Sioux literary devices, Standing Bear uses his four books to live out his chiefly role in his attempts to lead the Lakota and non-Indians to an understanding of the value of traditional Lakota culture and to preserve that culture for future generations.

The chapter on Gertrude Bonnin as writer Zitkala-Sa examines her writings in a modernist context, as well. Parallel to Eastman's quest to live modern life as a Sioux warrior should, Bonnin fulfills her feminine Dakota role by seeking to pass on her Dakota heritage. Despite the brevity of her writing career, Bonnin exhibits sophisticated use of Sioux symbolism and mythology, combined with Western mythology, to create passionate stories reflecting her political and social concerns for Indians.

As an anthropologist and a writer, Ella Deloria's works are valuable resources for discovering common literary elements stemming from the Oyate literary tradition. This chapter discusses the problem of a lack of value by scholars for works reflecting oral literary traditions from ethnic writers, and compares Oyate literary elements from several of the traditional tales in *Dakota Texts* with similar elements that appear in *Waterlily*, an eloquent interstitial modernist novel.

Because *Black Elk Speaks* is one of the most popular and most discussed books written by a transitional Sioux, the chapter on Nicholas Black Elk focuses mainly on the controversies surrounding the text, while attempting to validate the book as a *literary* text that Black Elk chose to compose. In choosing John G. Neihardt as his collaborator, Black Elk made a conscious decision to allow Euro-American literary traditions to be reflected in the text. Yet, the Sioux literary traditions, which Black Elk exercised in reciting his story to Neihardt, are so strong that not even Neihardt's intense Euro-American literary training can greatly alter them. In creating the text with both Sioux and Euro-American literary techniques, Black Elk accentuates the collage effect begun by Eastman, creating a vivid, and highly important, modernist literary text. In the process, Black Elk's work demonstrates that a writer does not have to speak English to have an impact on American literature.

Perhaps other scholars doubt that a Sioux Literary Renaissance happened at all. Instead of using the concepts of having to move from a time of "dark ages" wherein little or nothing creatively hopeful happens into a period of "renaissance" wherein a seemingly sudden intellectual spark ignites a wave of creativity as the definition for renaissance, I adhere to the word's literal translation as a rebirth. The Sioux, or Oyate, Literary Renaissance is a rebirth in two senses. First, most moderns believed traditional Sioux life was dying, would vanish from the earth forever, so that many of the transitional Sioux writers began writing to preserve that life, in essence, giving it a new form of life. Second, the new birth comes from the hybridization of two literary traditions. The coupling of Sioux and Euro-American literary traditions created a new literary tradition that eventually gave birth to Kenneth Lincoln's now famous treatise, *Native American Renaisance*. I do not believe there was ever a dearth of literary events, whether storytelling, singing, or chanting, within the Sioux nation, although there were few *recorded* events in traditional life before 1890, except in memories, which both Eastman and Standing Bear refer to as the Sioux form of libraries.

As Sioux, the native culture often seen as the last stronghold against Euro-American insurgence, they were profoundly affected physically by shrinking hunting grounds and buffalo numbers, by subsequent laws prohibiting intertribal skirmishes, by being forced to rely on often irregular government subsistence. Affected spiritually by confinement to reservations, the devastating massacre at Wounded Knee, and the suppression of various Indian religious ceremonies—around which their culture focused— and even socially and economically by the enactment of the Dawes Act, they fell to increasing pressures for Indians to be educated in Euro-American ways, and to experiments in changing Indian names to ones more palatable to the Euro-American legal system. All these changes created factionalism among the various members of the Sioux nation, especially between what has since been called the progressives, who see assimilation or adaptation as the way to survive, and the traditionals, who want to maintain traditional cultural values and lifestyles. I will also examine how each writer faced and dealt with her or his experiences in this profoundly important transitional period, wherein they came to see themselves not only as individuals, but also as modern American Indian citizens and modern American Indian writers.

Indians' perceptions of themselves underwent forceful pressure from the dominating Euro-American culture. The writings—including retold legends, fiction, and autobiographical works—by these five Sioux not only anticipated contemporary audience views, inadvertently helping project impressions of Indians still prominently accepted today, but also successfully used both Sioux and Euro-American literary traditions in ways not unlike the currently recognized literary modernists. In fact, I will argue, it is important to recognize and value the work these writers, and other of their Sioux contemporaries, accomplished, noting the probability of a phenomenon we can call the Sioux Literary Renaissance.

This study is just the beginning.

Charles Alexander Eastman (Ohiyesa)
From Eastman's *From the Deep Woods to Civilization*,
University of Nebraska Press, 1977

2

THE BRAVE THING TO DO

Charles Eastman's Warpath to
the Creation of a New Literary Form

For decades now, scholars have seen Charles Alexander Eastman as one of the foremost examples of Native American writers in this century. Like society, literary studies assign hierarchies. Interestingly, many scholars ignore or are ignorant of particular facts. Many in their attempts to justify their views overlook his complex heritage, and the contributions both preceding and contemporary Indian and non-Indian writers made to his work. Eastman's autobiography, *Indian Boyhood,* is often held up as *the* influential autobiography that set other Indian writers to work putting down their life stories. A. LaVonne Brown Ruoff asserts, for instance, that "Eastman's autobiographies inspired other Sioux writers, such as Luther Standing Bear and Zitkala-Sa, to write their personal narratives" (1990, 57). Although Ruoff could be correct in specifying that Eastman influenced later Sioux writers,[1] she overlooks other pre-Eastman Indian personal narratives, many of which are not unlike Eastman's autobiographies. For instance, a quick scan of the publishing chronology I provide in Appendix A

---

1. It is debatable that Eastman influenced Gertrude Bonnin (Zitkala-Sa), eighteen years his junior, because she was already a noted orator and writer when Eastman began writing. Although both began publishing their essays at roughly the same time (see the dateline in Appendix A), it is possible Bonnin read Eastman's essays in *St. Nicholas* and *Popular Science Monthly* before penning hers.

reveals that Eastman borrowed an already familiar title from Chief Tahan Joseph Griffin, whose book *Tahan: Out of Savagery into Civilization* was published the year before Eastman's *From the Deep Woods to Civilization*. Similarly, Arnold Krupat, arguably one of the more thorough and more vehemently outspoken American Indian autobiography scholars, points out that "the earliest Native American autobiography . . . is . . . by the Reverend Samson Occom, a Mohegan , who produced a short narrative of his life in 1768," although it was not published until 1982.[2] However, "the first extended autobiography by an Indian to attract a relatively wide readership" was by a Pequot, a Methodist minister, Rev. William Apess, in 1829. The book examines "the christianized Indian's relation to Euramerican religion that thematically dominates the early period of autobiographies by Indians" (Krupat 1994, 5).

In essence, Tahan and Apess—and their literary progeny[3]—set the standard for Eastman to follow. Perhaps, though, Spencer's social evolutionism, which was a well known and strongly believed notion at the beginning of Eastman's popularity,[4] simply would not allow Eastman to be known as anything less than the best of his kind, who were, in his words, "the highest type of pagan and uncivilized man" (1902, preface). He has become, then, to many scholars, the quintessential turn-of-the-century Indian, conveying for scholars and general readers alike a particularly safe and identifiable version of the assimilated Indian.

Eastman is certainly one of the most important Sioux writers of the transitional era, and is arguably the writer who was at the beginning of the tremendous surge of publishing that marks the Sioux Literary Renaissance. Setting out as a writer to imprint a legacy for his children by conveying his life story to them, Eastman ends up being one of the most modernist

2. Eastman mentions "that great Indian, Samson Occum" (1902, 65). Krupat also points out that "the first-person life history [was] only recently, in 1808, named autobiography by the British poet Robert Southey" (1994, 5).

3. See H. David Brumble III's *Annotated Bibliography of American Indian and Eskimo Autobiographies* for a fairly complete listing of Indian autobiographies ever published in the United States, up to the bibliography's publication date, 1981.

4. See Curtis Hinsley (1981) on how social evolutionism not only affected anthropological and ethnographical studies at the Smithsonian, but also affected Americans in general.

Indian writers. He is forced, through the educational systems he encounters, to move away from his traditional Dakota past, altering or abandoning many of its beliefs and customs to fit his new life, and spends the remainder of his life trying to maintain a balance between that past and his modern life based primarily on Euro-American values and customs.

This balance appears in his writing cloaked in both traditional Sioux symbols, legends, and traditional Dakota literary techniques, as well as Euro-American literary conventions and Christian beliefs. To create such a balance, he must experiment with the traditional autobiographical forms (both Dakota and Euro-American), parody anthropological forms, and introduce Sioux literary traditions to his mainly Euro-American audience, proving once and for all that Euro-Americans are not the only people who can eloquently use narration and writing, showing, in effect, there is no such thing as "white writing" (Murray 1991, 80). To be one of the first Indians to accomplish these literary goals required uncommon circumstances for the turn of the century.

To many people, to do something one fears most is a sign of bravery. Leaving the comfort of family and tribe as they went off to boarding school became a test of bravery for many American Indian children of the nineteenth and early twentieth centuries. Ohiyesa, young Charles Eastman, felt that leaving his family and tribe was a test of his courage. His faith in his father, in other people, and in his spirituality were all tested when he allowed, first, his father, then the people he studied under at various schools to change his appearance, his lifestyle, his language, and his religion. When he set off for boarding school, he did so as a Dakota brave, prepared to face death on this warpath, if he had to (1977, 32).

Eastman left the Santee Dakota people, whom he had known since his birth in 1858, several years before the Ghost Dance religion (1888–91) swept through numerous western and northern Plains tribes. In fact, he left for boarding school when "Sitting Bull and Crazy Horse were still at large, harassing soldiers and emigrants alike, and General Custer had just been placed in military command of the Dakota Territory" (1977, 30). His father, originally Many Lightnings, who became Jacob Eastman after converting to Christianity, taking his dead wife's surname as his own (Wilson 1983, 16), first persuaded Ohiyesa to try acculturation by speaking to him in terms a young warrior would understand and embrace: only the brave would succeed in the white man's world; those who did not try would be as doomed as the traditional Indians' ways of living surely were (Wilson 1983, 20–22).

Something not frequently examined is Eastman's father's conversion and subsequent steps toward acculturation, without which Eastman himself might never have changed. It is probable that Many Lightnings, during his isolation from his family and tribe as he served a prison sentence for his participation in the Minnesota Uprising of 1862, was more easily converted to Christianity because of the separation from his cultural support group. Such cultural separation and isolation would be practiced by Indian educators for decades, who often forcibly removed children from their families and tribes to more readily have them accept Euro-American standards of living. Eastman notes that "it was because of [Jacob's] meditations during those four years in a military prison that he had severed himself from his tribe and taken up a homestead . . . [declaring] he would never join in another Indian outbreak, but would work with his hands for the rest of his life" (1977, 15).

Although such a separation did not affect every Indian ever imprisoned, it probably affected many. His own separation from his tribe, coupled with the Sioux belief in stoic bravery while facing an enemy and their deep respect for the wisdom of elders—especially parents—probably quickened Charles's own acculturation. Eastman would have also seen this type of separation when he encouraged Indians to educate their children at boarding schools and when he embraced the principles behind the Dawes Act, which hoped to encourage individualism—that ever pervasive and often socially destructive American ideal—by forcing nuclear families, a clearly Euro-American concept of the family unit, to separate from the nearby support of their kin, thus severing tribalism. Eastman, by this time immersed in what he saw as American ideals, failed to see an age-old war tactic—divide and conquer.

Early on, Ohiyesa had been encouraged to think of himself as a member of the best family of the best tribe of the best Indians. Even before Spencerian social applications of evolution became familiar to Indians, such a belief was not extraordinary for many Sioux. The stories by Eastman, Gertrude Bonnin, Luther Standing Bear, and Nicholas Black Elk, as well as those by Ella Deloria and Marie McLaughlin, corroborate the fact that, to the Oyate, being the best possible person at a given task was all the honor one should seek. For instance, an Oyate warrior with an excellent fighting reputation honored the enemies who confronted him, as well as honored the people he protected. Eastman, naturally then, set his goals on becoming the best Dakota brave he could by becoming the best acculturated and assimilated Indian within the dominating Euro-American culture—the brave path, as he saw it, he chose to travel.

Although rarely ever critical of the process of his Euro-American education or of the method by which he adopted aspects of Euro-American lifestyle, Eastman himself admitted that "perhaps my earlier training had been too Puritanical" (1977, 73), referring to the fact that his conversion to Christianity was by accepting a very conservative form of Protestantism, which affected his perspective ever after (Stensland 1977, 199). Born three-quarters Sioux, one-quarter Euro-American,[5] Eastman's first fifteen years, as chronicled in his first book-length autobiography, *Indian Boyhood*, were spent under the tutelage of his paternal grandmother, Uncheedah, "the woman who taught [him] to pray" (1977, 32). Uncheedah fully intended to raise little Hakadah—Eastman's birth name—as a Sioux warrior fit to revenge what everyone in the tribe thought was his father's death for his participation in the Sioux Uprising of 1862 (1902, 18; Wilson 1983, 15).

Miraculously, his father returned, as from the dead, desiring to have his son accept the Euro-American way of life, especially in converting to Christianity and in seeking education in white schools. Because of his father's surprising "resurrection," Eastman was probably awed by the power of the Christian god, now worshiped by his father, which seemingly

---

5. Eastman's father, Many Lightnings (Ite Wakanhdi Ota), fooled Mary Nancy Eastman (Wakantankanwin, or Goddess) into eloping with him. Mary Nancy died from complications, shortly after giving birth to Eastman (b. Hakadah, or the Pitiful Last) in February 1858. Mary Nancy was the daughter of Capt. Seth Eastman, a topographical engineer at Fort Snelling, and Stands Sacred (Wakan inajin win), daughter of Chief Cloud Man (Mahpiya Wichasta, who established Eatonville, Minnesota, and was one of the earliest supporters of assimilation, believing in the superiority of Euro-American civilization until he died) (Wilson 1983, 11-13).

possessed the *wakan* power of returning the dead to life. As David Murray points out, Eastman uses his father "to represent a rupture rather than a continuity but a rupture which is the creation of his new self, a scene repeated as the end of one book and the beginning of the next" (1991, 80). Just as Christ is the separation figure between the Old and New Testaments, between the unfortunate sinfulness of humanity and salvation, Many Lightnings ruptures the pattern of Eastman's life, sending him down a new path. Resurrected with his father are Eastman's Dakota sense of kinship and progenical obligation, yet instead of slaying his father's murderers, he will be learning the ways of his father's "saviors."

Significantly, however, Eastman knew himself as a child without biological parents—a "motherless child," as he called himself—for more than ten years of his formative life. Although his uncle and grandmother were his closest "parental" roles in the traditional Dakota ways of child rearing, the idea of being an orphan would have probably been completely foreign to him, although the idea that he was motherless was impressed on him at a very young age since his birth name, Hakadah, means "pitiful last." Yet, later, as an acculturated and Christianized Sioux he would have come to know the Euro-American concepts of family, including what it means to be "orphaned." His early experiences, he would have come to learn, were as an orphan whose savior father returned and sent him down a new path, commissioning him to be a kind of savior for his people, a theme reflected repeatedly in his writings. As Anna Lee Stensland points out, "the poor, unpromising orphan boy who becomes the savior of his tribe or the recipient of the stories of the tribe is a common characteristic in the Indian myths of many tribes" (1977, 203). At least two Oceti Sakowin mythical characters are such orphans—Little Boy Man and Stone Boy, both of whom withstand natural and supernatural elements to save people they love (Stensland 1977, 203). Together, Eastman's two most autobiographical works, *Indian Boyhood* and *From the Deep Woods to Civilization,* reflect the essences of these mythical boys and their sacred quests in Eastman's patterning of his life story.

Eastman's father was influential in Ohiyesa's life, not only as the sagacious, almost wakan, elder, but also in his appreciation for things Euro-American. Jacob seems to have instilled in Eastman respect for the awe-inspiring ability of "the white man . . . to preserve on paper the things he does not want to forget" (1977, 28). This idea of preservation returned to Ohiyesa when he began to pen his recollections of his childhood for his children. He realized as an adult what the fifteen-year-old, who had asked, "'Why do we need a sign language, when we can both hear and talk?'" (1977, 17), could not foresee—to *preserve* a culture, one must preserve its defining parts, such as its traditions, its beliefs, and its lore. Eastman set out to save his people, his primary culture, at least on paper. He felt that "if his White readers could only understand the beauty and truth of the Indian way of life and learn to emulate the quality of truth found in it, a higher, more sensitive morality would eventually prevail in the larger American society" (Miller 1978, 64).

Perhaps this same sense of the need to preserve the valuable aspects of traditional Indian life and to educate Euro-Americans about that value is what also motivated him to accept a commission later in 1910 "to search out and purchase rare curios and ethnological specimens for one of the most important collections in the country" (1977, 166), one job to which not even his biographer, Raymond Wilson, refers. According to David Reed Miller, Eastman was paid by "the University of Pennsylvania Museum to conduct several months of fieldwork collecting folklore texts and museum artifacts" (1978, 63). Not the first time he would be shortsighted—a human failing, after all—in what was best for Native Americans, Eastman details out how he procured many sacred items from various tribes by means of "indirection" (1977, 166). Using his knowledge of other native cultures, which he picked up as a child, to his advantage, he was even able to obtain an Ojibway Sugar Point band sacred war club—a club so important to the Sugar Point band that they attributed to it all their success in war and to their safety from the encroachment of white civilization (1977, 171). It is possible that, as David Murray points out, "Eastman seems here to play the exploitative white with no awareness of the irony of his position" (1991, 78). Perhaps, as the antiwhite youth he had once been, he would have noted the significance of removing sacred artifacts from their owners, but as his mostly Puritanized adult self he only lauds his own cunning, a kind of cunning he might have used on enemies on the warpath.

For some, this casual acquisition might be an indication of the degree to which Eastman acculturated and assimilated Euro-American culture and values. But, because the Ojibway were traditional enemies of the Santee Sioux, because Eastman's religious views had shifted to embrace the "Christ ideal," and because Eastman believed there was no stopping the invasion of white people and values into Indian life, he probably had no second thoughts about acquiring artifacts—even sacred ones—for private museum ownership. The artifacts and legends he collected were for a higher purpose—preservation; they are relics, tokens of the free past that was, and, just possibly, spoils of war for a worthy warrior.

Before Jacob sent young Charles on his journey to the Santee Training School in Nebraska, he told Charles it was as though he were sending the young man on his "first war-path" (1977, 32), a path so important for a young Sioux, based on how well he performed, that it could determine the outcome of the rest of his life. On this first trip to Santee, Eastman was tempted several times to either return to his new home with his father or to his old home with his uncle in Canada. While he longed to return to his devoted grandmother's care, he remembers his father's parting sentiments "that if [Eastman] did not return, [Jacob] would shed proud tears"—tears for a warrior who died meeting the foe head on (1977, 34).

The image of himself as a civilized warrior, one who accepted, as he called it, the "Christ ideal," yet maintained the pursuit of preserving his Indian identity amid the savagery of civilization, was how Eastman would primarily see himself for the rest of his life. Like many modern, Euro-American-educated Indians, he desired to be known as an example for other Indians to follow, as well as for non-Indians to make note of. For most scholars, the fact that Eastman seemed either never able to wholly choose between the two cultures, Indian or Euro-American, or, at least, never wanted to choose one completely over the other has made him appear to be a man in constant conflict with himself. Many scholars, in fact, focus a great deal on this seeming inability to decide once and for all *what* he was;[6] some critics go so far as to overlook Eastman's Euro-American

---

6. Wilson, for instance, indicates that Eastman "struggled for his own identity" while he became "an acculturated Sioux rather than an assimilated one" (1983, 36). Later, however,

blood and subsequent heritage altogether, as is often done with people of mixed blood in America.

More important, Eastman himself often negates the idea that he as a genetic product, as well as a cultural one, of both cultures. He never fully acknowledges, for instance, that his mother was a half-breed, instead calling her "the handsomest woman of all the Spirit Lake and Leaf Dweller Sioux" (1902, 4), whose features, he had been told, "had every feature of a Caucasian descent with the exception of her luxuriant black hair and deep black eyes" (1902, 5). He hints to his readers that she is of "Caucasian descent," but leaves the possibility also open that, though she was Indian, she *looked* white, possibly raising her value to his Euro-American readers.

Eastman seemed to accept this hierarchical view of himself. The foreword to his first memoir, *Indian Boyhood* (1902), calls North American Indians "the highest type of pagan and uncivilized man," and says they "possessed not only a superb physique but a remarkable mind" as well. By implication, because this book contains the stories of one of those Indians who lives a "thrilling wild life," Eastman is also telling us that he is a sample of those human beings with superb physiques and remarkable minds.

Eastman extends the social evolutionary hierarchy to an analysis of Indian spirituality, clearly showing himself as having become elevated in his conversion to Christianity. In *Boyhood*, his spiritual yearning to please the Great Mystery is seen through critical eyes as a pagan mythology, especially because Eastman himself repeatedly calls it superstition,[7] such as in his descriptions of the Bear Dance (1977, 169–77). He even refers to

---

Wilson acknowledges Eastman's quest for hybridization of cultures: "There is little doubt that Eastman believed Indians should adopt white ways; however, he did not favor total rejection of past customs and traditions. He supported many of the old customs but realized that Indians were doomed if they clung to the past and did not alter their ways. As a subjugated people, Indians had to acquire the more advanced aspects of white civilization to survive and then to compete in white society" (1983, 145). What Wilson does not make clear is what exactly the "more advanced aspects" are that Indians should acquire.

7. It is difficult to determine Eastman's exact definition of "superstition" because it was often used, according to the publishers of Ella Cara Deloria's *Waterlily*, to mean "common belief" even up to the time Deloria wrote her novel, about 1944 (1996, xi).

Uncheeda as a "superstitious old woman" (1977, 24). Yet, many scholars overlook Eastman's underlying desire to believe in the workings of the Great Mystery, such as is illustrated in his comparison of native worship of Wakan Tanka to Christianity and in his condemnation of many Christians' superficial attitudes in *The Soul of the Indian*. His need to understand and appease his people's religion is repeated several times in *Boyhood*, with Eastman going so far as to point out times when Sioux prophecies have come true (1902, 177 and 253). Although Anna Lee Stensland expresses concern that Eastman's conversion to Christianity and his acculturation of many Euro-American values colors Eastman's telling of his stories, especially the traditional Dakota myths (207), Erik Peterson cautions us not to assume that just because Eastman left his tribe and adopted Christianity that he somehow became less Indian (1996, 174).

Martha Lynn Viehmann attempts to balance such viewpoints when she argues that "while acknowledging the pain of the loss of the old freedom and independence and while honoring many of the values embedded in that way of life, Charles Eastman . . . also embraces the possibility of change, of transformation of life 'from the deep woods to civilization' without total loss" (1994, 79), even though she later asserts that, when Eastman appeared dressed in his native clothing, he is merely responding "to intense pressure to appear as an Indian. By putting on the 'garb of honor' of his tribe, Charles Eastman also puts on a mask" (1994, 103). But was putting on Indian attire any more of a masking of who Eastman was than his donning Euro-American clothing? Why should Eastman's acceptance of some aspects of Christianity be any more superficial, or any less real, than his belief in Wakan Tanka?

Eastman, in fact, equates the Sioux beliefs with Christian ideals in a positive way repeatedly in *Deep Woods*, even though he points out near the end:

From the time I first accepted the Christ ideal it has grown upon me steadily, but I also see more and more plainly our modern divergence from that ideal. I confess I have wondered much that Christianity is not practised by the very people who vouch for that wonderful conception of exemplary living. It appears that they are anxious to pass on their religion to all races of men, but keep very little of it themselves. (1977, 193)

His conflicting point of view—attracted to the ideal, but repulsed by those who fail to practice what they preach—complements those voiced by writers of the high modernist movement, such as T. S. Eliot, whose epic poem *The Waste Land* has come to symbolize the failure of modern morality. Although this skeptical view alone does not necessarily make Eastman a modernist, many of his texts point up the conflict between religious practice and belief repeatedly.

Eastman argues that working Euro-American concepts of Christianity rely on seeking large numbers of converts rather than enhancing individual religious experiences, so that its followers are weaker practitioners of spiritual ideals, ideals that are like those with which he was raised (1977, 141). He devotes a whole chapter, "Civilization as Preached and Practiced," in *Deep Woods* to comparing Indian concepts of spirituality and religious reverence with Euro-American ones, lauding the parallel concepts, while admonishing Christian hypocrites: "My effort was to make the Indian feel that Christianity is not at fault for the white man's sins, but rather the lack of it" (1977, 149). Had Euro-Americans practiced what they preached, they would have taken the time to understand Indian cultures instead of degrading them simply to justify attempts to annihilate or subjugate Indians to justify acquisition of their lands. Christianity, as Manifest Destiny, was a misused and twisted conception of the spirituality of the "Christ ideal," as Eastman saw it.

In the chapter "Civilization as Preached and Practiced," the story that seems to best symbolize Eastman's views on Indian spirituality and Christianity as a cultural practice is one he relates about his visit to a small Sac and Fox tribe in Iowa. After being eloquently admonished by an old chief for trying to convert his people, Eastman notes that he

was even more impressed a few minutes later, when one of his people handed [him his] pocket book containing [his] railway tickets and a considerable sum of money. [He] had not even missed it! [He] said to the

state missionary who as at [his] side, "Better let these Indians alone! If I
had lost my money in the streets of your Christian city, I should probably have never seen it again!" (1977, 149)

In many ways, his indictment of white Christians who fail to practice
Christ's ideals clarifies not only Eastman's view of American society, but
also his view of himself within both Indian and Euro-American cultures,
especially when contrasted with a quotation he relates from an older man
who participated in a Bible study group:

> "I have come to the conclusion that this Jesus was an Indian. He was
> opposed to material acquirement and to great possessions. He was in-
> clined to peace. He was as unpractical as any Indian and set no price
> upon his labor of love. These are not the principles upon which the
> white man has founded his civilization. It is strange that he could not
> rise to these simple principles which were commonly observed among
> our people." (1977, 143)

Clearly, Indian values, when compared with similar Christian ones, are
superior because Indians, in Eastman's view, practice, even without knowing them, Christ's ideals. If Christ, the primary focus of modern Western
culture through Christianity, can be an Indian in practice, then Indians
can be the better Christians. Because similar values are found in both
religions, Eastman seems to stress, why not take the best from both?

Originally, Eastman hoped to use his Euro-American education to
help Indians, what he and others often, and usually without question,
called his people.[8] One reason he chose to become a physician was that it
seemed one of the best capacities in which he could serve his people. At
first, there seemed no limit to his wish to use his medical training to aid

8. It is another racial bias to insist on categorizing people by race when they are of
more than one race. Eastman himself varies in his references to both Indians and Euro-
Americans, sometimes calling them "they" and sometimes including himself in either race's
numbers by referencing them as "us" or "our." Critics, confused or frustrated or both by his
inconsistency, simplify the dilemma by exaggerating Eastman's inability to be wholly Euro-
American or wholly Indian, when neither racial or cultural stereotype would have satisfied
him.

Indians, but halfway through *Deep Woods* a limit appears. He tells us, "I had laid my plans carefully, and purposed [*sic*] to serve my race *for a few years* in my profession, after which I would go to some city to practice" (1977, 86; emphasis mine). Thus, native generosity temporarily takes the foreground, only to be followed by the Euro-American desire for *private* medical practice. Yet, native virtues such as generosity never leave Eastman, even if they seem tainted by Euro-American desires, such as Eastman's quest for more and more money to support his growing family.

In *Deep Woods*, Eastman asked himself what the differences were between Euro-Americans and Indians. Along with other founding members of the society for American Indians, he believed Euro-Americans keep "the old things and continually adds to them new improvements," while Indians are "too well contented with the old" (1977, 64). What started as a warpath for Eastman becomes a religious pilgrimage. He becomes a composite, the flesh equivalent of Beloit College, which "cover[s] the site of an ancient village of moundbuilders . . . show[ing] to great advantage . . . the neat campus, where the green grass was evenly cut with lawn mowers" (1977, 52). He seems to build his understanding of civilization from a base of native sensibility, which he sees as inherent in the "Christ ideal," upon which he couples his strategies from both Indian and Euro-American frameworks. It is important to realize that neither culture would ever fully satisfy the adult Eastman.

Although some scholars are quick to label writers of different races different in their approaches to self-writing,[9] few examine similarities to the extent that fully explains why a writer such as Eastman can bridge two cultures to *his own* satisfaction. Some, in fact, refuse to believe that Eastman was capable of writing his autobiographies in the manner they were written, crediting his wife, Elaine Goodale Eastman, with getting his works

9. Krupat nicely slices the racial pie thus: "Whereas the modern West has tended to define personal identity as involving the successful mediation of an opposition between the individual and society, Native Americans have instead tended to define themselves as persons by successfully integrating themselves into the relevant social groupings—kin, clan, band, etc.—of their respective societies. . . . These conceptions of the self may be viewed as 'synecdochic,' i.e., based on part-to-whole relations, rather than 'metonymic,' i.e., as in the part-to-part relations that most frequently dominate Euramerican autobiography" (1994, 4).

printed.[10] Hertha Dawn Wong, in fact, nearly equates Elaine with Nei-hardt, Black Elk's collaborator, although she steps back from such a bold assertion after she hints at it. Like Wong, many assume Elaine was "the force guiding [Eastman's] work into print" (1992, 141), or at least "his prin-cipal editor" (Wilson 1983, 131), because Eastman did not publish any of his writings after their separation (Ruoff 1991, xii). Such scholars overlook other possibilities for Eastman's lack of publication after his separation from Elaine. Eastman, significantly, lost someone readily available to type his work. The cessation of Eastman's publishing could be attributed to the mere fact that many of his publishing contacts, people who possibly chose to remain loyal to Elaine in sympathy to the trauma she experienced from their separation, were hers to begin with. As David Reed Miller points out in a footnote, among Elaine's papers housed at Smith College, "ironically Charles's name is conspicuously absent" (1978, 70, n. 3). Why would she, or her family, take such pains to remove his name, especially if they did, indeed, collaborate on all his works? If Elaine had been such a close col-laborator with Charles, why are most of the works she published after his death completely unrelated, or only indirectly related, to the Sioux?

Regardless of the lack of hard evidence, Wong, like others, also sees Elaine's influence in the educational messages of Ohiyesa's works (1992, 141), and in the fact that many of his descriptions of Indian life read as though written by an observer, not a participant (1992, 143). Ruoff goes even further to see Elaine's "purple prose," a reflection of her "poetic incli-nations," in Eastman's fiction in *Old Indian Days* (1991, xviii). What is most interesting about these scholarly perspectives is that Elaine seems to be the principal source of information for the view that she had an extensive hand in developing Eastman's writings, a belief perpetuated by each critic quoting each other. Both Wong and Ruoff, for instance, get much of their information from Wilson's biography of Eastman, wherein Wilson quotes a letter from Elaine to Harold G. Rugg dated April 19, 1939, three months

10. I cannot use the word "published" here because recent scholarship on writing and publishing argues that even giving a speech or telling a story publicly is a form of publica-tion. It is difficult, if not impossible, to ascertain if Elaine ever helped Eastman write his speeches.

after Eastman's death, in which Elaine claims, "'Dr. Eastman's books left his hand . . . as a rough draft in pencil, on scratch paper.' From these, she would then type copies, 'revising, omitting, and re-writing as necessary,' the same procedure undoubtedly employed in getting his articles ready for publication" (1983, 131). In the last clause, Wilson himself extends his speculations about Elaine's sphere of influence. Yet, and only later, Wilson reveals the fact that Eastman "despised" Elaine's insistent meddlings into his writings (1983, 191). Never is Eastman's irritation with Elaine's attempts at editorial manipulation mentioned by anyone as a possible reason for their divorce.

Perhaps the source that started most of the speculation about how much influence Elaine had over Charles's writing came from Miller's essay in which he quotes one of the Eastmans' nieces, Grace Moore, who reported that while working on *Red Hunters,* Eastman

> would walk the woods alone in the mornings. . . . Carrying a small note pad, he would jot notes of ideas as inspirations came to him. Returning around noon, he would explain his ideas to his wife, who then, under Charles' supervision, developed the ideas into prose, typing a draft for additional corrections and polishing. *Elaine was indispensable to her husband's writing: after his separation from her in 1921, he published nothing new.* (1978, 66)

The last line of speculation, which I have emphasized, is Miller's—the rumor that has since been passed from scholar to scholar. Because he does not quote directly from Moore, we cannot be certain his paraphrasing is accurate either. Later, in his own essay, he discusses how Eastman's inability to type, which delayed his ability to turn in his reports as a U.S. Indian inspector, was one of the primary reasons he was forced to resign that post (1978, 69). Elaine, obviously, typed Charles's manuscripts for him, but Miller's phrasing leaves clarity behind. Did Elaine develop the ideas into prose? Or did Charles do it as he dictated changes to his notes? Who did the additional corrections and polishing? Miller makes it clear that Eastman's notes from his investigations and inspections were typed by a stenographer, when he could find one, into a final report. Why should we suppose, just because she typed his notes for his manuscripts, that Elaine was significantly more important in his writing than as a stenographer and creative consultant?

In fact, it is doubtful Elaine had as much of a hand in her husband's writings as she claimed, although she undoubtedly had some. His earliest writings were probably relatively untouched by Elaine because it was only *after* he had written them that she learned of them, read them, and encouraged him to publish them in the magazine that had published her work, *St. Nicholas* (Wilson 1983, 131), although she paints herself as the self-sacrificing wife, when, in her memoir, she writes, "I had always something of a one-track mind, and for many a year every early dream and ambition [of mine] was wholly subordinated to the business of helping my talented husband express himself and interpret his people" (1978, 173). Interestingly, in writing for publication, she makes herself the supporting actor, suggesting she pushed Eastman with a "dint of much persuasion" to write *Deep Woods* (1977, foreword), and going so far as to pointedly list her publications—*Little Brother o' Dreams* (1910), *Yellow Star* (1911), *Indian Legends Retold* (1928), and *The Luck of Oldacres* (1928)—in *Sister to the Sioux* (1978, 174). But in her personal correspondence, she was collaborator. Elaine *is* credited with collaboration with Charles on compiling *Wigwam Evenings* in 1909, and he dedicates *The Soul of the Indian* to his "wife[,] Elaine Goodale Eastman[,] in grateful recognition of her ever-inspiring companionship in thought and work and in love of her most Indian-like virtues." If he can do that much to admit her assistance, what would have prevented him from acknowledging she had a larger hand in all his writings?

For clarity's sake, we should also acknowledge that Elaine claims to have "urged [Eastman] to write down his recollections of the wild life, which [she] carefully edited and placed with *St. Nicholas*. From this small beginning grew *Indian Boyhood* and eight other books of Indian lore, upon all of which [she] collaborated *more or less*" (1978, 173; emphasis mine). Eastman himself, in a book supposedly edited by Elaine, if we believe her claim, says that "when my wife discovered what I had written, she insisted upon sending it to *St. Nicholas*. Much to my surprise, the sketches were immediately accepted and appeared during the following year. This was the beginning of my first book 'Indian Boyhood,' which was not completed until several years later" (1977, 139). Historically, Elaine would not be the first wife who, with few substantial claims to personal fame other than through marriage, creates an image that makes her appear as important as, or important because of, her spouse—one of the few avenues of prestige open to women of the late nineteenth and early twentieth centuries.[11]

Had Eastman been Euro-American, it is possible that scholars would have made other observations about reasons for his occasions of "purple prose," the educational qualities of his works, and his use of "objective" narration, instead of trying to find reasons to question the authenticity of his work. Ella Deloria points out, for instance, that "the Yankton style in both oratory and storytelling is markedly vigorous, plain and terse, as compared to the Teton which is flowery, and often weakened by padding and needless romancing" (1978, 76, n. 1). Deloria does not mention the Santee speaking style in particular, but she does say that "Santee art is floral rather than geometric, like that of the rest of the Dakotas. In thought, too, and in ceremonies they resembled their Chippewa neighbors more than their fellow tribesmen to the west" (1944, 17). And we should remember that Eastman lived a great deal among the Teton Lakota, so that his language style could have become like theirs, "flowery" and romantic.

This preoccupation by scholars with how much of Eastman's writings are Elaine's is undoubtedly due to the amanuensis factor that clutters much American Indian scholarship with its obsession on deciding how much is authentically Indian and how much is Euro-American intrusion. The question of how much a text shows Sioux influences versus how much it demonstrates Euro-American influence becomes moot when it comes to writers such as Eastman, because he has undoubtedly been influenced as a writer by both. To redirect the question, we should examine Eastman's writings as products of both cultures, melding literary traditions to create a new one, instigated I believe by Eastman's writings. Such interstitiality is prominent throughout the Sioux Literary Renaissance.

11. See Nerburn's edition of *The Soul of an Indian* (1993) (not to be confused with Eastman's *The Soul of the Indian* (1911), although there are excerpts from the letter text in the former).

How, after all, can a scholar such as Ruoff claim unquestionably that more poetic descriptions are probably Elaine's, such as, "Long shafts of light from the setting sun painted every hill; one side red as with blood, the other dark as the shadow of death" (Eastman 1991, 124), or "the warrior's ambition had disappeared before it like a morning mist before the sun" (Eastman 1991, 51), or, the one she pinpointed as Elaine's writing, "the robust beauty of the wild lily of the prairie, pure and strong in her deep colors of yellow and scarlet against the savage plain and horizon, basking in the open sun like a child, yet soft and woman-like, with drooping head when observed" (Eastman 1991, 182; Ruoff 1991, xviii). Admittedly, it is easy to pick out phrases written by *Doctor* Eastman, such as, "water to be fetched in bags made from the dried pericardium of an animal," even though such uses of medical terms are few (1991, 175). But, until Eastman's handwritten manuscripts and Elaine's typewritten ones are discovered, if they exist, scholars do more disservice to Eastman as a writer to assert that his writings were not wholly his own.

One possibility few consider for Eastman's writing is that he uses the third-person references to Indians or Euro-Americans as rhetorical or literary devices to make his descriptions appear more scientific, more anthropological, thus perhaps more believable, or, to the more sophisticated reader, as a modernist parody of the common anthropological style used in as-told-to narratives about Indians. It is also possible Eastman felt a need to distance himself for emotional reasons or for his audience's sake. Having learned well from oral storytellers such as Smoky Day in *Boyhood*, and purposely writing, at least at first, for his and for Euro-American children, Eastman would have been very conscious of his audience. But such consciousness would never have stopped him from making his works as literary as possible because, as Anna Lee Stensland puts it, "a good story is far more important to Eastman and to other tribal Indians than accurate history" (1977, 201).

One major difference often noted between oral storytelling traditions and written ones is that oral stories, because of their spontaneity, are often nonchronological/tangential and are usually seen as circular because speakers must return to the original thread of the tale after each digression. Because one has time to straighten out such tangles through editing, written stories are often more linear, with most stories and autobiographies usually having straight chronological movements. Because *Boyhood* has a somewhat more linear structure, organization of the book can be seen as an alternative to the typical (thus usually seen as Western) maturation story, a sort of bildungsroman where the young man, to discover his individuality, leaves home. Yet the book's movement is not strictly linear, and could possibly be loosely patterned after the Old Testament.

Neither *Boyhood* nor *Deep Woods,* which follows sequentially, adhere strictly to the traditional chronological format of Euro-American autobiography, being "more topical" as Stensland puts it (1977, 200). *Boyhood* has twelve sections, some of which are broken into smaller, individually titled stories. The first section includes five stories largely about Eastman's childhood, wherein Eastman moves deftly from describing the second winter after the Minnesota Uprising back to events that had to happen before that fateful rebellion (Stensland 201). These are the genesis chapters of Eastman's life. The second section is only one story, which is largely anthropological, accompanied by Eastman's uncle's lectures on little Hakadah's training. The third section includes three more personal stories, and the fourth section is the only personal one told in the anthropological third-person point of view. Much of the remaining eight sections (an intermixing of Proverbs and Prophets?) includes observations and experiences intermingled with legends told by Smokey Day, the band's storyteller, or stories told by some member of Eastman's family; the very last section is Eastman's reflections, from his Dakota perspective, on civilization, the last sentence anticipating *Deep Woods:* "Here my wild life came to an end, and my school days began" (1902, 289). As the title of the second book implies, Eastman makes an "exodus" from the deep woods. Although *Deep Woods* adheres more stringently to traditional autobiographical chronology, Eastman manages to interject commentary about the differences and similarities between Indians and Euro-Americans throughout, ending with a commentary about "The Soul of the White Man." If we follow the biblical parallel, the book moves from the appearance of one savior and the education of another, through the description of the work done by the latter to his "Revelations" about human relations.

Creating such categories of difference (in religion) and assimilation (in

writing style) seems to give credence to what most scholars assume is
Eastman's biculturality—parts of his story are seemingly distinct in their
influences by both Indian and Euro-American cultures. As William F.
Smith Jr. asserts, the mere fact that Eastman wrote these books without
the intervention of a Euro-American editor "is an initial sign of the extent
to which [the books were] influenced by two cultures" (1975, 242).

But, as Brumble puts it most nostalgically, "in some sense most Indian
autobiographers seek to return [to their homeland]—if only by the workings of the memory, if only by mounting a memorial in words" (1988, 165–
66). The conflict imposed on Eastman to choose between what was seen
(then and often now) as separate and unequal Indian and Euro-American
worlds is painfully revealed in the opening chapter of Boyhood: "What boy
would not be an Indian for a while when he thinks of the freest life in the
world? This life was mine." The speaker presents his readers with an idealized vision and immediately sobers the tone: "This life was mine" (1902, 3).
The tone is made even more somber and nostalgic if the reader has taken
the time to read the two-paragraph preface in which Eastman speaks of his
"thrilling wild life" and the "remnant" Indians on the reservations who, for
him, are only "a fictitious copy of the past" (1902, preface).

Few autobiographers, of any culture, escape such nostalgia. Perhaps
what evinces most strongly the sense that Eastman, though recounting a
way of living unfamiliar to his readers, is more human being than a creature of a specific culture, is his tale "Hakadah's First Offering." But, to
establish this understanding, to lead us to this story, Western ideals of
autobiographical chronology get set aside so that the reader is forced to
piece together aspects of Eastman's youth. The first ninety-eight pages
discuss Eastman's birth and childhood. In the first chapter of Boyhood, we
learn that Eastman was called Hakadah, which means "the pitiful last,"
because his mother died soon after he was born. The story just before
"Hakadah's First Offering" is our first introduction to Hakadah and his
dog, Ohitika, Dakota for "the brave," as hunters—successful, yet accidental
hunters when they kill a fawn by frightening it to death. In chapter five
(which is the last chapter of the first section of the book), we witness the
ceremony and contest that wins him his name Ohiyesa, "the winner." Interestingly, the fourth section of the book, which contains only this one
story, "Hakadah's First Offering," is written in the third person—the only

story in the third-person point of view in the entire book, indeed, *the only autobiographical story in Eastman's entire oeuvre written exclusively in the more anthropological third-person point of view,* and is one of the many stories that reveal the circularity, as opposed to linearity, of the tale-telling in the book's structure.

This shift in narration, however, is important, especially given the nature of the story. Why would Eastman choose, first of all, to include in his memoir a story about himself told in the third person? Why imitate the more common type of Indian narrative, which filters its "indianness" through an anthropologists's point of view? Why would he, in fact, choose to write this story in the third person at all?

A drawing of an Indian boy stroking his dog by E. L. Blumenschein precedes "Hakadah's First Offering." The full importance of this picture does not become clear to the reader until midway through the story. The story itself involves how Uncheedah, Eastman's grandmother, takes it upon herself to see that eight-year-old Hakadah performs his first ritual sacrifice for the Great Mystery. This is a traditional tribal initiation ceremony for the Dakota, with variations from tribe to tribe within the larger Sioux or Oceti Sakowin nation. The ceremony involves several days' preparation, usually by the grandmother because she is usually responsible for the children's moral upbringing. The child is expected to choose his or her most valuable possession to sacrifice to the Great Mystery in demonstration of the child's awareness of the need to sacrifice oneself—even to giving one's life away—for the betterment of the whole community.

Eastman tells us how Uncheedah has been planning this ceremony for days before telling Hakadah that he is to sacrifice whatever is dearest to him. One possible reason for the third-person point of view becomes obvious early in the story. It allows us to enter Uncheedah's mind: "She believed that her influence had helped regulate and develop the characters of her sons to the height of savage nobility and strength of manhood" (1902, 102). Because her sons had gained honor as celebrated warriors and hunters, Uncheedha "had not hesitated to claim for herself a good share of the honors they had achieved, because she had brought them early to the notice of the 'Great Mystery'" (1902, 102). She prepares to do the same for her parentless grandson.

After thinking about it, Hakadah volunteers to give up his best weapons, his set of paints, and his best necklace. But Uncheedah is not satisfied with his suggestions and prompts him to consider again, wanting him to realize what it really is he values most—his dog Ohitika:

> But Uncheedah knew where his affection was vested. His faithful dog, his pet and companion—Hakadah was almost inseparable from the loving beast. She was sure it would be difficult to obtain his consent to sacrifice the animal, but she ventured upon a final appeal. "You must remember," she said, "that in this offering you will call upon him who looks at you from every creation. In the wind you hear him whisper to you. He gives his war-whoop in the thunder. . . . In short, it is the Mystery of Mysteries, who controls all things, to whom you will make your first offering. By this act, you will ask him to grant to you what he has granted to few men. I know you wish to be a great warrior and hunter. I am not prepared to see my Hakadah show any cowardice, for the love of possessions is a woman's trait and not a brave's." (1902, 105–6)

Once it becomes clear to Hakadah that he must sacrifice his dog Ohitika, Hakadah "was simply unable to speak. To a civilized eye, he would have appeared at that moment like a little copper statue. His bright black eyes were fast melting in floods of tears, when he caught his grandmother's eye and recollected her oft-repeated adage: 'Tears for woman and the war-whoop for man to drown sorrow!'" (1902, 107). The ritual is then described in cursory detail, with Hakadah bravely performing most of it, except the killing of the dog, which is a task that falls to an uncle. The story ends with Uncheedah offering a prayer to the Great Mystery to make the boy a great warrior and hunter.

There are several possible reasons why Eastman chose to write this story in the third person besides the fact that it allows him omniscience as a narrator. Perhaps he originally intended the story for separate publication, or he desired to avoid alienating his non-Indian audience with a strange, possibly repugnant ritual. Perhaps he was compromising with Elaine's editorial suggestions. Conscious of a literary audience, he could have been aware that through third-person narration, the author (autobiographer, remember) can not only "objectively" illustrate, without seeming phony in the moment's emotional power, how important such a gesture is to the boy, his family, and the tribal community, but also distance himself from the painful memory of having to sacrifice his own dog. Perhaps, since this is the only story that shows Eastman himself performing a Dakota ritual, he tries to reduce the "weakening" of the power of the ritual, thus perhaps weakening his own personal ties with the Great Mystery, by telling it in the third person.

Regarding the possibility that he was considering publishing the story separately, instead of in the book, it is important to note that "Hakadah's First Offering" was published in *Current Literature* in January 1903, a year after the book was published. But although the essay was probably written concurrently with the rest of the memoir, other articles published by Eastman freely use his experience as reference, so even if he were considering simultaneous publication it would not necessarily require the essay to be written in the third person. Editing concerns—especially the ability to alter texts for particular audiences—were not as easily handled in 1902 as they are today, but nonetheless would not have been so overwhelming that Eastman could not have altered the story for publication with the book. Because *Current Literature* cites Eastman's book as the source of the story, and because the story appears identically in the magazine as it does in the book—even with Blumenschein's picture of the boy and dog—it is doubtful Eastman wrote the story separately from the rest of the memoir. So it is doubtful he was concerned about publishing the work elsewhere as his reason for writing it in the third person.

The idea of sacrificing animals for religious reasons, though not unknown to the predominantly Christian non-Indian audience he wrote for, was still not a practice commonly accepted in 1902 and would probably have not been a subject approved for children. And Eastman's primary target audience for *Boyhood* was Euro-American children, for whom the book was to be one of his first guidance texts, which preceded his helping to found Boy Scouts and Camp Fire Girls. As Robin Lakoff suggests, the use of third-person self-reference is "a way for speakers [and writers] to distance themselves and their interests from the discourse, suggesting that whatever is being talked about is of no consequence to them" (1990, 245). So Eastman, to be more accepted by his audience, could have been attempting to tone down the fact that this ritual sacrifice was *his* personal experience.

Because it is his personal experience, however, it would have been impressed upon Eastman as a child that this was *his* sacrificial ceremony, *his* tie to the Great Mystery. Among the taboos held by the Oyate is that one should never speak one's private name, which was usually bestowed by a wakan, or holy person, in recognition of a deed, for fear of losing one's own personal powers. Since the individual's name is so guarded, it is reasonable to speculate that an individual's personal ceremonies would also be considered sacred. The fact that it is Eastman's personal experience is significant, because Eastman shows no qualms about going into much more detail, describing even graphic mutilation in detail, in his descriptions of another sacred ceremony, the Sun Dance, in *The Soul of the Indian* (1980, 56–63). He also describes other religious rituals, such as the Mystery Feast, as well as the religious purposes behind various practices, such as the ceremonial use of the pipe and sweat lodge (1980, 78–84), so the fact that the ritual was sacred, in and of itself, is not enough to have deterred him from discussing it. If the power of his personal sacrifice to Wakan Tanka was indeed one of Eastman's concerns, it clearly demonstrates that, despite his conversion to Christianity, he never stopped believing in the validity of his earlier Dakota religious training.

The idea of selflessness would not have been unfamiliar or repugnant to his audience, because he often wrote about the Indian ideal of self-sacrifice for the good of the community as part of the founding idea for the Boy Scouts and Camp Fire Girls. But he probably was very conscious of the fact that killing an animal as a sacrifice to the Great Mystery would be considered heathen, and he probably did not want that prejudiced belief projected onto him as the writer.

Interestingly, Eastman does not describe the *complete* ritual to his audience. As Ethel Nurge first pointed out, Eastman completely leaves out the fact that, after the dog is killed and used in the ritual as though still alive, he is later made to eat the cooked flesh of the dog to complete the ritual (1970, 37, n. 2). Although eating cooked dog meat was often part of Dakota ceremonies, because the dog is considered the most faithful creature to human beings and eating its flesh passes on that undying sense of loyalty and selfless love, it was already a pejorative to refer to the Sioux as the dog eaters in 1900, so that, too, was an image Eastman wanted to avoid.

Yet, Lakoff points out the power of third-person self-reference to retrospectively justify dubious past actions, and create dazzling personae for future use. . . . A device that is ostensibly distancing is utilized to create exciting drama. The third person allows the creation of characters; the connection with the first person provides an aura of authority and verisimilitude. Together they weave a spell, first catching the audience's attention, then gaining its trust. (1990, 253)

The use of the imitated anthropological third-person point of view does function to check the sentimentality readers might perceive in Eastman's descriptions of sacrificing his dog. Although Eastman arguably mixes the literary third person with the anthropological, the anthropological tone and diction stand out, clearly in parody: "Hakadah breathlessly gave a descriptive narrative. . . . The concluding sentence fairly dilated the eyes of the young hunter, for he felt that a great event was about to occur, in which he would be the principal actor. But Uncheedah resumed her speech" (1902, 103–4). Elsewhere, Eastman uses a more conversational, less stilted tone. But from his frequent references to more formal descriptions—such as "savage nobility," "to execute" (instead of sacrifice), and "a perpendicular white cliff"—we clearly feel that this narrative, though not unlike anthropological descriptions of Indian life, is several steps removed from the cold science of an anthropologist's pen. Literary scholars also tend to consider the third-person point of view more "objective," a modernist concern (Wagner-Martin 1990, 5), thus somehow more credible as well. Although we primarily have only Elaine's insistence that she had a hand in all of Eastman's writings, both she and Eastman would have been conscious of wanting to appear as objective and believable as possible in the piece. Eastman, especially later in his life, did act as an amateur anthropologist; as he went about conducting government business among Indians he took the time to "collect" artifacts for museums, so perhaps here he is trying out that role. It would be nearly impossible to prove that Eastman was aware of the modernist movement, which was *just* getting under way, and its concerns with objective narration.

His desire *might* have been to help his audience relive the experience as completely as possible, but he also has to weigh the effects his details might have on the reader. He does not want to alienate his readers. Perhaps, though, the grief Eastman felt in losing his best friend—even some thirty years later—was too great. It is, after all, *the only story in this entire oeuvre* that is autobiographical, yet written in the third person.

Eastman builds identification in the same way, layer upon layer. By the time we get to "Hakadah's First Offering," we know he is Hakadah, but he *removes* the adult personae from the story as much as possible. We still know he is in control of the story, but, by focusing on the small boy's experiences, he redirects our sympathies; whereas we would question, as an adult in retrospect does, Eastman's point of view about the sacrifice if he were narrating it as the adult Charles Eastman, we accept what the child learns and does and do not require him to comment on the sacrifice's appropriateness or on the possible lack of development in a culture that stipulates such a ritual.

"Hakadah's First Offering" becomes a symbol for Charles Eastman's continued self-sacrifice. He sacrifices his active *presence* in the story by writing it in the third person. He caters to his audience's desire to *know* more about his culture—its customs and religion—in an anthropological sense, rather than a personal sense. Although he seems to be putting the concerns for his audience's sensibilities foremost in writing this story, he can also distance himself somewhat from feeling the full impact, again, of the sacrificial experience.

The picture of the boy and his dog, then, becomes an important representation not only of the personal impact of the boy's coming-of-age sacrifice to the Great Mystery, but also of the intimate bond with his readers Eastman is willing to forgo for his larger audience's needs and expectations. In fact, he compensates for their ignorance and prejudices by making it appear—especially if the story is read only in *Current Literature* and not in the context of *Boyhood*—as though this experience were not his own.

Because this story is the only switch to third-person narration without adopting a character-speaker to accompany it, it is evident that, even while writing this story, the memory of the event is probably still a powerful operative in Eastman's psyche—so much so that he has to completely remove himself from the tale to tell it. In fact, some critics speculate that Eastman's book, which includes several recounted tales from Indian storytellers, has been padded with these secondhand stories "to supplement the [absent and probably unpleasant] reminiscences" of his life, especially encounters with whites and instances of Indian customs he or his editors felt his white readers might not understand (Murray 1991, 77).

With all these possible reasons for not writing the story, why did Eastman choose to tell it at all? Was he merely demonstrating how ingrained is the notion of self-sacrifice to a Sioux child? Is he trying to prove that such self-sacrifice is an—if not the—important element in successful tribal/community living? Or is he merely justifying his view of the "Christ ideal," because little Hakadah must choose to give up his best friend, thus has to appreciate that his dog has sacrificed himself for Hakadah's benefit, just as Christ did for Christians? Conceivably, "Hakadah's First Offering" works as the Dakota version of Christ's sacrifice for sinful humanity. What creature is more loyal and continues to love without question no matter what happens to it than a dog? Another possible reason Eastman chose to leave out the information about his eating the dog's cooked flesh is because, literarily, it would not work within the confines of the Christian symbolism—excepting, of course, in the symbolism of the Eucharist wherein Christians eat and drink the "body" and "blood" of Christ. Equating Christ directly with a dog would probably, in fact, only undercut what he has so carefully constructed here, and would have altered his subtle connection of his "savior" father with Christ.

"Hakadah's First Offering" also serves as a marker in the "progression" of Eastman's life. As a child, he was ready and willing to set aside his rather carefree life to partake of a ceremony that conveys to his people that he had come of the age to formally pay respects to the spirits of the world, and would remember ever after, because of his obligations and ties to those spirits and his people, that he should consider them before he thinks of himself. By the end of Boyhood and the beginning of Deep Woods, even his Euro-American readers would be prepared to see Eastman forgo his desires to follow in the direction his newly resurrected father chose for him.

As Eastman probably soon learned, such subtlety in paralleling his father and his faithful canine companion as figures of his "Christ ideal," especially in such an unexpected place as a book by an Indian, would elude most non-Indian Americans. Eastman wrote some quite sophisticated prose, and I will argue that his was much more sophisticated, much more subtle than his wife's writing. Although he refers to the Animal People in several of his stories, his collection of short fiction, *Red Hunters and the Animal People* (1904), possibly the first collection of short fiction by an Indian (Ruoff 1991, ix), is quite sophisticated in the development of the stories and in the descriptions of the characters—both human and animal.

Just as James Welch will do later in his historical novel *Fools Crow* (1986), Eastman places his audience alternately into the mind-set of the Indians and the Animal People, with often dramatic, yet sympathetic descriptions of what they experience. For instance, when Igmu, the female puma, is out hunting, she sees a man ride by, not on a pony, but on "a long-tailed elk" (1904b, 8); when she listens for danger signs, she knows that "at that time of the day no people talk except the winged people" (1904b, 10), and when she catches a grizzly eating the cached kill, he is "the old root-digger" (1904b, 16).

In the stories in *Red Hunters*, Eastman seizes opportunities to explain various Sioux myths or customs, intertwining stories with a fairly subtle didactic example probably once told to him as a child. "The River People" is an elaborate story from both the beavers' perspective and the Indians'. Eastman assures us that "the beaver people are considered the wisest of the smaller four-legged tribes, and they are a people of great common-sense" (1904b, 179). Chapawee, the female beaver who resides as prime lodge builder and lore teacher, tells her gathered children the stories of how their band came to be and why they reside at the Great Pipestone Quarry, what was formerly Yankton Nakota territory. The buffalo people, a possible metaphoric parallel to Euro-Americans, destroyed the beavers' original lodges in their clumsiness because "they do not respect the laws and customs of any other nation" (1904b, 182). So Chapawee's family—her mother, father, and two brothers—move on, only to be separated by a great spring flood. Persevering alone, she eventually meets Kamdoka, who becomes her lifelong mate. They choose to live and raise their successive generations in the Pipestone Quarry because the Indians come for pipestone only in the summer, when they are not interested in beaver pelts (1904b, 190).

After providing this beaver clan's lore, the story then switches perspectives to the Red Hunters who work for the American Fur Company (1904b, 193). The hunters observe the beavers' homes and actions for several days, taking the time to weigh "the full dignity and importance they had given to their intended massacre of a harmless and wise people" (1904b, 195). In a dual movement, Eastman manages, first, to dignify the Indian hunters' objectives for killing the beavers by noting that they are careful to leave four young beavers to carry on the next generation and to care for the two elderly beavers so "their spirits [do not] follow us" (1904b, 199), and, second, to create a parallel between the beavers and American Indians who are massacred or conquered, whose strength leaves them, leaving the narrator to wonder "who would care in such a case to survive the ruins of his house?" (1904b, 199).

Similarly, the other stories in the collection also draw possibilities of such parallels, with the primary theme being how the Oyate, the People, related to and copied manners and customs from "the best animal people" (1904b, 210). In the process, he explains legends, beliefs, and customs, such as how Wounded Knee Creek came to be called by that name (1904b, 119), why the elk represents virile young manhood (1904b, 211), and how regaling one another with stories not only teaches the young (1904b, 236), but also persuades opponents (1904b, 244).

Eastman even uses authorial intrusion to mimic the typical as-told-to anthropological narrative and to inject humor, such as in "A Founder of Ten Towns," about Pezpeza, whose "biographer and interpreter tells thus of his wonderful frontier life and adventures" (1904b, 125). Such parody, like that in "Hakadah's First Offering," is at once modernist (Wagner-Martin 1990, 5), as well as reminiscent of Victorian authorial intrusions. The two books, *Red Hunters* and *Boyhood*, were published only two years apart, but, as "A Founder of Ten Towns" demonstrates, Eastman has refined and strengthened his sense of literary parody. Whereas the mimicked anthropological tone is only periodic in "Hakadah's First Offering," the imitation scientific point of view carries "A Founder of Ten Towns," with even the minutest of events explained in analytic detail, with the animals serving as "native" substitutes: "Every day some prairie-dog left the town in quest of a new home. The chief reason for this is over-population—hence, scarcity of food; for the ground does not yield a sufficient quantity for so many" (1904b, 128); and the Indians as scientific observers:

> Pezpeza's town was now quite populous. But he was not the mayor; he did not get any credit for the founding of the town; at least as far as

the Red people could observe. Their life and government seemed to be highly democratic. Usually the concentration of population produced a certain weed which provided abundance of food for them. But under some conditions it will not grow; and in that case, as soon as the native buffalo-grass is eaten up the town is threatened with a famine, and the inhabitants are compelled to seek food at a distance from their houses. This is quite opposed to the habit and safety of the helpless little people. Finally the only alternative will be the desertion of the town. (1904b, 133-34)

Eastman subverts the anthropological language and the condoning, parental attitude often found in anthropological reports of the time by applying them to prairie dogs, at the same time playing off the Siouan belief that animals *are* simply other forms of people and deserve the same respect shown to human beings.

In fact, Eastman's Animal People are very much like the animals in Western fairy tales, fables (such as Aesop's) and folk tales (such as Joel Chandler Harris's Uncle Remus stories), and even the personified animals in Greek and African myths. But unlike many of the non-Indian tales, these near-traditional American Indian stories raise animals to a spiritual and physical plane equal to the Indians, indeed all human beings, themselves. Eastman was the first Indian writer to openly describe and explain such ties to his primarily Euro-American audience, putting the Sioux beliefs into a form non-Indians could understand and accept.

In "A Founder of Ten Towns," for instance, the prairie dogs are directly linked to the ancient Mound Builders as a possible explanation as to where those ancient people went when they disappeared (1904b, 124). The parallel Eastman draws here demonstrates the Sioux belief in the powers of transformation and the duration of the soul, as well as giving one specific reason why many traditional Indians saw animals as people.

Most of these stories successfully elicit feelings of respect for the animals from the reader. When the old chieftainess, the white buffalo cow, dies and is "reborn" in the baby white buffalo, readers are assured of the duration of the soul and the power of the white buffalo woman—who brought the seven major Oceti Sakowin rituals including the peace pipe— to the Sioux. More difficult to accept is the ritual capture and killing of the newly born white buffalo calf, which for the Sioux is "the token of plenty and good-fortune" through her preserved hide (1904b, 105). For the buffalo, she had represented a new powerful leader. Here, then, the needs of the Sioux prevail over the needs of the buffalo, because "'it is the will of the Great Mystery'" (1904b, 105), just as the needs of Christians prevail over Christ's existence, with the white buffalo hide becoming a clear parallel to Jesus' cross.

The needs of the Indians for survival are not the justifications of the Red Hunters when two men spend hours hunting a big sheep ram in "The Gray Chieftain." Instead, they note admirably his fine qualities of bravery and cunning in evading them, making him a worthy opponent who will bring them great honor. Instead of sparing his life, they rejoice at having had the ability to kill him: "'He is dead. My friend, the noblest of chiefs is dead!' exclaimed Grayfoot . . . in great admiration and respect for the gray chieftain" (1904b, 158). Because the Indian calls the mountain goat "my friend," Viehmann asserts that "this moment of affinity between man and beast, reinforced by the similarity of the names Grayfoot and gray chieftain, symbolizes the interconnection of human and animal life" (1994, 77). The interconnection demonstrates, through animals for humans, that one should sympathize with one's opponents and nobly accept death when it comes, including the sacrifice of one's life for another, as the ram does for the Indian (Viehmann 1994, 78). Such demonstrations reemphasize Eastman's self-sacrificial, yet honorable, approach to life—it is far more honorable to fight a worthy foe or to accept a worthy challenge than it is to merely accept the easiest thing available.

Eastman claimed that "the main incident in all of [the stories], even those which are unusual and might appear incredible to the white man, are actually current among the Sioux and deemed by them worthy of belief," acknowledging that only "here and there the fables, songs, and superstitious fancies of the Indian are brought in to suggest his habit of mind and manner of regarding the four-footed tribes" (1904b, vii). Even though *Red Hunters* is a very important book in Eastman's oeuvre, and even though the book is clearly a predecessor to more contemporary literature as well as a book worthy of consideration by modernist scholars, it is, unfortunately, the only book of Eastman's no longer in print. Like his other works, *Red Hunters* ends prophetically for itself on the note of sadness Eastman felt in the imminently predicted disappearance of the Indian because of the intrusion and annihilation by Euro-Americans (1904b, 245).

Although Eastman acknowledges his biases against whites as a child, especially toward the end of *Boyhood*, they are carefully tempered with equal praise and awe-filled impressions of the wonders of Euro-American civilization, probably so as not to make his white readers too uncomfortable, as well as to assert for himself that he has made the right decision in following his father's wishes to acculturate. Though seemingly less worried about offending Euro-American readers in *Deep Woods*, he reminds them on several occasions of his former ignorance of white ways, such as when he retreats into the woods for solace from the Great Mystery because he "knew nothing of the white man's religion [and thus had to follow] the teachings of [his] ancestors" (1977, 26). But, through the extent of his writings, it is clear Eastman was far from ignorant about either culture, and chose, when the need suited him, to claim allegiances to both.

So much attention has been paid, instead, to Eastman's supposed conflict as a man caught between the two cultures, with one critic calling Eastman "bifurcated" and afraid that his "inner betrayal is too great for him to endure" (Nerburn 1993, 62), that critics have tended to focus on the trivia of Eastman's writings, instead of its strengths. Some argue directly that Eastman has appropriated English, but could not use it well. David Murray, for instance, asserts that Eastman "vacillates from one spurious 'identity' to another, rather than think with the terms available . . . with the result that he can only simplify a complex process into a series of crude oppositions" (1991, 78-79). In fact, Kent Nerburn's criticism and concern for Eastman's possible struggle with his possible feelings of "liminality" prompted him to alter Eastman's texts, eliminating both third- and first-person references when he saw fit, which was more often than not, to make Eastman solely Indian in his references.[12] The dilemma, it seems to me, lies in the fact that scholars and critics have the need to categorize Eastman as solely the prototype of the kind of Indian he tried to convince

12. See, for example, the stories in *Red Hunters and the Animal People*. Not only do many of Eastman's Indians speak in racial stereotypes, but the author also equates rattlesnakes with "the negro in the South—he was permitted to dwell in the same town, but he must not associate with the other two [races] upon equal terms" (1904, 126). Later, the rattlesnake family is described as always loafing about (1904, 129). Clearly, African Americans were not equal to Indians in Eastman's view.

us he was not, completely ignoring his Euro-American heritage, preferring to excise any Euro-Americanness as though it pollutes Eastman's writings.

Nerburn's liberties with Eastman's texts bring us to another dilemma, unanswerable here, in regard to the ownership of Eastman's texts. Because no living heirs have renewed Eastman's copyright, his works are now in the public domain. In fact, four of his books are now part of Project Gutenberg on the Internet, which makes common ownership texts available to anyone with access. In many ways, such free and common access to his texts is good. Now more people can benefit from Eastman's insights. But such freedom also allows people such as Nerburn to rearrange Eastman's texts as they see fit, completely altering the pattern of stories that Eastman had originally chosen, thus changing their reception and their message. Perhaps such alteration does not harm, but it is a concern worth investigating.

Was Eastman a conquered Indian—a man overwhelmed so much by Euro-American values that he could not overcome them to remain an "authentic" Sioux? Or was he a man of two cultures, two cultures so distinct from each other to most people that they assume he had to make a choice and accept one or the other? Or was he bicultural, a hybrid, if you will—a product of more than one culture, a man who could blend the two and their literary traditions to create a new literary form?

Eastman would probably opt for being called bicultural. Eastman was no longer the traditional Dakota, nor was he merely an "apple"—red on the outside, white on the inside. Eastman was a man who could have survived in either world, and did, going on to merge the cultures in the best way he could for himself, and, in the process, doing what he could for his primary Sioux culture. He accepted many Euro-American values, but he never fully assimilated into the mainstream culture, having "found a new sense of identity and spiritual renewal as an 'Indian'" when he conducted his anthropological fieldwork for the University of Pennsylvania Museum (Miller 1978, 63). He seems to have realized, at least by the time he was older, that he liked being an Indian as much as he enjoyed being "American." Repeatedly, in *Deep Woods* and other works, he parallels similar beliefs and values held by the two cultures. Peterson argues that Eastman and George Sword, another Sioux writer, forged a "*different* narrative pattern" that is "initially Sioux" but which "draw[s] on both Christian and Lakota beliefs to demonstrate the syncretisms of the two" belief systems (1996, 181), and, as I extend Peterson's argument, to create a modernist collage-like, interstitial literary tradition from the Sioux and the Euro-American traditions. Eastman, after all, was not that much unlike contemporary European immigrants, who acculturated by choice, often losing languages, religious practices, and fashions in favor of what they saw as "American." Often unknowingly, however, natives and immigrants alike influenced changes in American perceptions and values, even in literature.

Eastman desired such influence through his writings and speeches not only on Euro-American perceptions of Indians, but also on Indian perceptions of Christianity and civilization. But first he had to convince himself of his own desired images of these things. Thus, he must acknowledge the multiplicity of both cultures, so that both Indians and whites have savage capacities, as well as are capable of being noble spiritualists and teachers, using, of course, the stereotypes of his day. In *Deep Woods* he achieves this complexity most effectively, although *The Soul of the Indian* is Eastman's only book that rivals the religious/spiritual popularity of *Black Elk Speaks*.

September 1876, when Eastman reached Beloit College, was "less than three months after Custer's gallant command was annihilated by the hostile Sioux." Notably, the Seventh Cavalry is gallant and the Sioux hostile, even though two of Eastman's uncles were participants in the fight. Yet, while at Beloit, because the townspeople mistakenly believe Eastman is Sitting Bull's nephew, he is followed in "the streets by gangs of little white savages, giving imitation war whoops" (1977, 53).

It seems ironic, later, that Eastman would argue that he needs to switch colleges because Beloit has accepted other Sioux as students and he feels "that [he] might progress faster where [he] was not surrounded by [his] tribesmen" (1977, 58). He never completely justifies this reasoning, although it seems quite probable that Eastman needed to be *the* Indian on campus to feel secure in his importance, mentioning later that he was able to have protracted discussions about "the Indian standpoint in sociology and political economy" because he was then *the* expert on the subject (1977, 68). Despite possible resentments or fear of contemporary Indian scholars—which he does not seem to exhibit in other of his writings, such as those in *The American Indian Magazine,* which was edited by Bonnin—he credits his uncle as being "a positive genius" in his observations about natural history (1977, 68).

Although spiritually he thought it best to seek enlightenment "in silence, in the deep forest or on the height of the mountain," as is the Sioux way (1977, 26), he also felt merely thinking and speaking in English made him act like a white man (1977, 58). Even though he admitted to "some disadvantages connected with this mighty civilization" (1977, 62), such as letting the poor and elderly lose "their self-respect and dignity" (1977, 147), he also, like Bonnin, admires its literature (Eastman 1904a, 592). Although he balks at the self-respect and dignity taken, for instance, from a "pretty Dakota maiden" forced to attend Dr. Alfred L. Riggs's school in Nebraska against her will—a scene that made Eastman's "blood boil" (1977, 45)—he is awed by the realization that "nations, tongues, and civilizations, as well as individuals, have lived and died" and are brought to life again through books (1904a, 592). Eastman accepts acculturation as his particular path in life, but, naturally, detests seeing someone else forced against her will to accept the same life.

As a civilized warrior, Eastman's first encounter as "an object of curiosity . . . was not a pleasant feeling" (1977, 21). Yet, later, he deliberately switches colleges so he can remain a unique phenomenon and be an object of curiosity. Even in 1890, when he becomes "a 'white doctor' who was also an Indian [he is still] something of a novelty" (1977, 76). Eastman saw himself as *the* representative of the Dakota people, throwing himself fully into the role as the warrior in full battle regalia, which he often wore to speaking occasions. Even though Eastman probably began to enjoy such attention, accepting the title of the best of the best, he became aware of the responsibilities involved in being *the* best example of an acculturated Indian. One responsibility was giving his audience what it wanted.

Hertha Wong claims that Eastman's use of metaphors of nature, as comparison of how he felt in the stages of his acculturation, "emphasize[s] his Sioux identity" (1992, 146). While such an emphasis does come across, Wong fails to realize that these metaphors are more than a natural comparison for the man who was once a "wild" Indian who lived outdoors. She also fails to acknowledge that the use of natural metaphors is not uncommon in other cultures. They are, though, devices most contemporary readers would have stereotypically expected from an Indian writer (and sometimes still do). Eastman, a man who believed the culture he was raised in was vanishing from the face of the earth, would also have been compelled to preserve for his children, his original audience, the aura, if not the essence, of what it felt like to be an Indian, one who had "missed the demoralizing influences of reservation life" (1977, 59).

He does cave in occasionally to the stereotypical expectations brought about by dime novels about the West. Some of his Indians say "ugh" and "how." And he often refers to them as savages with savage minds. But the word "savage" may have meant several things to Eastman. He often touched on what he called "the racial mind," contact with which was refreshing for him compared to the tunnel vision he often found in non-Indians (1977, 150). In fact, Eastman found and admired this same type of racial mind in the "Yankees of the uneducated class," because they were "very Indian-like in their views and habits; a people of strong character, plain-spoken, and opinionated" (1977, 66). Gerald Vizenor argues that Eastman was teasing "the antiselves of evolutionism" when he describes Indians as savage and uncivilized (1994, 49), which can also be seen as further proof of Eastman's deliberate parody of anthropological writing.

He also wanted to capture for his children, who must live in this new era for the Indian, the sense that they belonged, as mixed in culture as they must have felt, to this world. Eastman reflects at Dartmouth: "thinking of the time when red men lived here in plenty and freedom, it seemed as if I had been destined to come view their graves and bones. No, I said to myself, I have come to continue that which in their last struggle they proposed to take up, in order to save themselves from extinction" (1977, 65). Eastman realizes, profoundly in the vein of doom in which most of his contemporaries viewed Indian culture, that history exists and civilizations rise and fall, so that, as he studies literature and history, "civilization began to loom up before [him] colossal in its greatness" (1977, 69), even as he assumes "the day of the Indian had passed forever" (1977, 62).

Eastman would not completely give up the Indian culture that had nurtured him, and he worked to preserve it for his children, all the while convincing his contemporaries and future generations that Indians were not that unlike Euro-Americans, thus not a threat, but an asset, to American society. His stories and essays bring the Dakota way of life, in particular, directly home to his readers, so that they might experience a bit of Indian life to develop an appreciative taste for it. His articles, such as "My People: The Indian's Contribution to the Art of America" and "What Can the Out-of-Doors Do for Our Children?", and his nonfiction books, such as *Indian Heroes and Great Chieftains* and *The Indian To-Day,* describe Indians and their cultures in more authentic detail than non-Indians probably would have read, thus helping signify the importance of an authentic view of Indian life. And this two works of fiction, *Old Indian Days* and *Red Hunters and the Animal People,* though racially stereotypical in some ways, bring out the traditional Indian views of life and make vital the native connection with the natural world and among one another, preparing paths of acceptance for more complex views of Indian life from later Indian writers.

Eastman set out on the warrior's path, intent on learning the white man's ways. Learning to use Euro-American words and publishing media, including Euro-American/Dakota forms of public speaking, to spread an appreciation of the culture of his childhood, to ease Indian transitions into Euro-American culture, and to demonstrate that there are similarities in values between the two cultures seems to have justified his Dakota name, Ohiyesa, "the winner." Ray Wilson, Eastman's biographer, views Eastman's life more pessimistically. After the failure of his marriage and other ventures, "Eastman withdrew—a very Indian thing to do. He could no longer live the expectations of others in the white world; he could no longer return to the deep woods. He lived instead alone and on an island, his most symbolic act" (1983, 193).

But interest in Eastman has been rekindled. A very influential modern Indian writer—present at the beginning and very influential throughout most of the Sioux Literary Renaissance—Eastman was an appealing and sought-after orator in his day, and an appealing writer today. Eastman is also important as a human being, a Dakota fighting the seemingly endless battle for the preservation of his first culture by combining its literary traditions with Euro-American ones. He was the fire starter of the Sioux Literary Renaissance, even as he followed in the footsteps—sometimes taking two or three strides where predecessors took one—of earlier Indian autobiographers and writers. In the light of that fire, Eastman's writings, his legacy to us, for us, can now be better appreciated.

Luther Standing Bear
From Standing Bear's *Land of the Spotted Eagle,*
University of Nebraska Press, 1978.
Courtesy University of Nebraska Press

3

"AS LONG AS YOU THINK I CAN'T,
I WILL SHOW THAT I CAN"

Luther Standing Bear's Quest for Honor

*I*t is highly probable that Luther Standing Bear had either read or heard about the writings by Charles Eastman. There are several reasons for such an assumption. Standing Bear's memoir, *My Indian Boyhood* (originally published in 1931), imitates Eastman's *Indian Boyhood* (1902), while clearly differing from it; whereas Eastman's is a generic title that could imply anyone's Indian boyhood experiences, Standing Bear's is clearly his own. Standing Bear counters Eastman's descriptions of games, feasts, and ceremonies with more specificity. His *Stories of the Sioux* (originally published in 1934) concern more "firsts," like those in Eastman's autobiographies, reflecting one of the most common Lakota themes, which stems from the honor carried by counting first coup on an enemy. Standing Bear's writings demonstrate his deep concern for upholding his Lakota honor, attempting to clearly prove that he deserves the title of chief. While Eastman was more creative in his writings, Standing Bear's anthropological details, assisted in part by Prof. Melvin Gilmore and Warcaziwin in *Land of the Spotted Eagle* (1978) and by E. A. Brininstool in *My People the Sioux* (1975), are more thorough, although not always more accurate, than anything Eastman provided. Excerpts from Standing Bear's works are quoted almost as extensively as those from Chief Seattle's speeches and *Black Elk Speaks*. Perhaps because his writings are not as literarily dextrous in Euro-American literary views, his writings do strongly demonstrate literary traditions among the Lakota. His works are well worth examining in the light of the strength of his authority and the strengths of his Sioux literary traditions.

Standing Bear takes the time to separate his works from Eastman's, because it was important to him that he not only be believed, but also be known as the best authority on Sioux culture. To procure that sense of authority, he emphasizes the Sioux storyteller's need for corroboration, and highlights the Sioux concerns for honor and prestige, asserting in a traditional Lakota manner that he, like Eastman, is from a family of good reputation and importance among the Sioux, even though he claims his writings were not done "with any idea of self-glory" (1975, preface). Although he freely gives information about typical Lakota practices, he practices the Sioux art of indirection when speaking about his family, especially about his wives and his parents' separation.

Even though his works are the least literary in Western terms of the five Sioux writers in this study, Luther Standing Bear's books are important primarily for what they show us about the Sioux literary tradition and about traditional Lakota values, which inform that literary tradition. Because he had less Euro-American-style education than his contemporaries Charles Eastman or Gertrude Bonnin, Standing Bear's approach to writing his books exhibits fewer Euro-American influences, therefore allowing his Lakota values and his knowledge of Lakota literary traditions to come to the foreground. Most important to Standing Bear in his writings are that he comes across as a worthy authority on his subject (carefully tallying Story Sticks in his favor), that he weds his audience to the belief of his authority through indirection and imitation of anthropological objectivity, that he emphasizes what is important through repetition, and that he proves himself worthy of the title of chief.

In his introduction to Standing Bear's *My People the Sioux*, Richard N. Ellis brings up several questionable points about Standing Bear's various claims, such as the facts that Luther repeatedly calls his father a chief, that he credits his father with talking the "hostiles" who retreated into the Badlands after the Wounded Knee massacre into surrendering,[1] and that

---

1. According to James Mooney in *The Ghost Dance Religion and Wounded Knee*, which was

he also gives his father credit for preventing the "hostile" chiefs, Spotted Tail and Red Cloud, from killing Crazy Horse. None of these claims, Ellis admits, are verifiable. The real controversy about them is that there is no historical evidence to substantiate the claims (1975, xv–xvi). Nor are there any but firsthand accounts, much like his own, to discredit them.

Similarly, we have only Standing Bear's word that he was made a chief after his father's death. Why is it important for Standing Bear that his reading public believe he is a chief, as well as believe he is the son of a very important Sioux chief? How does he go about convincing us he is truthful, at least as truthful as his memory allows?

First of all, it is highly probable that Luther's father was really a chief— at least a band chief,[2] meaning he was responsible for the welfare of a small group of families, probably no more than twenty to thirty family groups, although Standing Bear's own estimation of band size ranges

---

first published in 1896, the elder Standing Bear had been part of a party, along with American Horse and Little Wound, that had persuaded Striking Bear and Short Bull, who had fled to the Badlands with their people when frightened by the sudden insurgence of more than three thousand soldiers (1973, 850), to return peacefully to the Catholic mission near the Pine Ridge agency about one week before the Wounded Knee massacre (1973, 868). As Eastman points out, information corroborated by Mooney, the overly nervous Pine Ridge agent, D. F. Royer, newly installed in October 1890 at his post, had unnecessarily called in the troops, which Eastman believed "would be construed by the ghost dancers as a threat or a challenge, and would put them on the defensive" (1977, 98). Royer was described by Herbert Welsh, then president of the Indian Rights Association, in *Scribner's Magazine,* according to Mooney, as "a person . . . 'destitute of any of those qualities by which he could justly lay claim to the position—experience, force of character, courage, and sound judgment'" (1973, 848). Both Eastman and Welsh were correct in their assumptions, and Royer's paranoia caused the panic of most of the Sioux, ghost dancers and others, and led to the resulting hostilities. Luther could still be right about his father's participation in persuading the post-massacre refugees to turn themselves in, because most sources tend to list only a few chief names and gloss the rest with "and others." However, because he wrote *My People the Sioux* when he was at least sixty—nearly forty years after the massacre—he could be confusing his father's participation in persuading the initial "hostiles" held out in the Badlands with the postmassacre ones.

2. Richard N. Ellis asserts that Standing Bear's "father was undoubtedly a band leader" (1993, 142).

"from thirty or forty families to one hundred or more families, [with] a band of one hundred tipis or so being considered a large band" (1978, 120), perhaps exaggerating to further claim honor for his father. The elder Standing Bear, a Brule Sioux half-breed (1978, xiv–xv), was a member of the Wears Salt band (so called because a blind grandmother accidentally used salt instead of flour to make paints for the faces of a group of children (1978, 122–23). The struggle over whether he was indeed a chief primarily comes from non-Indian prejudicial beliefs—older than contact itself[3]—that there can be only one leader, one chief, to a tribe, when in fact there were several chiefs, each with separate (although sometimes overlapping) responsibilities. These responsibilities became more evident as the bands broke up into smaller units to increase foraging ranges, such as in winter when game was scarce. Paula Gunn Allen asserts that there were, at a minimum, always two "chiefs," or leaders, per band, the red or war chief and the white or inside chief, who, at least for the Indians of the Southwest, was usually a woman with the primary responsibility of moving and setting up camp efficiently and seeing to domestic situations should they arise (1992, 18–19). Leaders, emphasizes Marla Powers, accrued personal power and tribal respect because they exhibited the qualities, "generosity, fortitude, bravery, and hunting ability," that visibly demonstrated their connection to and respect for the spirits (1986, 26). Although there were leaders, most tribal decisions were made in council, where everyone who demonstrated such personal power and honor could freely speak after appropriate ceremonial pipe smoking, which often calmed nerves and cleared heads (M. Powers 1986, 127).

Important to Standing Bear is that his readers understand early on in *My People the Sioux* the importance of his father in the band. Standing Bear is meticulous in his descriptions of tepees and their varying sizes, pointing out that a poorer family, with fewer horses, could transport only a smaller tepee that required "only about two horses . . . on the move." A large tepee required at least six horses to move, so that "if a man wanted a large tipi,

3. Marla Powers reminds us that "the term 'chief' was not indigenous to the Oglalas; rather, it was a Euramerican term. Among the Sioux no leader existed who was supreme in all aspects of life" (1986, 29).

he must first be sure he had horses enough to move it." Standing Bear puts the equation before us: having many horses is considered being wealthy, because having more horses means the privilege of having a larger tepee, which in turn can accommodate more family members, such as multiple wives. Standing Bear the First's "tipi was the largest in our tribe." In fact it was so large that "when we made camp, all the rest of the tribe would camp at a distance, as they were afraid the wind might get too strong in the night and knock our tipi over them" (1975, 13). All this physical evidence is supposed to corroborate Luther's claim that his father was an important Lakota chief—one worth dealing with and hearing about.

If all this "factual" information is not enough, Standing Bear also includes a heroic story about his father in *Stories of the Sioux*, entitled "Standing Bear's Horse." The story is simple, but difficult to believe. His father, Standing Bear the First, as he calls him, encourages ten other warriors to accompany him on the warpath to "punish the enemy and to make them return to their own land" because they have been harassing the Sioux (1988b, 32). The part that is difficult to believe is that only Standing Bear the First chooses to ride a horse on this mission. The eleven warriors have a difficult time finding the enemy because "they wanted no open fights with the Sioux, who they knew were the bravest of brave fighters" (1988b, 32). As a result, the war party has to travel all the way to the edges of Sioux territory to engage and repel the enemy. On the way back, they discover the plains have been stripped of all life because of a prairie fire. Exhausted and starving, unable to go farther, the other warriors ask Standing Bear the First to kill his horse so they can eat it. After praying, Standing Bear the First climbs a hill with his horse only to discover a lone buffalo in the valley below. He quickly kills the buffalo and the warriors feast. The story ends with "In later years Standing Bear the First showed Standing Bear the Second the exact spot where the Great Mystery had placed the buffalo," which enables Luther to bring himself into the story, as well as adds a sense of "truth" to this story mixed in among Sioux legends. Truly, his father was a legendary figure to Luther.

Although touting one's heroic achievements was expected of Sioux warriors, hunters, and sacred men, allowing one man to rule their lives was an alien concept. The Euro-American insisted upon dealing with one over-

all chief or with a few major chiefs, such as for treaty agreements, oversim-
plifying the more complex tribal system under which the Sioux lived. It is
important to note that the Sioux, like most other tribes, were forced to
appoint a representative or group of representatives to act as head chief(s)
in a position of mediator—the negotiator for his people with the United
States government. Although such leadership was an alien concept to most
tribes (M. Powers 1986, 29), it eventually became the norm. The gradual
weakening and elimination of these chiefs led to the lessening and near
negation of the Sioux political voice, which Richard N. Ellis calls one of
the most important "method[s] of reducing cultural integrity" (1975, 144).
As a result, it was important for Standing Bear to reassert the power and
the voice of the Sioux Nation through his inherited standing as a chief. To
do so, to become the spokesperson for his people, Standing Bear has to
prove his worth for such a role, and his books, especially *My Indian Boyhood, Land of the Spotted Eagle* (originally published in 1933), and *My People the
Sioux* (originally published in 1928) are his testimony.

Standing Bear is carefully laying out for us devices like what the
Lakota called Story Sticks. Traditionally, when Lakota men gathered in the
council hall, or Tipi Iyokihe, for some leisure, men who were known to
have had exceptional adventures were asked to tell their stories. As each
man finished his story, "a tally-stick taken from a bundle kept in the Tipi
Iyokihe for that purpose . . . was stuck in the ground upright, the narrator
being entitled to a stick for every adventure which he could truthfully
relate" (1978, 127). The man with the most stories to tell was most revered
because "in this way the listeners lived over the thrills of the adventurous
ones and indelible records were printed in the minds of the youths" (1978,
127). This type of storytelling—*woyakapi*, or true stories (Wong 1992, 125)—
involves a narrator conveying important information to an audience that
needs the information to live productively after hearing (or, in this case,
reading) the content, which illustrates the significance of a particular person, event, or place (Allen 1983, 46). Standing Bear's *woyakapi* expands to
discuss not only himself, but also his father, their people, and their
homeland.

So there are several possible reasons why Standing Bear might have
wanted to make his father appear more important to the Sioux Nation

than he might have been in actuality. Standing Bear was following, after all, in Eastman's literary footsteps—and Eastman had billed himself as the best Indian from the best family of the best tribe. So, not unlike many non-Indian cultures, part of a Lakota's reputation as a man of honor started with his father's reputation. In *My People the Sioux,* we are introduced to his father's important status very early on: "I was the first son of Chief Standing Bear the First" (1975, 3). This theme of being the first runs heavily throughout Standing Bear's books, from Luther's being the first Sioux boy to enter the Carlisle school grounds, to being the first Sioux to work in a position on the reservation "where he could compete with the white people" (1975, 243), who were the only people legally allowed to work for the government as Indian agents. He argues that his father "was the greatest chief who ever lived the lives of both the Indian and the white man" and "was the first man to see the need of day schools on the reservations" (1988a, 4).

Of course, his father's reputation also depended on that of his father, "One Horse, who was a great chief and [Luther's] grandfather" (1988a, 3). One Horse had captured so many spotted horses by the time of his son's birth, he named him Spotted Horse (1975, 3). Young Spotted Horse became the first Standing Bear after he gained the first coup on a Pawnee, and was also wounded by him, who was so brave and fiercesome that no one, at first, dared get close to him. After this brazen display of valor, the newly named Standing Bear, in honor of his bravery, was also made a chief (1975, 4–6).

Like Eastman, Standing Bear works very hard to establish the fact that he came from a very noteworthy family. Not only were his father and grandfather chiefs, but his mother was Pretty Face, who "was considered the most beautiful young woman among the Sioux at the time she married my father" (1975, 3). He elevates her to quite a status, not merely the most beautiful of their band or of Spotted Tail's tribe, but of the whole Sioux nation.

Although such aggrandizing posturing, albeit via the indirect route of connection with important individuals, might seem artificial and might seem to provide a reason to look askance at Standing Bear's grounding in reality, it is a traditional warrior touch—a way to get one's listeners to believe one is an authority because one is worthy of such respect. Traditionally, however, such a storyteller would have handy witnesses to corroborate the stories told and to uphold the speaker's authority (Brumble 1988, 26–27; Wong 1992, 122). It was important to the Lakota warrior that his deeds be publicized (Brumble 1988, 27), but it was vain for him to do so without being asked or without having verifiable witnesses, which was a sign of arrogance (1978, 129). As a writer, Standing Bear has no such authorizing support. He must resort to traditional autobiographical nuances to create his rapport of believability with his readers.

One such autobiographical validating touch is to prove someone else is in error concerning either the writer him or herself or about a concept close to the writer's expertise. Standing Bear denounces the Euro-American free and easy use of the word "chief" to describe any and every male Indian:

> Whenever an Indian leaves his reservation and comes among the white people to-day, either to go on the stage or in the moving pictures or with a Wild West show, he is always greeted with "Hello, Chief." This is most decidedly wrong. Suppose when you visited an Indian reservation, the Indians would say to you, "Hello, President," or "Hello, King." You would think it not only silly, but it would be most embarrassing. Then sometimes the white people call a woman of mixed blood "princess." How can that be right and proper when Indians have no kings or queens, and therefore can be no "princesses"? The highest title an Indian woman can receive is wife or mother. And where is there greater honor than that? (1975, 276–77).

By emphasizing how inappropriate it is to call all Indian males chief, Standing Bear wants us to believe he would never use the term lightly (he signed all the prefaces to his books Chief Standing Bear), going so far as to emphasize that, though there is great honor in receiving the title of chief, such an honor requires much self-sacrifice by the man who receives it (1975, 277).

Although Ellis and other critics do not consider Standing Bear's works "superb examples of literary art" (1975, xix), this passage concerning his opinions about non-Indians' casual ways of using titles for Indians is very

complex. Luther worked in movies and with Wild West shows, so he probably encountered being called "chief" often. How must this have made
him feel?

When Standing Bear worked for Bill Cody's Wild West show, his
father had already passed away (in 1898), leaving a "chief" gap for their
band. As the first son of Standing Bear the First, Luther should have been
in line for the position. Yet, he was not made a chief until after he returned in 1905. Why the delay? Perhaps he had to earn the title and because there were no more battles to be fought (other than legal ones),
Luther had to prove himself worthy some other way. He points out an
instance, in *Land of the Spotted Eagle,* wherein one man, who was designated
a chief by whites in Washington, did not *earn* the title from the Sioux
because he lacked "the traditional qualifications for a chief" (1978, 178).

In the passage regarding the misuse by non-Indians of the term
"chief," Standing Bear also elevates the status of chief, perpetuating the
erroneous belief that there was one chief over each tribe, possibly to put
the concept in terms his non-Indian readers would understand—president
and king. But, in doing so, he also elevates his status, thus his authority
and, hopefully, his believability. To Standing Bear, though, there seems to
be little difference between being a president and being a chief, comparing
Crazy Horse to the United States' first president by pointing out that
"George Washington gave England a lot of trouble, too" (1978, 178).[4]

Then, in the discussion on the misuse of the chief title, Standing Bear
reduces the status he just created by reminding his readers that the Sioux
have no kings, or queens, and thus no princesses. Both Eastman and Bonnin refer to young Indian women as princesses in several of their writings,
so that here Standing Bear is also counteracting a stereotype they helped
affirm. Because there is no such thing as an Indian princess (except in the
contemporary honorary sense at powwows and other tribal events), even

4. This comparison of a chief's status to that of the president's is not inaccurate, given
the fact that the U.S. government recognized Indian tribes as sovereign nations in 1830 when
"Chief Justice John Marshall [wrote] in the . . . Supreme Court case *Worcester v. Georgia* that
Indian tribes were 'distinct, independent, political communities' who retained at least limited rights of self-government" (Lazarus 1991, 17). Indian chiefs are, in effect, heads of state,
now that government limits each tribe to one leader.

though the men vie for positions and titles of honor, the women in traditional Sioux society had to settle for being wife or mother, according to
Standing Bear. In seeming anticipation of any New Woman's objections,
he then none too subtly challenges them to name a higher honor, failing
of course to note that being husband and father should also be enough
honor for men.

Certainly, part of Standing Bear's impulse to denounce the idea of
princesses comes from his need to assert his point of view is more correct
than previous perspectives on the subject. Zitkala-Sa used the term in
"Shooting of the Red Eagle" to refer to a chief's daughter (1985, 99). But
calling Indian women princesses is only one thing that he refutes. He also
tries to dispel the belief that women did anything more than defend their
homes and children. Although Eastman does assert that certain things,
such as walking on the hide of bear, wolf, or wildcat, are taboo for women,
the second half of Old Indian Days is devoted to telling women's stories,
with the women's deeds ranging from superior selflessness and modesty
(as are expected), to deeds of valor from warfare. To counter Eastman,
Standing Bear acknowledges that women could ride horses well (1978, 103),
that some women are so wakan that they are "allowed to make and decorate war shields for the warriors" (1978, 140), and that women are the
founders of peace (1978, 202) and symbols of sacredness and purveyors of
traditions, such as through the "Holy Woman," as Standing Bear calls
White Buffalo Woman, who brought the peace pipe and its ceremonies to
the Sioux (1978, 221). Yet, he argues that women never were warriors. At
most, in Standing Bear's stories, women are accidentally heroic, such as in
"The Woman Who Killed the Owl," in which a woman cooking an evening meal gets annoyed by a hooting owl, throws a bone at it, and kills a
Crow scout in doing so, and in "Grandmother and the Bear," in which a
woman protects herself and children who are picking turnips by pointing
an iron rod at a bear, which thinks the rod is a gun. It seems to have been
very important to Standing Bear that people believe his version of the
"truth" rather than Eastman's or Bonnin's.

While Standing Bear may have lost his appeal to some women readers
by limiting women's roles in Oyate life, he has spent considerable time
anticipating their, and his other readers', concerns about his sincerity.

Above all, he wants his readers to see how he always speaks with honor and proper decorum, as is expected of a Lakota. So he attempts, somewhat clumsily, to develop a sense of sympathy or at least an understanding within his readers to instill a belief that he is worthy of the title of chief.

For instance, the image of his first wife, Nellie DeCory, a newborn daughter, Alexandra Birmingham Cody Standing Bear, as a display for the Wild West show in England creates reader sympathy for them: "the work was very light for my wife, and as for the baby, before she was twenty-four hours old she was making more money than my wife and I together" (1975, 266).[5] Here is a mother and child, less than a day out of childbirth, working as a sideshow. Did, perhaps, Standing Bear, and Buffalo Bill Cody, believe the English would be impressed by the Indian woman and child's stamina?

Within four pages, however, little Alexandra dies—the first really sympathetic heart tug for readers—but Standing Bear does not dwell on her death, managing to cover her illness, her death, and her funeral in one paragraph (1975, 270). Then Standing Bear is in a train wreck and seriously wounded, which prevents him from joining the Wild West show for a second year (1975, 271–72). Upon his return home, his first son, little Luther Standing Bear the Third, dies (1975, 272) and Standing Bear must take his son's honored position as council drum-keeper, collecting sacrifices offered at dances. As when discussing the deaths of any of his male relatives, Standing Bear makes an effort to point out his son's generosity to validate "the great mourning throughout the tribe" at his son's passing (1975, 272). In a time-honored tradition, Standing Bear praises males/warriors for their sacrifices and nobility.

After these three tragedies, Luther is made chief. It is doubtful that many readers, despite his stereotypical oversight in regard to the importance of women, would have begrudged him his title of chief after witnessing his stoic grief. Through his selfless and untiring work as official interpreter and as an Indian manager for Bill Cody's Wild West show, in his quest to provide for his family despite the physical harm he endured, in

5. Such live "anthropological" exhibits were very popular in Victorian England and America. Revisit the discussion of these in the introduction.

his stoic, but appreciative sense of loss over his children, and in his generosity toward his people by having given away more than a thousand dollars of goods on the day he was made chief (1975, 276), he proved himself a man worthy of being a Lakota chief.

As both Eastman and Standing Bear emphasize, trying one's best to obtain such honor and respect was the primary emphasis in a Sioux boy's life skills training and social education. According to Marla N. Powers, the four virtues that were most important to the Lakota were generosity (wacantognaka), bravery (cante t'inza), patience (wacintanka), and wisdom (ksabyahan opiic'iya) (1986, 60). Demonstration of these four things would guarantee an individual the honor and respect Sioux children, both male and female, sought, so Standing Bear attempts to exhibit all four. He has to prove himself better than Eastman, for instance, because Eastman had, after all, been lauded by Euro-Americans as the best his culture had to offer modern America decades before Standing Bear rose to popularity. If he can prove himself more worthy of honor than Eastman, he will have proven that, even though less formally educated than Eastman, he is the better Sioux.

Unlike Eastman and Bonnin, Standing Bear's autobiographical accounts revolve around him primarily with very little description or development of the people with whom he associated, other than his father, accompanied by largely anthropological information about Lakota culture. He only occasionally brings in his first wife and children for emotional effects, and never mentions his second wife at all. His attention is primarily focused on the male aspects of being a Lakota, although in *Land of the Spotted Eagle,*[6] he spends considerable time describing kinship and gender-based roles.

Perhaps in his eagerness to "correct" information Eastman had given, such as Eastman's assertion that women's roles were more diverse than

---

6. The title *Land of the Spotted Eagle* refers both to the plains area where the Sioux traditionally lived, and to the land where the dead dwell in happiness. Many traditional Lakota believed the spotted eagle is the animal that carries the *wanagi,* or spirits of the dead, to this land of happiness and plenty, which is always located to the south (1978, 122).

were stereotypically depicted in Western novels and movies by giving several accounts about women's roles as warriors and chiefs, Standing Bear ends up contradicting himself on occasion. For instance, when discussing proper courting conduct, Standing Bear asserts that "good courting manners in Lakota youth forbade his calling at a young woman's tipi . . . and no presents were given until an engagement took place" (1978, 98). Yet, while describing how a young man might catch an opportunity to speak to the young woman, he describes how young men often followed girls home from ceremonies, with the mother passing "food to all the young men who stood or sat outside the tipi door waiting to speak to the girl" (1978, 105–6). Further, he notes that even while courting, young hunters "would go hunting and bring a buffalo to her father and brother"—a token present that proved the hunters could provide for a woman and her family (1978, 104). Eastman, in a much more brazen account, depicts a man inside a young woman's tent, "bending over her and gently pulling her robe, as a suitor is permitted to do to awaken his beloved" (1991, 46). Perhaps the difference marks the distinctions in customs between the Dakota and the Lakota, with the Dakota allowed inside the woman's tepee and the Lakota remaining respectfully outside.

What is further ironic about Standing Bear's negligence in providing details about specific women's lives, especially concerning his wives' or even his mother's influence on him, is his lament for the loss of "mother authority" among the Sioux because of Euro-American social influences. Traditional Lakota mothers were the only authorities who could sanction marriages, says Standing Bear, "being the nearest interested person. Had an utter stranger . . . been asked to receive the vows of the young people and sanction their marriage, it would have been an act without meaning to them" (1978, 109), clearly indicating a distrust of the Euro-American practice of being married by a priest or judge and giving credence to the stereotypical assumption that seems to occur in many cultures that mothers' ties to their children are stronger than the fathers'. Mother authority for the Lakota, according to Standing Bear, reflected social authority. Emphatically, Standing Bear argues that women should remain the sole educators of children:

Today mother-power is weak, scattered to many places—taken over by
the teacher, preacher, nurse, lawyer, and others who superimpose their
will. This loss applies also to the white mother, for she, too, is blinded
and confused by the intricacies of the society in which she lives. And the
incongruity of it all is that the child has not become individualized, but
has become stamped with the ideas of others. Few today are the youthful
individual thinkers and doers who dare step out of the ranks, for the
ranks close about them and try to force them to conform. (1978, 109)

Standing Bear's claims that Lakota children are much more individually oriented than Euro-American children would probably have been
highly contested in his day. As he admits, Lakota "boys were to be future
warriors and the girls were to be future mothers" (1978, 117), which would
seem to be a very rigid and narrow range of social expectations for both
genders. But what Standing Bear means by his references to individuality
is clarified later:

Though each person became individualized—could be as truthful, as
honest, as generous, as industrious, or as brave as he wished—could even
go to battle upon his own initiative, he could not consider himself as
separate from the band or nation. Tribal consciousness was the sole
guide and dictator, there being no human agency to compel the individual to accept guidance or obey dictates, yet for one to cut himself off
from the whole meant to lose identity or to die. (1978, 124).

A nonconforming individual within the group, especially in such a small
group as a band of fifteen or fewer families within possibly hostile territory, could upset the social balance, endangering everyone.

Mari Sandoz's observations on how the Sioux raised their children
corroborate Standing Bear's assertions about individuality. Sioux children,
according to Sandoz, learned to be independent by being adopted by a
second set of parents, who helped see the children's proper training and
kept them from being too emotionally attached or dependent on their
biological parents. They were thus provided with the extended support of
the second family, as well as all the "siblings" that came along with it.
Such a broad range of personal experiences allowed the Sioux child to

learn to make personal decisions at an early age, because, as Sandoz asserts, "no Sioux could tell anyone what to do" (1985, 36).

As for why roles were designated so clearly based on gender, Standing Bear simply says that "the division of labor [depended on] the best experience of the people," so that women tended to home matters—food, shelter, and clothing preparations—and men tended to more dangerous pursuits—hunting, scouting, and warfare (1978, 127). Most Sioux writers corroborate Standing Bear's assertions regarding the proper training of the genders for their roles within the community. Indirectly, Standing Bear's assertions about proper gender roles point toward his training as the son of a chief, who killed his first buffalo, but never made it to the warpath.

To assert that traditional Lakota training is an education, and to counter the argument that those who are not educated in schools are ignorant, Standing Bear points out the irony in the differences between Indian and non-Indian educational systems several times in his books:

> An [Indian] education could not be confined to a certain length of time nor could one be "finished" in a certain term of years. The training was largely of character, beginning with birth and continued throughout life. True Indian education was based on the development of individual qualities and recognition of rights. There was no "system," no "rule or rote," as the white people say, in the way of Lakota learning. Not being under a system, children never had to "learn this today," or "finish this book this year" or "take up" some study just because "little Willie did." Native education was not a class education but one that strengthened and encouraged the individual to grow. When children are growing up to be individuals there is no need to keep them in a class or in line with one another. (1978, 15)

While non-Indians learned in organized groups citizenship duties that required them to act as a group and to be conscious of commonalities, Lakotas learned customs, mores, survival skills, and spirituality as individuals, usually as a child at a parent's or grandparent's knee (Deloria 1996, 24). Although the individuals within each culture tested their strengths, especially in games, with other individuals, for Euro-Americans the competition was typically geared toward obtaining power and influence over others; for many Indians the competition was typically geared toward winning honor and respect, not necessarily power, from others.

The primary difference between the two educational philosophies, both of which called for several forms of self-sacrifice, was that the individual-based education for the Sioux youth was to ensure the survival of his people, and the group-oriented education of the Euro-American youth was to ensure his individual survival and, often, his monetary success. Whereas the Euro-American might sacrifice sleep and self-respect to climb the corporate ladder, the Indian sacrificed his worldly goods, which sometimes meant his family's food, to see that all in his band survived and lived as comfortably as possible. These beliefs are inherent in the two culture's religious ideals, as well. In Christianity, one must seek salvation, have an individual relationship with Christ as the foremost thing in her or his life, as an individual, to reap the rewards of heaven. In traditional Lakota religion, "beliefs concerning a hereafter . . . range from a belief in an unspecified place in which the spirits of human and animals live in a world reflective of the 'real' world, to the idea that there is no hereafter, but that all spirits reside visibly and invisibly near the place of their kinsmen" (W. Powers 1977, 51).

This oversimplification of the cultures glosses over much, however, because a larger difference that should be noted and conceded is that traditional Lakota life revolved around the transience of a hunter/gatherer tribal society wherein the accumulation of goods was impractical, and which allowed the whole tribe to move to where food or goods could be obtained when supplies ran low; meanwhile, Euro-American life revolved around establishing a permanent residence, which allowed and possibly encouraged the accumulation of material goods, partly from fear of less productive times when food or goods would be harder to obtain. As Standing Bear and others attest repeatedly, Indian wealth was measured not only in how much they could afford to give away to others, but also in how much they were able to keep. Horses, tools, clothes, tepees, wives, and numbers of living children all contributed to the tribe's image of an individual male. Many tepees surrounded by many horses attested to the wealth in game and foraging of the surrounding environment, as well as the hunters' abilities to provide food for the large number of people. Such a large gathering could not be sustained long before game shied away and the grass became eaten or trampled. But, while such a group was together, few enemies dared invade.

However, "the fame of a band rested upon its braves and honored men rather than upon the number of tipis, horses, or other goods it might possess" (1978, 132). Men who were honored for their deeds and good judgment were allowed to influence or to sway the band's decisions, although that influence could be removed if the advice given proved dangerous or costly in some way. The primary sense of honor is thus primarily gained through what a Lakota does for others.

For both Sioux and Euro-American cultures, obtaining these goals—influence through power or respect through honor—meant achieving that culture's status as a responsible adult. As Standing Bear admits,

> I thrived upon the thought of achievement and approval and I do not think that I was an unusual Indian boy. Dangers and responsibilities were bound to come, and I wanted to meet them like a man. I looked forward to the days of the warpath, not as a calling nor for the purpose of slaying my fellowman, but *solely to prove my worth to myself and my people.* (1978, 14; emphasis mine)

This goal—providing his worth to himself and to his people through bravery, *cante t'inza*—compelled him to take up a role that seemed lost—being a chief to his nation. Although Standing Bear left the reservation to live elsewhere and do other work, such as act in movies, he returned, later in life, to the reservation to witness the deplorable conditions into which his people had fallen.[7] This visit to Pine Ridge convinced him to do what he could under the circumstances to guide his people—both the Sioux with whom he was born and the Euro-Americans with whom he lived and worked—into a better understanding and, he hoped, a better life. To do so, he had to draw on his Lakota training.

Clearly differentiating between the two culture's educational systems

7. Richard Ellis says, "Standing Bear was shocked by the physical and mental status of the reservation Sioux. If his visit did not serve as a catalyst for the writing of [this book], it undoubtedly confirmed and strengthened previously formed opinions . . . and convinced him of the need to educate the American people about the strengths of traditional Sioux culture" (1975, i).

is important for Standing Bear, who, like Eastman, experienced both culture's educational practices. As Ella Deloria describes in *Waterlily,* and as
Standing Bear emphasizes in *Spotted Eagle,* Lakota teaching methods were
aimed at teaching by pointing out "the rules of behavior toward one another" and supplying examples, not through humiliation (Deloria 1996, 34).
Indirectly demonstrating appropriate behavior, instead of exacting punish-
ment to create a sense of humility, starts even before children can speak,
with the parent or grandparent redirecting an older child's behavior as an
example for the toddler (Deloria 1996, 36).

Not until Standing Bear attended Carlisle did he experience humiliation. The Carlisle teacher demanded the student, when reading a passage
written in English, read the passage until it was read correctly. Instead of
praising their efforts, the teacher questioned each student's reading, asking
the student if she or he thought the passage had been read correctly. Still
uncertain of their command of the language,

> One after another the pupils read as called upon and each one in turn
> sat down bewildered and discouraged. My time came and I made no
> errors. However, upon the teacher's question, "Are you sure that you
> have made no error?" I, of course, tried again, reading just as I had the
> first time. But again she said, "Are you sure?" So the third and fourth
> times I read, receiving no comment from her. For the fifth time I stood
> and read. Even for the sixth and seventh times I read. I began to tremble
> and I could not see my words plainly. I was terribly hurt and mystified.
> But for the eighth and ninth times I read. It was growing more terrible.
> Still the teacher gave no sign of approval, so I read for the tenth time! I
> started on the paragraph for the eleventh time, but before I was through,
> everything before me went black and I sat down thoroughly cowed and
> humiliated *for the first time in my life* and in front of the whole class! (1978,
> 16–17; emphasis mine)

Standing Bear effectively makes his readers bear the humiliation as well,
forcing us to follow his efforts numerically through each reading. In such a
laborious way, he helps us achieve at least a small sense of what he went
through during the class session, exhibiting not only his bravery, *cante
t'inza,* but also his patience, *wacintanka.*

Later, when he attended the weekly Saturday school meetings, Luther still feared reprimand. He thought Captain Pratt would announce his failure before the student body. Standing Bear was surprised when Pratt proclaimed that Luther had read his teacher's reading test eleven times in succession and correctly every time. Luther was elated at the praise because he "truly liked General Pratt[8] and words of praise from him meant a good deal. . . . But in spite of the praise that I received that day and the satisfaction I have had in all these years in knowing that I was a good student, I still have the memory of those hours of silent misery I endured in childish misgivings" (1978, 18).

Yet, the students were not the only ones humiliated by the Euro-American educational system designed for the Indians. Before any of the children learned English, a woman tried to teach them how to play reeded "horns." Though she attempted to communicate by gesture, when she demonstrated wetting the reed, the boys misunderstood and began spitting into their instruments. The teacher got so frustrated and discouraged that she ended up crying, while the boys sat and "waited for her to get through" (1975, 148).

To Standing Bear, such misery endured by people at the mercy of a social construction not geared toward empowering individuals is questionable policy, and not a demonstration of wisdom, *ksabyaban opiic'iya.* Yet, he does not directly say so, only implying his viewpoint through the indirect use of examples. Only later, in the latter part of *Spotted Eagle,* does Standing Bear fully confront the wrongs he feels Euro-American culture has imposed on American Indians.

The primary good that Standing Bear seems to have acknowledged in having attended Carlisle was twofold: experiencing non-Indian ways of living to compare them with Indian living in order to arm himself for the future, and being able to meet children whom he would have, at an earlier time, considered enemies, such as the Pawnee boy Luther befriended after he was captured, and whom he met again later at Carlisle. This twofold

---

8. Standing Bear refers to Captain Pratt as General Pratt, perhaps because of a lapse in memory, but also possibly because the higher rank makes words of praise from Pratt more important.

experience benefited Indians who were going to have to deal with attempts at forced assimilation, because it equipped them with knowledge of how non-Indians think and live, and it forced them to join with other Indians, leading to the pan-Indian movement of the early twentieth century.

The further one reads in *Spotted Eagle,* the more one notices Standing Bear's tone becoming increasingly condemning of things Euro-American. In one of his most biting indictments of Euro-American culture and its assumption that Indians are better off assimilating to it, Standing Bear asks, "Has the white man's social order been so harmonious and ideal as to merit the respect of the Indian, and for that matter the thinking class of the white race?" (1978, 251). This was a legitimate question, which had not been asked before, at least so openly. Such a direct attack or challenge is also very Sioux-like. Warriors often used tales to taunt or challenge their peers to draw out confessions or to goad others into action to prove the challenge wrong (Brumble 1988, 29). Here, then, Standing Bear challenges Euro-Americans to right their wrong way of thinking and acting toward Indians.

More directly than any of the other Sioux writers examined herein, Standing Bear argues for a return to tribal ideals, including customs, religion, and dress, all of which, he points out, have survived the attempted extraction or elimination of them by the dominating race: "Had the Indian been as completely subdued in spirit as he was in body he would have perished within the century of his subjection. But it is the unquenchable spirit that has saved him—his clinging to Indian ways, Indian thought, and tradition, that has kept him and is keeping him today" (1978, 190).

In many ways, Standing Bear's imitations of anthropological accounts are corrections of the more objective, thus not personally connected or socially accountable, anthropological narratives popular among ethnologists at the turn of the twentieth century. As Brumble points out, many Indians believed anthropological narratives made Indians merely "artifacts . . . of the dominant culture" (1988, 22). To keep anthropology from stealing humanity from Indians, Standing Bear works hard in his books to not only justify how the Lakota think and live, but also to demonstrate the worthiness of such thought and actions.

One way of demonstrating and clarifying Lakota values is when

Standing Bear repeatedly confronts language as it is used by Euro-Americans in a Sioux-like indirect way, such as his discussion of the words "chief" and "princess." When defending "'going back to the blanket'" as a viable approach to living in modern America, Standing Bear says that "the Indian blanket or buffalo robe, a true American garment, [is] worn with the significance of language[;] covered beneath it, in the prototype of the American Indian, [is] one of the bravest attempts ever made by man on this continent to rise to heights of true humanity" (1978, 191). The significance of language, for Standing Bear, is not just what is written in books, because "countless leaves in countless books have robbed a people of both history and memory" (1978, 27). Language, as the basis for communication, reflects culture and status; in the case of the blanket, something that had to be traded for either from Southwestern Indians or Euro-Americans, the more elaborately woven and more brilliant the colors, the more the blanket spoke of the significance of the wearer because he would have had to pay dearly, such as with a horse, for it. Even though Standing Bear uses writing to communicate with Indians and non-Indians alike, recognizing the ability of the written word to transmit information at a distance, he still feels the most important stories are those recorded in memory "of interest or importance, some happening that affected the lives of the people" that "taught the virtues" and conveyed ideas "of pure fancy," because "a people enrich their minds who keep their history on the leaves of memory" (1978, 27). Standing Bear recognized that, as Indians became more increasingly educated in Euro-American schools, their sense of value for their native cultures would be diminished by the assertion of Euro-American values for written literature over the merits of oral tales. Because of Standing Bear's admiration for oral literature, much of the tone of his books, even when he is being anthropological, is informal and conversational, with several attempts at directly addressing his audiences, both Indian and non-Indian.

Even though many scholars dismiss Standing Bear's works as being of no literary importance, more so than the other writers of his time, Standing Bear uses the traditional Lakota indirect approach to assert his authority, to validate his claims, and to create interest and, he hopes, belief in his subject. Parts of all his books are anthropological. Because of this anthropological stance, which sometimes seems to overwhelm his autobiographical attempts, he reveals in fact very little about his personal life, especially of his experiences post-Carlisle. Unlike Eastman, however, Standing Bear's use of the "objective" anthropological third-person point of view is not an attempt to parody anthropologic writings, but to validate his own point of view, demonstrating he can view Lakota culture objectively, to correct misinformation, and, more subtly, to eliminate the need to discuss matters he feels should remain private.

Nowhere in any of his books does he discuss the fact that he married more than once, for instance. Even early on in *My People,* he downplays significance of his mother's choosing to leave his father after Chief Standing Bear the First takes two more wives—an event we learn about indirectly:

> One day my mother went to see her mother, who lived some little distance from us. . . . When night came and she did not return for supper, I did not cry. Some other women came to our tipi, and they were very good to me. . . . Some days afterward, one of my uncles . . . took me to see my mother. . . . She never mentioned to me about going back to my father, and, in fact, never thought of returning. One day, when I was playing outside, my father called for me. I went home with him, and he gave me a horse and all the things necessary to make a man of me. When I went inside the tipi, the two women were still there, and they both called me "son." (1975, 28)

In a very traditional way, no one makes an issue out of Pretty Face's decision, although the families seemed to continue to manipulate Luther between the two camps with both sides offering him gifts and pampering. Also in this indirect way the reader learns about family structures, because Standing Bear points out that all his stepbrothers and stepsisters, as well as his cousins, are called brother and sister (1975, 29).

Standing Bear's discussions of his first wife, Nellie DeCory, are brief and rather cryptic,[9] possibly because of Lakota standards of decorum in which one never reveals or shares private information, such as what animal

---

9. Richard N. Ellis also points out "impotant gaps in [*My People the Sioux*], particularly relating to his marriages and to his activities in Los Angeles" (1993, 151).

is one's spirit guide, any private song created for private occasions (such as love or medicine songs), and even one's name. It is possible that he did not dwell on their life together because he was writing about her while married to his second wife, May Splicer (Ellis 1993, 149). For whatever reason, he encapsulates the courtship with Nellie: "There was a half-breed girl in the camp of whom I began to be very fond. We took many long walks together. She was very gentle and quiet" (1975, 198–99). He takes more time to illuminate her parentage, as is Lakota custom, and her father's wealth, which would make her more appealing, I assume, to his white readers:

> Her mother was a full-blood Indian woman, who could neither read nor write. Her father was a full-blood white man[, De Cory, who] was one of the men who gathered up all the things the Indians threw away, not realizing their value. But De Cory did, and he sold them, and in that way made considerable money . . . one of the wealthiest men on the reservation. (1975, 199)

Standing Bear later emphasizes his father-in-law's generosity:

> He came to the house one day with his wagon loaded with all kinds of food and greases, such as we used in making Indian fried bread. One whole hog was killed and dressed for us, and we were very busy getting it in shape so it would not spoil. . . . [He] gave us five head of cows to start with. Then he picked out a very fine team of matched horses and two mares. (1975, 202)

He also emphasizes that Nellie's Indian mother raised all her children "as 'white' as she knew how" (1975, 199), perhaps to show his readers that his wife was almost as acculturated into a Euro-American lifestyle as he was.

But most of Luther's attention is focused not on his new bride but on the controversy entailed in his choice of bride, because the two widows of Chief Spotted Tail try to force him into also marrying "their daughter Grace," because they are concerned that Nellie would not know how to take care of him properly because she was not brought up in the traditional Brule way (1975, 200). Standing Bear passes over his connections with Grace in *My People,* except to relate this incident. When he refuses, and has to have the women evicted from his house by the reservation police, Grace's brother becomes infuriated at the insult (1975, 201). To soothe Grace's brother, the elder Standing Bear gives him a few horses to save Luther any further trouble with the young man (1975, 202).

Significantly, this struggle with Grace and her mothers helps create the sense that Luther was in demand as a potential husband—one of the "best" catches, so to speak. In *Spotted Eagle,* Standing Bear describes his courtship with Grace. One evening he walked home from church with Grace and one of her mothers, who discreetly disappears inside while Grace and Luther talk under the cover of his blanket (the most discreet way for Lakotas to court). Customarily, when another suitor wants to spend time with the young woman and the previous suitor is taking too long, the one waiting indicates impatience by brushing the back of the courting blanket. When Luther gets this signal,

> Grace doubtless wanted to have some fun with me, so she wrapped her hand tightly in my watch-chain, as I was wearing civilian clothes under my blanket. Thus I was detained longer. But in a few moments I was forcibly reminded of Lakota courtesy by a decided kick on the back . . . that caused me to sway slightly forward. Here was a case where only the young lady could keep the others from piling on me, which she did. (1978, 101)

Exactly what Grace did to keep the other suitors at bay is a mystery, however, because Standing Bear discreetly returns to his discussion of courtship. The fact that she was highly sought after speaks to the importance of Luther's success in commanding her attention, however.

It is through *indirection* that Standing Bear achieves the creation of his status, and its believability, with his reading audience. He cannot directly assert his authority or importance, because, to the Lakota, "bragging was a social sin" (1978, 104). Standing Bear uses a traditional Lakota belief that showing one's "industry and worth" is far more believable than talking about it (1978, 104) to convince his readers of his credibility. He layers information about this custom for his readers in a gradual way.

Most important, Standing Bear takes his time in building up his collection of personal Story Sticks, the traditional Lakota way of validating his authority. He proves to his readers he has lived this life. He also emphasizes his worth, as a husband, as a father, as a manager for the Wild West show, and, especially, as a Lakota chief.

Standing Bear attempts, through his four books, to wield his chiefly powers by reminding his people what traditional Sioux life was like and why it has enough inherent value to be worth maintaining. Because chief power has been eliminated by the government on the reservations, and because Standing Bear sees nothing but depression and despair at Pine Ridge and Rosebud upon his return there, he feels the need to live up to the title bestowed on him by his band and his tribe. Through his books, because of their reflection of his values, because of his intimate knowledge of Sioux life, as well as his belief in it, because of his demonstrated worth as a chief, and because of the apparent need for leadership to guide the Sioux back to self-sufficiency and self-worth, Standing Bear assumes that responsibility, attempting to use his chiefly authority to resurrect the Oyate culture. Primarily because this sense of this authority is so strong in his writings, Standing Bear has become one of the most quoted American Indians, next to Chief Seattle and Black Elk. Because of this authority and because his writings clearly demonstrate some important aspects of the Sioux literary tradition, he is one of the most important transitional era Indians to examine.

Zitkala-Sa (Gertrude Bonnin)
From Zitkala-Sa's *American Indian Stories,*
University of Nebraska Press, 1985

4

WEAVING A MAGIC DESIGN

Gertrude Bonnin Creates a
New Literary Tradition as Zitkala-Sa

*I*f Charles Eastman can be seen as carrying out one of the dominant male Sioux roles by directing his life as though he were on the warpath, Gertrude Bonnin works to carry out her "feminine Dakota heritage" (Susag 1993, 8) by passing on, thus continuing, Oyate cultural values (Susag 1993, 21). Although scholars tend to focus on "the turmoil, hurt, anger, and frustration felt by a sensitive, talented American Indian woman" (Picotte 1985, xv), Zitkala-Sa's writings demonstrate the power and passion Indian women felt and exhibited in their lives and artwork. As Kelly Morgan points out, the onset of forced reservation life affected both men and women, but men were more greatly affected by the elimination of the hunting and warring traditions in their typical Oyate roles, whereas women continued to care for and influence their families, even though their individual spiritual, economic, and educational choices directed their "roles as culture bearers, as women" (1997, vii).

Bonnin drew on the powerful kinship influences with which her mother defined her early life and her inherited understanding of Indian symbolism and mythology, as well as her acquired knowledge of Western myths, to create a literary art form that helped her balance the passions and concerns she felt for both Indian and Western cultures. Although her writings reflect fewer Euro-American values than Eastman's, Zitkala-Sa demonstrates through her stories how the Sioux had already assimilated into their daily lives Euro-American goods and tools, such as writing, which complemented their culture.

Despite the brevity of Bonnin's literary career, especially when compared with Eastman's or Deloria's, she managed to combine Sioux literary traditions with Euro-American ones as effectively as, if not more thoroughly than, either Eastman or Deloria. Like Eastman, Bonnin at first wrote both autobiographical essays and short stories, later merging her literary talents with political rhetoric to write more blatantly political open essays and appeals, seeking equity and suffrage for Indians. Her earlier essays and fiction, however, as Dorothea Susag argues, "contradict the myths of powerless victimization, language inadequacy, and feminine impotence" believed of Indians in general and Indian women in particular (1993, 21), and incorporate Oyate cultural values and literary traditions to alter "Judeo-Christian discourse and ideology," upon which Western cultural values and literary traditions are based (1993, 22), creating a modernist type of collage. Much as literary scholars had to become familiar with such myths as the Fisher King to understand the less obvious meanings in T. S. Eliot's epic poem *The Waste Land*, scholars must learn about aspects of Sioux culture—such as its myths and legends, the importance of Indian women's symbolic art, the strength of kinship bonds, and the early material impact Euro-American culture had on Sioux living—to truly appreciate Bonnin's works.

Academic studies of Bonnin's life and works, like Eastman's, insist on seeing Bonnin's life in turmoil, as is reflected in her early writings. Mary Ann Stout claims that "Zitkala-Sa's life and writings are filled with confusion and contradiction" because she tried to remain wholly Dakota,[1] es-

---

1. As Dorothea Susag notes, Bonnin descends from the Nakota dialect–speaking branch of the Sioux, but always called herself a Dakota, as do contemporary residents of the Yankton Reservation (1993, 22, n. 2). It is possible that Bonnin, like many Sioux, saw the entire nation as a collective, despite dialectical differences, because her chosen pen name, Zitkala-Sa, is Lakota for red bird. Margaret Lukens unsuccessfully attempts to argue that Bonnin's choosing a name from the Lakota dialect instead of the Nakota dialect, which is the least dominant of the three dialects, "indicates a more profound dislocation from her origins" (1991, 168). To simplify concerns of proper labeling of Bonnin's heritage, I will alternately call her a Sioux, a Dakota, or a Yankton Nakota.

pousing values inherent in things Indian, especially Siouan, but advocating some assimilationist policies (1992, 16–17). Stout, like other scholars, cannot accept the idea that one can be Indian culturally—while taking a political stance for recognition of the values of Indian cultures have to offer—and still be wholly American. After all, what American fits the description of or *is* completely satisfied with everything "American"?

In a similar dichotomous stance, Deborah Welch assumes Bonnin "was increasingly being brought to a point where she would have to make a choice—the Indian world or the White," even though Zitkala-Sa sought compromise (1985, 13), a compromise that began for the Sioux as a nation when they first began trading with Euro-Americans and adopted Euro-American tools into their lifestyles. For Dexter Fisher, "language became the tool for articulating the tension [Bonnin] experienced throughout her life between her heritage with its imperative of tradition and the inevitable pressure of acculturation" (1985b, 204). According to Fisher's dissertation, Bonnin was

> Controversial to the end . . . an enigma—a curious blend of civilized romanticism and aggressive individualism. To many traditional Indians, she was somewhat suspect because she took bits and pieces from various tribes where it suited her, as exemplified in the eclectic dress she wore for public speeches which combined Sioux beadwork with Navajo silver. To whites, she was irritating because she was efficient and unpredictable. . . . She often ridiculed the blind adherence of Indians to outmoded traditions of a past era; yet, at other times, she would vociferously defend their right to retain and preserve their culture. (1979, 25)

Perhaps, taking cues from Hazel Hertzberg's seminal work, *The Search for an American Indian Identity* (1971), Welch and Fisher seem to be reacting more to Bonnin's assertive personality, which inevitably caused conflicts with people unaccustomed to dealing with a strong-minded and strong-willed woman—let alone an Indian woman—than they are to her writings. Fisher calls Bonnin "headstrong and independent" (1985, xi); Welch believes Bonnin had "personality handicaps" (1985, 164); and Hertzberg has characterized Bonnin as needing to be a "one-woman show" (1971, 208). All three may be highlighting the vital urgency in tone founding many of

Zitkala-Sa's writings and speeches, but they appear to be paying more attention to biographical concerns, such as other people's reactions to Gertrude Bonnin, one of the primary political voices for transitional era Indians (Hertzberg 1971, 138). Fisher, for instance, oversimplifies the conflicts this way: "To her mother and the traditional Sioux on the reservation where she had grown up, she was highly suspect because, in their minds, she had abandoned, even betrayed, the Indian way of life by getting an education in the white man's world. To those at the Carlisle Indian School . . . she was an anathema because she insisted on remaining 'Indian'" (1985a, viii).

Fisher's dualistic description of the prejudices Bonnin faced as both a traditionally educated and a school-educated Indian overlooks several important points about Bonnin's life. First, she returned to the Yankton Reservation several times where the primary conflict Bonnin faced on the reservation was between herself and her full-blooded, older, half-brother, Peter St. Pierre, who inherited Gertrude's land allotment from her mother. Although the inheritance slight was primarily a familial falling out, Bonnin believed it was racially based, because she was possibly fathered by the Euro-American whose surname, Simmons, her mother took, although Fisher asserts she was fathered by a man named Felker (1985a, ix). St. Pierre was apparently successful in developing her mother's prejudices against Euro-Americans into a bias against Gertrude and her other half-brother, David[2] (D. Welch 1985, 61). The schism with and final rejection by her mother, Ellen Simmons, Tate I Yohin Win, only highlighted other rejections she had experienced in her life—from former fiancé Carlos Mon-

---

2. Fisher quotes a letter from Bonnin to Montezuma in which she calls David her half-brother, although Deborah Welch indicates they probably had the same father, Simmons (1985, 4). Bonnin recalls an incident, probably told to her by her mother, with her father, whom Fisher earlier said was Felker, a man who had deserted the family before Gertrude was born (1985a, ix): "Once my father scolded my brother, and my mother took such offense from it—that eventually it resulted in a parting—so as I grew I was called by my brother's name Simmons. I bore it a long time till my brother's wife—angry with me because I insisted upon getting an education—said I had deserted home and I might give up my brother's name 'Simmons' too. . . . Then I chose to make a name for myself—and I guess I have made 'Zitkala-Sa' known—for even Italy writes it in her language" (1985a, x).

tezuma, who told her her writings would make no difference (D. Welch 1985, 38), from influencial Carlisle founder Captain Pratt, who called her writings "'trash' and their author 'worse than pagan'" (D. Welch 1985, 27), and from officials of the Bureau of Indian Affairs who refused to provide Bonnin with a teaching position on the Ute Reservation while her husband was stationed there (D. Welch 1985, 73). These were the *personal* conflicts that affected Gertrude most profoundly.

It is unfortunate that scholars would choose to label Bonnin "schizophrenic" (Stout 1984, 71) and ambivalent (Fisher 1979, 204). Fisher even goes out on a limb to blame Bonnin herself for her inability to remain comfortably living on the reservation after her taste of schooling: "Gertrude Simmons *tried to convince herself* and her mother that the bit of education she had received made it impossible for her to fit comfortably back into the traditional customs of her tribe" (1985a, xi; emphasis mine). In making this claim, Fisher ignores the plethora of agonizing, personal stories told by Indian children who had been removed at young ages from their families and taken for two to three years to boarding schools, where many died. Luther Standing Bear remembers,

> I soon began to see the sad sight . . . of returned students who could not speak their native tongue, or, worse yet, some who pretended they could no longer converse in the mother tongue. They had become ashamed. . . . The boys came home wearing stiff paper collars, tight patent-leather boots, and derby hats on heads that were meant to be clothed in the long hair of the Lakota brave. The girls came home wearing muslin dresses and long ribbon sashes in bright hues which were very pretty. But they were trying to squeeze their feet into heeled shoes of factory make and their waists into binding apparatuses that were not garment, but bordered on some mechanical device. (1978, 235)

Such cultural reprogramming, in isolation and far from home, like Eastman's father, was difficult to overcome upon returning home. The children became aliens to the parents, and the parents became undeveloped and backward people to the children. Furthermore, the drastic changes in environment were so stressful that Standing Bear estimates "nearly one half of the children from the Plains were dead and through with all earthly schools" in the three years he was at Carlisle (1978, 234). Fisher does Bonnin an injustice when she blames her solely for her inability to return to traditional Yankton life.

Gertrude, or Gertie as she was known on the Yankton Reservation, was not unwelcome there (Picotte 1985, xv). There, she met her husband, Raymond Bonnin, who, according to Deborah Welch, was "a man eight years her junior, her inferior in education, a man who stood in admiration of her accomplishments. In short, it was a marriage in which she could have some assurance of being the dominant partner, and of maintaining charge of her own life" (1985, 66). Although such a practice of finding an "inferior" mate has been standard for men, Welch chooses to condemn such a preference in Zitkala-Sa, one example of how well-meaning scholars bring inbred, probably unconscious, prejudices against independent, self-directed women.

The major social conflict on the Yankton Reservation, with which the Bonnins got themselves embroiled, arose between two groups—one with fraudulent claims to land rights, the other with legitimate ones—seeking control of the reservation to control the sale of lands (D. Welch 1985, 172). Zitkala-Sa would witness more fraudulent scams against Indians in her Oklahoma investigations as a representative of the General Federation of Women's Clubs, eventually publishing a report entitled *Oklahoma's Poor Rich Indians: An Orgy of Graft and Exploitation of the Five Civilized Tribes Legalized Robbery* (D. Welch 1985, 184). She would learn from both of these experiences that the government had the power not only to dictate policy, but also to cover up wrongdoings. Later, she and Ray joined forces with their opposition, who surreptitiously gained power, on the Yankton Reservation to fight policies of the Indian Bureau (D. Welch 1985, 218–23).

But Zitkala-Sa did not limit her ambitions to work on reservations. After working for the Society of American Indians, which eventually disintegrated but was the first pan-Indian organization in the United States, as well as creating influential writings for its publication, *The American Indian Magazine,* she worked with other political groups, such as by investigating the graft and land fraud in Oklahoma for the Indian Welfare Committee of the General Federation of Women's Clubs, later founding her own pan-Indian group, the National Council of American Indians, of which she remained president until her death (D. Welch 1985, 201). As Fisher admits, Bonnin

> became known to Indians and government officials alike as a persuasive public speaker and an effective, if relentless, mediator. She had, at last, found the way to use her education and skills of expression to aid her people, not to be an object of suspicion to them, and in doing so, she became the champion of the underdog Indian and a scourge to irresponsible Indian agents. (1985a, xvi)

To give credit to all the critics who are so quick to focus on schisms instead of bridges, it is difficult to fully separate the political Mrs. Bonnin, who helped secure Indian voting rights, from the originally idealistic writer Zitkala-Sa, who wrote to influence public opinion about Indians and Indian culture, including finding value in native literary traditions.

Zitkala-Sa's stories are meant to influence and *change* Euro-American opinions about Indians, opening their eyes to abuses, such as land fraud. Two stories, "The Widespread Enigma Concerning Blue-Star Woman" and "The Badger and the Bear," are designed especially to teach Euro-Americans about how easy it was to manipulate Indians out of their lands. The title of "Blue-Star Woman" with its larger, more difficult words "Widespread Enigma Concerning" immediately signals that this is not an ordinary children's story. "The Badger and the Bear," on the other hand, is structured in fablelike form, specifically for indirect educational purposes.[3]

"Blue-Star Woman" begins with "fields of golden sunflowers facing eastward, greeted the rising sun" (1985, 159), symbolizing the promise of sustenance and endurance. An old Indian woman contemplates her lack of kinship ties while she cooks fry bread and coffee—foods given her

---

3. The tales contained in *Old Indian Legends* are often compared with the ones Ella Cara Deloria collected in *Dakota Texts*, with Deloria's tales being called the more "scientific" (Stout 1992, 41; Picotte 1985, xviii), even though Deloria combined tales from different tellers (which Bonnin must have done as well) creating a synthesized, idealized, and generalized collection of folk tales (DeMallie 1988, 237). Zitkala-Sa's tales, undoubtedly, were "embellished" as Stout calls it, which was her writer's prerogative. But I would argue that she maintained the original purpose of such stories—to educate by example—just as Aesop's fables and countless other tales for children have been meant as educational tools.

by a generous neighbor, in a giveaway not unlike what the "Pilgrim Fathers" received (1985, 162). Zitkala-Sa reverses the Thanksgiving giveaway, however, because the foods are distinctly Euro-American in origin, as the Oyate had neither flour nor coffee before contact with Euro-Americans; most Sioux, in fact, never saw them before reservation rations began being distributed (Standing Bear 1975, 22 and 71–72). Because she was orphaned at a young age, Blue-Star Woman is uncertain whether she is Sioux or not. Her enigma, then, is that she cannot prove to authorities that she deserves a land allotment on this reservation. The old woman also faces a dual dilemma because of cultural ignorance—she must openly speak her name— a name she is proud to write because it is "her individual name," one she would not lose in marriage as most Euro-American women do (1985, 163), as well as the names of her dead parents, to government authorities. The Sioux taboo against speaking personal names aloud, which "was probably a means of protection in the days of black magic" (1985, 160), means nothing to non-Indians who want to legally assign her a portion of the reservation lands. Not only does she not know her parents' names, because no one spoke the names of the dead, but also because she has always lived alone on the edges of the tribe, "her *reincarnation* had passed unrecorded in books" (1985, 161). In other words, when Indians were reassigned Euro-American names in place of their Sioux names, hers was never recorded on the rolls. Because of the practices of the two cultures, she has become a *persona incognita.*

Two "nephews," strangers she associates with Iktomi,[4] the Sioux trickster, come to her morning meal and leave after devouring all her food, like Iya,[5] the devourer, and after they persuade Blue-Star Woman to allow them

    4. Iktomi, the spider trickster, was once the spirit of wisdom, Ksa (Dooling 1984, 35), who, through believing the words of others began to find enjoyment in fooling others, pointing up the difficulty in knowing whether one is following folly or wisdom (Dooling 1984, 34). Because he repeatedly tried to fool the spirits, Iktomi was banished from their realm.

    5. Iya is the son of Unk, the spirit of passion and jealousy, who seduced Inyan, the rock—the original being from which all the other spirits originally came. Iya is a foolish and evil giant, given to rages, in which "he is known as Ibom, the Cyclone, who is the Spirit of

to help her gain a land allotment in return for half of the land. They convince her that "half a crust of bread" is better than none at all. To cinch her agreement, they point out that their trickery for getting her allotment is like using a backfire to fight a raging prairie fire: " 'In just the same way, we fight crooks with crooks. We have clever white lawyers working with us. They are the back-fire' " (1985, 169).

The story then switches point of view. Chief High Flier is informed of Blue-Star Woman's allotment. He knows that because she is Indian she is entitled to allotment somewhere, but he is convinced her land should not come from his reservation. In angry determination, he has his grand-daughter write a letter to "a prominent American woman," asking for her assistance in stopping this illegal claim (1985, 173). As he rides his horse to the nearest post office to mail the letter, he thinks over the situation, be-coming convinced that his well-meaning friend will only turn his letter over to Washington bureaucrats where it will get no response. A disem-bodied voice tells him his conclusions are right, so he stops his horse in sight of the government buildings to which he was riding to burn the letter with a fire of "dry grasses and the dead stalks of last year's sunflowers," believing the woman in Washington would get the message "on the wings of fire" (1985, 176). As he is riding home, however, Indian police overtake and arrest him for attempting to set fire to the government buildings. The superintendent, who is given supreme authority on the reservation by the Bureau of Indian Affairs, convicts the old man and sends him to prison. In his desolate prison cell, he has a vision wherein his Euro-American woman friend becomes "a vast multitude of women, with uplifted hands" (1985, 179), gazing upon the Statue of Liberty, whose light "penetrate[s] Indian reservations" (1985, 180). The power of the vision of Euro-American women sustains him until his release. Immediately after returning to the reserva-

---

disaster" (Dooling 1984, 8). Iya was condemned by Skan, the spirit of the sky, after he spoiled the spirits' first feast, so that "he shall be forever hungry with a hunger that cannot be satisfied, so he shall eat filth and his breath shall stink" (Dooling 1984, 11). Later, Unk mates with her son, Iya, and gives birth to Gnaski, the demon, who delights in manipulating people with superficial flattery to make them look foolish (Dooling 1984, 9).

tion, where the hills are empty of any sign of sunflowers (1985, 180), he is confronted by the two "nephews" who ask for his thumbprint signature. When Chief High Flier asks his son why they want his authorization, his son simply replies, "'I pledged to pay them half of your land if they got you out of jail'" (1985, 182).

Clearly, the sunflowers that are mentioned several times in the story are dying away and disappearing, like the Sioux and like their life-sustaining traditional way of life, for Zitkala-Sa, possibly forever. Symbolically, the sunflower and the sun it represents on earth have multiple meanings, from the fertility provided by Wi, the sun spirit, to the promise of continuity as the sun returns each morning. The onset of drought, mirrored by the one in Eliot's *The Waste Land,* which was published the following year, brings desolation to the Sioux. The promise of a restoring rain is as distant in the story as it was during the drought experienced in South Dakota in the late 1800s.

Surprising to most readers might be the image of the Euro-American legion of women who are to come to the Indian's rescue. According to Mary Stout, "the old chief's dream, acknowledges a hope that Zitkala-Sa always had. Her intensive work with the General Federation of Women's Clubs proves that she thought she had found a group who would listen to the story of the Native Americans; a group which even had enough political clout to right the wrongs she saw" (1992, 48). Knowing something of Bonnin's political career and her close ties to the General Federation of Women's Clubs, as well as knowing something of Sioux culture (the name taboos) and mythology (Iktomi and Iya) aids in reading "Blue-Star Woman." Also important is how Euro-American culture affected Indians— from forcing them to change their names to Anglicized ones, eliminating women's uniqueness by forcing them to take their husband's new surnames, to making the Sioux conscious of the need to wrangle legally to possess the land that had sustained them for centuries, even if only by obtaining small bits of it.

Personally for Bonnin, her research and legal battles on behalf of many tribes, including hers, her dealings with and her bitterness toward the Bureau of Indian Affairs, which chose only to acknowledge her when it needed her in desperation, her experiences with the unending tangle of politics in Washington, and her struggle with land graft all contributed to her distrust and suspicions, even of Indians who would use the system to their own advantage. Even without particular knowledge about Bonnin and Sioux culture and its Euro-American-imposed changes, the message about wanton land fraud is clear.

"The Badger and the Bear," because it is written specifically for children, is more subtle in its address of Euro-American and Indian relations than "Blue-Star Woman." The badgers can be seen as simply symbolizing American Indians, and the black bears are the encroaching Euro-Americans. The badger family lives in a well-kept underground dwelling, where father badger brings his bountiful hunting kills, keeping "mother badger very busy, and the baby badgers very chubby" (1985, 61). One day a large, but gaunt, black bear comes to visit, and "though he was a stranger and his strong paws and jaws frightened the small badgers, the father said, 'How, how, friend! Your lips and nose look feverish and hungry. Will you eat with us?'" as is the Dakota custom (1985, 63). The bear returns daily, so that the family anticipates accommodating him. But then, one day, his behavior changes and he remains standing instead of sitting on his usual fur rug in the Dakota place of honor near the door. When the father badger asks him what is wrong, the bear states that he, the bear, is very strong. Father badger quickly reminds him he got strong on their shared food, but the bear ignores the reference to his expected appreciation. When the bear demands the dwelling for his own home, father badger says, "'I fed you. I called you friend, though you came here a stranger and a beggar. For the sake of my little ones leave us in peace'" (1985, 66). But the bear tosses them each out without any provisions whatsoever.

Desperate because he cannot hunt without his weapons and his children are starving, father badger returns to the dwelling to beg for food. Again, the bear tosses him out, with "the little ruffian bears" hooting and shouting "to see the beggar fall upon his face" (1985, 69). Zitkala-sa effectively creates sympathy for the badgers who, like the Sioux, have been denied their traditional ways of living and must resort to receiving commodities from the government to survive, with thoughtless Euro-Americans calling them beggars. One little bear takes pity on the badger family, though, but only through trickery—a reverse Iktomi move wherein trickery becomes necessary—is able to obtain meat from his father, the now robust black bear, for the badgers.

The next day father badger again returns to beg. When he is thrown out this time, he sees a small blood clot in the grass, which he picks up and carries home. With this clot he prepares a sweat lodge for the blood clot and prays to the Great Spirit, who sends him a Dakota brave as an Avenger. The black bear, seeing the badger and the brave, feigns friendliness and offers, as is custom, something to eat. But the Avenger warns the bear that he must return everything to the badger or suffer. In fear, the bear family flees.

Read through the eyes of transitional Sioux life, the story is part wishful thinking wherein all Sioux lands, such as the Black Hills, would be returned to them, with all non-Indians, who only want to profit from what the Indians have by displacing them from their homelands, leaving them alone forever. But it is also largely truth, pointing out that Indians at first welcomed Europeans to this land, even helping feed and clothe them, only to be turned out of their homes once the whites outnumbered and overpowered them.

This story has interesting variants, however. Eastman's version, also called "The Badger and the Bear," appears in the only volume of his work, *Wigwam Evenings* (1990), directly cited as collaborative with his wife, Elaine. The plot of the Eastmans' story mirrors much of Zitkala-Sa's except that it leaves out the badger's magic, which brings the Avenger, as the Eastmans also call the miraculously appearing Sioux warrior, thus eliminating more of the Siouan literary elements than Bonnin's version. The Eastmans' version mimics the traditional European fable when it ends with a moral, "There is no meanness like ingratitude" (1990, 69).

Zitkala-Sa's version is followed immediately by "The Tree-Bound," which is a continuation of the same story. She separates the two stories in a Euro-American literary style because the point of view in the second story shifts to that of the Avenger, completely leaving behind the badgers. As Ella Deloria recorded the story, titled "Blood-Clot Boy," in both Lakota and English, there is no separation despite the shift in point of view. Comparatively, Deloria's retelling of Blood-Clot Boy's story is more distinctly

Siouan. The animals in Deloria's story, however, are a rabbit, who is immediately driven out of his home by the bear so has no chance to show the bear proper Siouan hospitality (1932, 113). As in Zitkala-Sa's version, the rabbit/badger character surreptitiously obtains the blood clot, from which the Avenger, Blood-Clot Boy, is magically created using the sweat lodge (1932, 114). Also like Bonnin's version, Blood-Clot Boy/Avenger can perform magic; however, Blood-Clot Boy kills the father and mother bear outright, ending up sparing only the baby bear who showed Rabbit pity by feeding him and his family (1932, 116).

Possible reasons for the differences in the story are many, and it must be recognized that each storyteller always adapts a story to her or his liking. But both Bonnin and Eastman probably sanitized their stories for their Euro-American audiences, because both books were originally targeted at younger audiences. Blood clots, to most Euro-Americans, were probably very disgusting things, so Blood-Clot Boy becomes the Dakota Avenger in Bonnin's and the Eastmans' versions.

Why, though, do the Eastmans eliminate the potency of the magic? In their version, the Avenger simply "sprang from a drop of innocent blood," which mirrors Christian ideals of purity and innocence and the power of blood, as in the Eucharist, to right wrongs (1990, 68), making his appearance more miracle than magic. Why, too, are the protagonists badgers in the Bonnin and Eastman versions? Again, different storytellers might prefer different animals. Badgers have reputations of ferocity and cunning, whereas rabbits are better known for their speed (and quick thinking?). But other stories modern children might have been familiar with, in particular Joel Chandler Harris's *Uncle Remus and His Friends* (originally published in 1892), were less than ten years old when Zitkala-Sa published *Old Indian Legends* (originally in 1901), nearly twenty years old when the Eastmans published *Wigwam Evenings* (originally in 1909). Two of the most popular figures from the Uncle Remus tales were Brer Rabbit and Brer Bear, also adversaries who attempted to trick each other. In Harris's stories, as in all the Sioux versions of "Blood-Clot Boy," the rabbit (or alternatively the badger) is always more cunning. Perhaps Bonnin and the Eastmans chose to use a badger in lieu of a rabbit to keep children from confusing their tales with the Uncle Remus ones.

Published in 1901, most of the stories in *Old Indian Legends* involve the trickster Iktomi and the eater/devourer Iya, who eats up whole villages and anything else he desires, and other would-be profiteers, all of whom can easily be seen as symbolizing infiltrating, deceitful Euro-Americans intent on obtaining Indian lands and absorbing Indian children into mainstream society. Yet, if this symbolism is the case, Zitkala-Sa lets us know that not all Euro-Americans are bad. The little bear in "The Badger and the Bear," who sympathizes with the badgers, is undoubtedly someone like James Mooney, Sen. Henry M. Teller, or Thomas A. Bland, who argued repeatedly that, although assimilation must take place, it should be "at a slower pace, in a manner to be determined by Indian peoples themselves within the bounds of tribal culture" (D. Welch 1985, 81). This ability to see the positive and negative attributes of both cultures often leads critics to label Bonnin ambivalent. What Bonnin recognizes, however, is that both cultures do affect each other, and that individuals from either culture can be unscrupulous. This balanced view of both cultures, also characteristic of Charles Eastman's views, is often misunderstood by critics who prefer to see transitional Indians easily and wholly acculturate as Euro-Americans or remain wholly Indian culturally.

While Eastman claimed to be preserving his early life experiences as something from a vanishing culture, Zitkala-Sa's autobiographical essays do "not showcas[e] her life as yet another artifact to be preserved" (Fisher 1985b, 206). Because she is more outspoken about her and her mother's feelings toward whites in her three major narratives, "Impressions of an Indian Childhood," "The School Days of an Indian Girl," and "An Indian Teacher among Indians," many scholars, such as Deborah Sue Welch, Mary Stout, and Dexter Fisher, overlook the stories themselves and concentrate more on her frequent "unreasonable attitude toward other people" (D. Welch 1985, 73) and her "tone of militancy" (Stout 1984, 73) and a perceived "pattern of ambivalence . . . as she alternates between a controlled rage over the mistreatment of Indians and a desire to convince Americans of the Indian's humanity" (Fisher 1985b, 204–5).

Why Fisher believes Zitkala-Sa's anger over the treatment Indians received at the hands of what she calls "hard-working, well-meaning, ignorant [people] who . . . inculcat[ed] in our hearts [their] superstitious ideas"

(1985, 67) is somehow unconnected to her insistence that Indians are human beings, too, is unclear. Indians were mistreated, after all, because Euro-Americans could comfortably place them in a category of "otherness" and often justified abuse because they believed Indians to be somehow less than human. By pointing out abuses toward Indians, both subtly and directly in her stories, Bonnin is highlighting the fact that Indians are deserving of the same rights other people take for granted simply because of the "race" and culture into which they were born. Although her outspoken comments were unusual for an Indian writer in the era in which she wrote, Zitkala-Sa's writing is more than militant commentary; it is literature. Of the four Sioux writers in this study who wrote their works unaided by another highly skilled and trained writer, Gertrude Bonnin exhibits, perhaps, the most creative, the most facile, literary talent, exhibited best by its integration of elements, both cultural and literary, which many consider diametrically opposed.

It needs to be pointed out, however, that in focusing only on the inevitable conflicts that come from one culture asserting its values over those of another, instead of recognizing that Bonnin's writings highlight the ongoing transitions—the give and the take—between the two cultures, scholars fail to notice that Zitkala-Sa becomes the epitome of a person who can and does *balance* the two cultures in her life and attempts to demonstrate in her writings the need and possibility for a balance in America as a whole. Even Dexter Fisher admits that Bonnin tried "to become the literary counterpart of the oral storytellers of her tribe" as well as "felt compelled to live up to the critical expectations of her white audience" (1985a, vii).

Dorothea Susag attempts to downplay the schism many scholars assume plagued transitional Indian writers. Searching for an initial theme, however, she incorporates Edward Said's descriptions of an exile who asserts difference and clings to memories of their past, where "the literary voice . . . *becomes the site of contestation* between two languages, two systems, two cultures" (1993, 5; emphasis mine), even though she ends up arguing that Zitkala-Sa successfully modified the two cultures (1993, 22), not only for herself, but also for future generations.

Few scholars seem able to connect the appeal literature, and other parts of Euro-American life, had to Bonnin's ingrained sense of the Sioux literary tradition—a tradition so tightly and actively interwoven into everyday Yankton life, unlike Western literature, that "being eloquent" (Stout 1992, 11) was a prerequisite for effective tribal communication (Susag 1992, 13–14). Being eloquent meant gaining the attention, and respect, of listeners, because cooperation was vital to tribal life in order to make equitable, and often lifesaving, decisions. The best speakers, then, were more often the most influencial people. Speaking metaphorically of her work—reading and writing—at college, Zitkala-Sa says, "By daylight and lamplight, I spun with reeds and thistles, until my hands were tired from their weaving, the magic design which promised me the white man's respect" (1985, 76). Eloquently, Bonnin translates one activity, writing (also dominantly a male activity at the turn of the twentieth century), into another, weaving (a traditional female activity)—symbolically paralleling cultural values, as well—weaving and writing as arts of expression, and traditional concepts of men's work as women's art. In effect, Bonnin crosses over two imposed boundaries, so that she modestly invades two territories: those of Euro-Americans and men, in particular.

In Western mythology, such a comparison of artistic, often gendered, expressions, in particular storytelling and weaving, comes as early as the Greek myth of Philomela. After being raped, having her tongue cut out, and then imprisoned, Philomela cannot tell her sister what happened to her, except through weaving an intricate tapestry (Hamilton 1942, 394–96). Perhaps, then, Bonnin weaves through the silence imposed on Indians, and most women, with her writings as Zitkala-Sa. Whatever the case, Bonnin recognized that being eloquent, no matter what the language or method of conveyance, garners respect and admiration. As the writer, Zitkala-Sa, Bonnin crafts works that combine Sioux and Euro-American literary traditions, reflecting values from both cultures and demonstrating one culture's effects on the other, to gain respect and admiration, as well as to influence opinions and decisions, from both cultures.

Even though being facile with language in order to explore its limits and possibilities is not limited to Euro-American writers, many literary scholars still seem unwilling to recognize literary capabilities, let alone traditions, in writers in transition between oral and written cultures. Although Dorothea Susag admits that "Zitkala-Sa has constructed a literary *voice* both from the rhetoric and value systems of the colonizers, and from a remembered Yankton/Dakota landscape, language, and story" (1993, 7), she hesitates to assert there was and is a viable Sioux literary tradition, hinting instead at a "tribal literary tradition" that she refuses to isolate from other generally recognized Indian oral traditions (1993, 9), and pointing out that Bonnin allows us to "see how Lakota *story* tradition, translated into English, has been woven into the Judeo-Christian tradition and rhetoric" (1993, 17; emphasis mine). While such an observation is heading scholarship over Bonnin in the right direction, it still oversimplifies what she does in her writing.

Even though Eastman, Standing Bear, and Black Elk also demonstrate combinations of Sioux literary traditions with Western ones, Bonnin's writings are different from theirs in several ways: she never assumes an anthropological point of view toward her Indian subjects; she does not shy away from pointing out weaknesses in Euro-American thought and actions; she never attempts to separate Euro-American influences—such as the adoption of materials goods such as beads, cloth, and metals—from contemporary Dakota life although she is critical of many practices imposed overtly on Indians, such as Christianity and boarding schools, and she was one of the first, if not the first Indian writer, to argue for being allowed to live as both Indian and American.

To assume that literary finesse—by which I mean the ability to tell stories facilely, deeply imbedding possible meanings, in multiple, sometimes experimental, forms—comes only with studying Western ideals of literature is arrogant and racist, to say the least. Imagination is a human trait, shaped by culture and experience. A literary or creative tradition becomes established when one speaker or writer influences others, but the products as each successive creator shapes them are never identical; yet, when they carry on or transfer specific aesthetics, themes, or forms, they are part of an ongoing, thus traditional, literary or creative experience. Analyses of several writers from one tribe, such as Julian Rice's *Lakota Storytelling* (1989), assist in establishing the fact that various Indian nations conceived and transmitted stories within culturally established forms, just as Euro-Americans have done.

Perhaps Bonnin's awareness of Western values of literary finesse can be credited to the fact that she began studying Euro-American concepts of literary quality at an earlier age than any of the men in this study. Perhaps such awareness of language's capabilities for eloquence not only comes from tribal necessity and her Euro-American-based literary training, but also comes from her finer sense of appreciation for abstract, metaphorical concepts like symbols, an appreciation that would have come directly from tribal elders and her mother, who "instructed her child in the Dakota way, expecting her to transmit to her children the same Dakota tradition" (Susag 1993, 4). Because of her initial grounding in the traditions that accompany a primarily oral culture, Bonnin possessed a charismatic finesse in oration that the men, too, seemed to have. Both Eastman and Standing Bear were popular speakers; and Black Elk mesmerized audiences with his demonstrations of Lakota rituals, songs, and dances at pageants for years.

Bonnin comes to writing, then, well fortified—possessing a deep appreciation for language's subtleties from her childhood training in Dakota literary traditions, from her experiences as a college orator, and from her education in Euro-American literary traditions. Compared with the male Sioux writers, only Eastman had a training close to, yet not quite comparable with, what Bonnin received. While Eastman did have his grandmother and other elders to teach him the cultural values of storytelling, Bonnin had her mother, who, judging by Zitkala-Sa's descriptions of her, was one of the most influential people in Bonnin's life.

Similarly, women are often noted as being the primary givers of power in many traditional Lakota stories, such as in the common legend of "The Stone Boy." Not only do Stone Boy's powers come from his mother, who lived among the Winds, but when he rescues his four Wind uncles from the buffalo people, he can do so only because of the spiritual/magical powers given him by the women he meets along the way (Walker 1989, 51). Almost all contemporary Oceti Sakowin writers, such as Luther Standing Bear, who discuss traditions of tribal art credit women with the most creativity because, unlike the men whose artwork was primarily restricted to painting tepee covers and adorning their weapons, women's artwork was also considered the more symbolic art, often using geometric designs in their artwork, as well as the totem images the men used (1978, 91).

It is important to note Paula Gunn Allen's description of symbols here. According to Allen, to Indians, symbols are not just concrete representations of abstract concepts. Instead of merely metaphorically representing an imagined reality (an idea), or an emotive reality (a feeling), symbols stand for "that reality where thought and feeling are one, where objective and subjective are one, where speaker and listener are one, where sound and sense are one" (1992, 71). So that, when Zitkala-Sa refers to sunflowers, as she did in "Blue-Star Woman" and which are replete throughout her writings, she at once refers not only to the idea of the flowers, which are scattered wildly across the plains, but also to the tribal emotionality and spirituality connected with the sunflower. In one of the primary dances of the Sun Dance, wherein young men begin dancing when the sun rises and continue dancing for three to four days without food or water, the dancers, who are adorned with leather sunflower symbols, do much the same sort of symbolic representation in their dance as Bonnin's sunflowers do in her stories. The sunflower is "the only flower that follows the sun as it moves on its orbit, always facing it" (1975, 120). It also looks something like the sun, known to the Sioux as a physical manifestation of the spirit Wi, so that as a symbol, both in the Sun Dance and in Bonnin's stories, the sunflower is a tribal way of all at once bringing the sun to earth in a physical form and connecting spiritually with the life-giving—and seemingly never ending—power of the sun, of Wi. The sunflower is, for the Sioux, then, a symbol of spiritual strength, which, at a deeper level, is necessary for tribal continuity. When we read Zitkala-Sa's stories, then, we must realize that the sunflower, and other natural symbols, are being used at multiple levels. When the sunflowers wither and disappear from the plains in "Blue-Star Woman," not only has the life-giving ways of traditional Sioux life been extinguished, in Zitkala-Sa's view, but the Sioux are on the verge of disappearing, spiritually, culturally, and physically.

That most of Zitkala-Sa's symbols are natural in origin is not surprising, given the fact that her earliest lifestyle, like most Indians of and before her era, provided her ample contact with and appreciation for the natural world. Margaret Lukens demonstrates how Gertrude's lessons from nature helped develop her problem-solving skills and her "scientific skills of experimentation [that are] necessary for life on the land":

> Knowledge of light and shadow was the way Gertrude would learn to tell time, to understand where to position a dwelling or plant vegetables, and to navigate on the trackless prairie. Zitkala-Sa narrates the young Gertrude's attempts to catch her own shadow, noting, "Before this peculiar experience I have no distinct memory of having recognized any vital bond between myself and my own shadow," illustrating the introduction of an important scientific concept into the mind of the youngster through playful interaction with the natural world. (1991, 170)

Her mother, herself trained to know life-giving and life-threatening plants and animals apart, as well as how to use their forms and parts in artwork, would have provided Gertrude's segue into understanding the symbolic aspects of nature, as well as the mythology that accompanied them.

When Skan, the sky spirit, created Wi, the sun spirit, he cast shadows on the earth, Maka, and decries, "'The shadow of each thing shall be its spirit and shall be with it always'" (Jahner 1989, 195). In Zitkala-Sa's story about chasing her shadow, her spirit in traditional Sioux belief, Gertrude pursues the shadow, which is always just ahead of her, until she is exhausted. To catch her breath, she sits on a rock, the physical manifestation of Inyan,[6] or the primal power that created everything (Jahner 1989, 194), and the shadow teasingly sits next to her (1985, 23). Gertrude's friends "planted their moccasined feet firmly upon [her] shadow to stay it" (1985, 24), but it cannot be held down, and slips away, always just ahead of her.

---

6. One version of the Oyate creation story (and there are many) says that Inyan, the rock, was lonely so created companions: Maka, the earth, made from the material of Inyan's being whose blue blood formed the waters of the earth; the power from the blue water separated from it to become the sky spirit, Skan, who gives power to all else (Dooling 1984, 3) and is the final judge on all matters (Dooling 1984, 4); Skan then took parts of himself and Maka to create Wi, the sun spirit, to give Maka warmth and to decorate her with life (Dooling 1984, 4).

Dorothea M. Susag equates this spirit[7] chasing with Bonnin's pursuit of her Dakota heritage, which always seems to be part of her but separate from her (1993, 16). Whatever Bonnin's reasons for incorporating traditional Sioux mythology into her autobiographical stories, she clearly demonstrates a command of abstract symbolism's power and potential.

Sioux women's creative outlets seemed to begin shrinking with reservation life. Standing Bear comments in *Spotted Eagle* on the increasing loss of traditional women's artistry because of the loss of natural flora to the region (being replaced by farmed vegetation), which were used for dyes and paints; because of the damage to the earth, as well as restrictions placed on native access to particular geographical areas, the soils of which were used for both clays and paints; and because of the ease of using beads instead of dyed porcupine quills in needlework on clothing (1978, 91). Standing Bear is the only one of the five Oyate writers in this study who comments on this phenomenon—the replacements of Sioux tools and commodities for Euro-American ones. The use of beads in Indian crafts seems "traditional" now, but the switch has been important to Sioux culture, demonstrating how easily Euro-American "things" have been synthesized into even "traditional" elements of Siouan life.

Marla Powers reports, for instance, that from the time "when the reservation was first established and up through the 1940s, traditional costuming flourished. It is often said that the Lakota people, once they no longer had to hunt for game and retired to the annuity system . . . began beading in great quantity simply because they had the time and the materials to do it" (1986, 137). She assumes, as do so many others, that "beading" is as traditional as "quilling" was. Standing Bear credits his mother with obtaining "the first beads ever seen by the Sioux Nation" (1975, 7). So why is it

---

7. Many traditional Oyate believe there are four "spirits" per person. In creating the first people, Skan "gave a spirit like that of the Sacred Beings but a little lower" to the creatures. From himself, he gave them "a *nagi*, a spirit that guides the conduct . . . to be their ghost or double. Then he gave to each the *nagila*, a particle of his divine energy. He commanded Tate [the wind spirit] to breathe into each image a *niya*, the breath of life, and Wakinyan [the thunder spirit] to give each a *sicun*, the spirit which gives power to produce offspring, and to give health and growth" (Dooling 1984, 11).

so easy for us to assume beading is traditional, but literary craft—facility
with narrative forms and symbolic abstractions—is not?

Writers, such as Standing Bear, Marla Powers, and Edward Lazarus,
point to the effect Euro-American culture has had on Sioux culture. In
fact, as Lazarus argues,

> the Sioux . . . had abundant reason to want tranquil relations with the
> whites. In the generation since Lewis and Clark's visit, the Teton had
> tripled in size to 10,000 members, testimony to the prosperous life they
> were enjoying. The Indians could credit their contact with the white for
> much of this prosperity. The introduction of firearms, cooking utensils,
> and a host of other items had drastically reduced the workload of their
> hunting culture and brought relative leisure to their nomadic existence.
> To an ever-increasing degree, the tools of western civilization were be-
> coming everyday necessities of Sioux life. (1991, 11)

Because the Teton were much farther west than the Yankton's, Lazarus is
speaking of an influence in the Far West that had already had a profound
effect on more eastern tribes like the Bonnin's Yankton Sioux. That depen-
dence on trade with whites for things such as cooking pots—which not
only made cooking easier, but could also be broken down and shaped into
metal arrow heads—would be only a temporary boon for the Sioux, and
for the traders themselves. As G. E. E. Lindquist points out, early trading
with Euro-Americans brought a kind of economic prosperity for Indians:
"That the fur trade increased the larder of the Indian as well as that of the
trader, few will question. Oliver Faribault, a noted fur trader, used to say
that he counted it a loss of five hundred dollars for every Indian who
learned to read and write" (1944, 67). The goods they trade for and the
Euro-American tools the Sioux come to appreciate, including literary tools,
are assimilated into their daily lives.

But the increasing desire for products from Euro-Americans began to
change not only the way the Oceti Sakowin lived, but also how they produced their own goods. Women's artwork changed from a nature-based art
form to a manufacture-based one using artificial paints and beads, and
woven cloth instead of leather. Ghost shirts—those sacred, bulletproof
shirts of hope for the Lakota—for instance, were made out of white cloth,

probably muslin (Mooney 1973, 790). Ironically, "the singular piece of craftwork that is the symbol of being Lakota in the modern world," is the Star of Bethlehem quilt design, brought back about the turn of the century to the reservations from, most likely, Carlisle Indian School in Pennsylvania as a skill the girls learned in school (M. Powers 1986, 138). A possible reason the star quilt appealed and still appeals[8] to the Sioux is that stars, especially the Morning Star, are sacred symbols representing the promise of dawn and the continuous rebirth of life-giving daylight, thus the continuous sustenance of the tribe. Stars often appeared as one of the many symbols painted on the Lakota Ghost Shirts (Mooney 1973, 790).

In Zitkala-Sa's short story "The Trial Path," stars become symbolic of the power of love, even from beyond the grave. The story is an *ohunkakan* story, or a tale "regarded as having some fictional elements" (Picotte 1985, xi), which was told "in the evening as everyone in the family went to bed, during the time between lying down and sleep" (Picotte 1985, xiv), which is also the time in which the story takes place. As two women talk at night, "a large bright star" peeps in through the top of the tepee at the granddaughter who listens avidly to a tale her grandmother tells. The granddaughter, reassured that the largest and brightest stars are wise old warriors and the smaller dimmer ones young braves, decides the star she sees "is my dear old grandfather" (1985, 127). As the girl states this, watching the star, a sort of time warp occurs wherein her voice traverses past the fall night air, "over many winter snows, till at last it cleaves the warm light atmosphere of her grandfather's youth. From *there* her grandmother made answer" (1985, 128; emphasis mine).

The story her grandmother then tells about the girl's two grandfathers, one of whom kills the other and must face a trial test to determine his fate,

8. To attest to the continuing popularity of the star quilt design, most of the stores carrying locally made crafts on both the Pine Ridge and Rosebud Reservations sold star quilts of brilliant colors in August 1995. For some Oyate, the Milky Way, the Wanagi Tacanku, or Ghost Road (W. Powers 1977, 93), is a pathway filled with the campfires of the dead on their way "to a place which is reflective of their life with *ni*," or breath (W. Powers 1977, 53), which is through a hole in the Big Dipper, where all souls are born and return (Goodman 1992, 22). Other Oyate believe one travels to an ideal land south on the backs of spotted eagles, which is why "to 'go south' is a metaphor for dying" (W. Powers 1977, 93).

is told as though that time were present time: "'It is the day of your grandfather's death. . . . How fast, how loud my heart beats as I listen to the messenger's horrible tale!'" (1985, 128–29). This kind of memory, according to medicine man Lame Deer, is called *waki-ksuya,* which means "to recall, to travel back into the past, to hold communion with the spirits, to receive a message from them, to bring to one's mind the dead friends, to hear their voices once again, even to the point of having a vision" (1991, 198). The stars, after all, shined upon that past time, as they still do the present, so become the vehicle for the story, for the two women's memories, and for the spiritual recurrence of the highly emotional event that took one husband from the elder woman and gave her another.

The story subtly explains connections, weblike and circular, between past and present, between kin—blood relatives and adopted, between humans and animals, and between storytelling and ceremony. The grandmother carries on the mental and emotional memories of her two husbands, both of whom are considered the granddaughter's grandfathers. The second husband, who passed his trial test by successfully riding an unbroken pony, forever ties the value of his life with that of the horse, who was named Ohiyesa, "the winner,"[9] so that when the man dies sometime later, the horse is killed at the gravesite so that "together master and beast will enter the next camp-ground" (1985, 135). Storytelling becomes a ceremonial act that ties the grandmother—and her memories—to the granddaughter, strengthening and redefining their kinship ties, as well as their cultural ones, providing the grandmother with continuance—"'I did wish the girl would plant in her heart this sacred tale,'" she says when she discovers the girl is asleep (1985, 135)—in thought, in emotion, as well as through heredity, through the granddaughter.

"The Trial Path" is imbued with Dakota values and beliefs—kinship ties so strong and vital that they last beyond death, the importance of the

9. Interestingly, both Bonnin and Eastman named their sons Ohiyesa. Eastman named his son after himself, of course, but why did Bonnin choose that name for her son? It is clear from this story that she liked the name, but could there be another reason? Bonnin was already nearly two months pregnant when she married Ray Bonnin (D. Welch 1985, 45), but there is no evidence that he is not their son's father. Could "The Trial Path" with the idea of two husbands for the grandmother be in any way autobiographical?

past in the present, the importance of carrying on information—especially familial tales—through storytelling, the power of storytelling to shape the beliefs of the young, thus of the continuing culture, and the importance of animal connections to human life. Many of these values and beliefs appear repeatedly throughout Zitkala-Sa's writings.

By the time Gertrude left Yankton for "the red apples" in the East, she would have witnessed her mother's creative efforts at home. In Bonnin's youth, her favorite pastime was to sit near her mother after dinner listening to the legends told by the elders who had been treated to her mother's hospitality (1985, 13). She adapted these oral stories "for the white man's papers," and for an early chance to make her voice heard (1985, 97). Like the women artisans whose creations change with the encroachment of another culture's influences, Bonnin combines the oral stories, and their various traditional forms that she grew up hearing, with Euro-American literary traditions formed from centuries of manipulating words on paper into a new form. Her firm grounding in oral traditions also helps her become an eloquent speaker, "a prized art among college students in the nineteenth century" (Welch 1985, 10).

Her early training in metaphoric symbolism provides a solid base for her sophisticated, modern prose. The sacred sunflower, which follows the sun's path dotingly across the sky, is a symbol for the reverent and steadfast Sioux. The persistent wind is a more intricate symbol. Her mother's name, after all, is Reaches for the Wind (Tate I Yohin Win), so that Zitkala-Sa uses it as both a symbol for her mother's influences and the persistence of Sioux culture (Susag 1993, 11). Bonnin also places herself in the mythic role of Wohpe, Skan's (the sky's) daughter, who comes to the earth as a falling star and becomes Tate's (the wind's) adopted daughter, taking the shape of a wind, who is "a mediator, moving among oppositions to create harmony" (Jahner 1983, 58 and 195). As Zitkala-Sa says so eloquently of herself, "My Indian nature is the moaning wind" (1985, 67). The hand-hurting reeds and thistles with which she weaves as symbols of pens and papers are the tools with which she tries to successfully and harmoniously merge two cultures, Sioux and Euro-American. From watching her mother do beadwork to listening to, and probably practicing or repeating, the elders' stories, Bonnin sharpens her literary finesse and success in addressing Euro-Americans with their own literary expectations, and working within Sioux literary traditions, becoming, indeed, a mediator between supposed opposites.

Having it considered effective, quality, *modern* literature, I believe, was one goal Bonnin had for her writings. Zitkala-Sa's major search in her works is for "those ears that are bent with compassion to hear" her words, which come "out as the low voice of a curiously colored seashell" (1985, 68), inviting the curious to pick her works up and listen closely to what she has to say. To reach a wider audience than those most modernist writers wrote for, or just those interested in the anthropological aspects of Indian life, Bonnin crafts her stories, both autobiographical and fictional, carefully, trying to attract more educated non-Indians to her works to educate them more effectively about the plight of Native Americans, as well as to demonstrate that, even as an Indian, she, too, was capable of writing sophisticated, modern prose, which has the power to sway feelings and opinions.

Repeatedly, she demonstrates the all-too-human need to have someone understand her pain and sympathize with her needs—as a human being. The fact that she is an Indian girl, manipulated into voluntarily leaving a life she knew and loved to try a strange way of living that had seemed to promise untold wonders for her innate curiosity, is almost incidental. In "Impressions of an Indian Childhood," she becomes *any* child who is taken away from familiar surroundings and has a new regimen of living imposed on her—because the damage is similar for any child who becomes *acculturated* to one way of living and then must remove herself, without the love and support of family and friends, from that way to adopt another.

To give credit to the scholars who are overpowered by Zitkala-Sa's powerful imagery of a child torn from home, Bonnin does emphasize her regrets at having left the surroundings of her first culture and her lack of finding little possibility of a satisfying way of living in the second. So that she finds herself "homeless and heavy-hearted" as she goes away to college and later begins teaching at the Carlisle Indian School where she "pine[s] for sympathy," as she seems to throughout the rest of the autobiographical essays (1985, 76). But I would argue that it is not self-pity Zitkala-Sa is

really stressing here, something even contemporary reviewers did not recognize, instead accusing Bonnin of having an "'over sensitive nature,'"
which has made her "'melancholy'" to the extent of standing in "'rebellion and bitter opposition'" to Euro-Americans and their culture, com-
plaints often lodged against other outspoken women writers of that time
(Susag 1993, 21). Instead, she uses her personal experiences to draw attention to the highly damaging impact that forced acculturation through
forced deculturation has on children and their sense of self.

Although Bonnin did feel and experience some extreme instances of
estrangement, compounded by feelings of guilt for having gone against her
mother's wishes not to leave the reservation, during her years away from
Yankton, she *chooses* as a writer to emphasize these feelings—feelings she
could have easily glossed over as did Eastman. As Deborah Welch points
out, "With her pen, Zitkala-Sa determined to reach a broad spectrum of
Anglo society, showing them that Indian peoples were human beings, with
fears, hopes, and dreams for their children, much like themselves" (1985,
18).

Even though the three essays were originally published separately in
their final book order in successive issues of *Atlantic Monthly,* they show
obvious signs of having been well thought out in their order beforehand.
The first chapter of "Impressions of an Indian Childhood" foreshadows all
that will happen in the rest of the stories as she begins with the scene of
herself as a child running carelessly across the prairie while her mother
cries over the "sham," the "paleface," who threatens to take away everything they have ever had. On the Yankton Reservation Ellen Simmons,
Tate I Yohin Win, is the wind, Tate, in Gertrude's hair, allowing her to
grow up free and confident (Susag 1993, 11). But the wind symbolically
demonstrates her passionate need to create harmony, like Wohpe, in this
case between her mother and Euro-Americans, of which Gertrude is part—
genetically and, later, culturally. Although her mother repeatedly cautions
Gertie about trusting the whites, the first essay ends with the eight-year-
old girl begging to be allowed to go east to the land of the red apples, a
reversal of the Garden of Eden myth. The mother acquiesces, reluctantly,
saying, "She will need an education when she is grown, for then there will

be fewer real Dakota, and many more palefaces" (1985, 44). Whereas her
mother is pessimistic, Zitkala-Sa is tempted away from this paradise in
South Dakota, mixing Sioux myth with Euro-American ones.

Unlike Eastman's father, who essentially forces his son to adopt white
ways, Zitkala-Sa's mother has implanted resistance in her daughter. It
should be noted, however, as Raymond Wilson does in his biography of
Eastman, *Ohiyesa: Charles Eastman, Santee Sioux,* that Eastman's grandmother
was largely responsible for his Indian education, thus encouraged resistance to the influence of Euro-American culture (1983, 13). Wilson also
demonstrates how important Eastman's father was to his acceptance of
Euro-American culture and quotes him as saying, "'Our own life, I will
admit, is the best in a world of our own, such as we have enjoyed for ages
. . . [but] the sooner we accept their mode of life and follow their teaching,
the better it will be for us all'" (1983, 20). Even Standing Bear's father
encourages him to learn Euro-American ways well, because "they keep
coming like flies" and Indians have "to be able to live with them" (1975,
151). The Sioux women demonstrate more resistance to acculturation than
do the men.

Although Bonnin laments the loss of her mother's respect, Luther
Standing Bear says that one of the major faults of Euro-American culture
and how it has modified Sioux culture is the loss of traditional mother
authority:

> Today mother-power is weak, scattered to many places—taken over by
> the teacher, preacher, nurse, lawyer, and others who superimpose their
> will. This loss applies also to the white mother, for she, too, is blinded
> and confused by the intricacies of the society in which she lives. And the
> incongruity of it all is that the child has not become individualized, but
> has become stamped with the ideas of others. Few today are the youthful
> individual thinkers and doers who dare step out of the ranks, for the
> ranks close about them and try to force them to conform. This process
> was not possible in Lakota society in tribal times. The Indian mother
> pointed the way, but she followed in her son's and daughter's path. She
> did not take from, but rather, added to, their strength by urging it to
> express itself. (1978, 109)

Standing Bear probably oversimplifies and overemphasizes the role of the biological mother, however. Ella Deloria and Mari Sandoz emphasize that children were considered community responsibilities among the Sioux, with a second set of parents often being designated to avoid overprotecting the children and preventing the mother from showing favoritism to her children over her husband (Sandoz 1985, 27). Often, the grandparents were particularly useful in aiding the parents in teaching the children social values (Deloria 1996, 32–33). But Zitkala-Sa emphasizes that it was "close beside my mother" sitting on a rug where she began her "practical observation lessons in the art of beadwork" (1985, 19), later having observed and absorbed enough to be able to impersonate her mother in play with her friends, imitating things they heard their mothers say and mimicking "their various manners, even to the inflection of their voices" (1985, 22).

It is perhaps an imitation of her mother's voice, as well as those elders who visited regularly to tell tales of Iktomi after the evening meal, that she affects in her stories. At least she openly reveals the importance of her mother in her life. Even if she occasionally became ill with guilt and anxiety, readers can also sense her adamant "refusal to remain the victim" (Susag 1993, 7). One of Bonnin's major regrets was, undoubtedly, losing her mother's respect (1985, 80 and 97). Yet, she strives, in her writings and political activities, to carry out the mission she saw necessary to remove her mother's sadness and fears—to halt the victimization of Indians by Euro-Americans—and to carry forth her Dakota woman's role—to perpetuate the culture she learned at her mother's side on the Yankton Reservation, while still becoming an American citizen.

As Welch asserts, "Fiercely proud of her Sioux ancestry, Zitkala-Sa sought acceptance in the Anglo world on her own terms, refusing to bend to the prevailing ethnocentrism of her time" (1985, v). But only when Zitkala-Sa realizes for herself how damaging her separation from her mother and their traditional Sioux life at such an early age has been on her current life does she begin to truly rebel against the "Christian palefaces" who marvel "at seeing the children of savage warriors so docile and industrious" (1985, 98). This realization comes at the end of the first essay, when Bonnin tells us that, as "the lonely figure of my mother vanish[ed] in the distance" (1985, 44), she "no longer felt free to be [her]self, or to voice [her] own feelings" (1985, 45). Here began her quest to find, and use, her voice, even if in childlike imitation of her mother's more powerful one, to free herself.

And her mother's voice and influence was powerful. An example of how much power Ellen Simmons had over her family is seen in her control of Gertrude's brother, David Simmons, who "returned after three years [at school] to take up life as a farmer, drawing an allotment in 1892, never to leave the reservation again" (D. Welch 1985, 6). The fact that Gertrude had persuaded her mother to let her attend boarding school later filled Bonnin with intense feelings of guilt and unhappiness because she became terribly homesick and lonely at school. Yet, she had to live with the fact that she was responsible for the sense of alienation she experienced, because her mother had warned her about trusting the palefaces (D. Welch 1985, 7–8). Perhaps, too, Gertrude felt some anger toward her mother for having been right. Naturally, she laments having given up what she had known, where she felt she had belonged: "I had arrived in the wonderful land of rosy skies, but I was not happy, as I had thought I should be. My long travel and the bewildering sights had exhausted me. I fell asleep, heaving deep, tired sobs. My tears were left to dry themselves in streaks, because neither my aunt nor my mother was near to wipe them away" (1985, 51).

Even though it is not just her mother she misses,[10] it is her mother's "powerful force," as embodied in her Nakota name, Tate I Yohin Win, reaches for the wind, which carries her through her autobiographical essays. Tate is the main Dakota wind spirit, which Dorothea Susag mistakenly conceives of as being female, who "moves in connection with the masculine Sky, Skan" (Susag 1993, 11). Susag argues that "in Zitkala-Sa's recollection and recording of [wind images], she acknowledged her mother's personification of this most powerful force, and she affirms the

10. According to Lame Deer, "Indian kids call their aunt 'Mother,' not just as a polite figure of speech but because that aunt acts like a mother," more evidence of the importance of the strength of kinship and communal ties, so that "Indian children are never alone" (1991, 184).

continuity between the Wind, her mother, and herself" (1993, 11). Although I would agree with Susag's insistence that the references to wind in Zitkala-Sa's autobiographical essays do in many respects symbolize Ellen's forceful nature upon Gertrude, her insistence that Tate is female is erroneous." A possible implication in Ellen's Dakota name, Reaches for the Wind, is that she reaches for the ephemeral, the uncatchable, the untameable. So that when Zitkala-Sa says, "I was as free as the wind that blew my hair, and no less spirited than a bounding deer. These were my mother's pride—my wild freedom and overflowing spirits" (1985, 8), it is at once a yearning for the kind of freedom Gertie feels as a child that Ellen reaches for, as well as a yearning to keep hold of Gertie herself.

So the connection with the freedom of the wind is ironic for both Zitkala-Sa and her mother, one of whom is caught up in dealing with acculturation forces, the other of whom is confined to a reservation. But the wind symbolically, primarily, stands for her mother's felt influences on Bonnin. As Zitkala-Sa steps down from the train upon her return from Carlisle where she has been teaching, again against her mother's wishes, "she's struck by a 'strong hot wind . . . determined to blow [her] hat off, and return [her] to the olden days'" (Susag 1993, 11). For Zitkala-Sa, the mother influence attacks her physically on the Yankton Reservation. But Bonnin did not ever openly disagree with her mother's assessment of Euro-Americans and their culture, possibly because she would have had to admit her mother had been correct in her judgment when Gertrude was eight and wanted to go to the land of the red apples.

As a child, secure in her personal identity, she had already analyzed and rejected many Euro-American customs, such as when through her educators' ignorance or outright rejection of Indian customs she is humiliated by having her hair cut. As Zitkala-sa says in "School Days," "Among our people, short hair was worn by mourners, and shingled hair by cowards!" (1985, 54). It is doubtful that Gertie had her hair shorn. The girls'

11. See James Walker's *Lakota Myth* (1989, 46), for instance; or Lame Deer's discussion of Tate's marriage to *"Ite*—the face—the most beautiful woman in the universe" who becomes Double-Face or Two-Faced Woman after having an affair with Wi, the sun (1991, 180–81).

hair was rarely cut, because long plaited hair was also in style for Euro-Americans. Zitkala-Sa is clearly demonstrating how the children must have wondered at and been terrified by this invasion of their persons, because they could not yet speak English and no one explained why the act was necessary in their own languages. Were they supposed to mourn or had they indeed been marked as cowards? The real tragedy for children such as Zitkala-Sa is that the Euro-Americans who assigned themselves the task of acculturating these children never seem to have asked or cared about what short hair meant to Indians. As Standing Bear laments, they never took the time to learn about the people they set out to change (1978, 241).

Effectively, Zitkala-Sa uses stereotypes in her autobiographical essays often reserved for Indians on non-Indian ideas, such as calling Christianity a superstition (1985, 62), and pointing out double standards, such as allow-ing an opium addict and an alcoholic to maintain positions they had no business holding to ensure their survival while the same whites ridicule Indian children with demeaning labels reminding them of their depen-dence on government financing for their educations (1985, 95).

The final chapter of "An Indian Teacher," in fact, most scathingly of the autobiographical essays exposes white injustices and prejudices against Indians, focusing most strongly on the phenomenon of visitors who come to the school as though to a zoo. With this caged image in the foreground, Zitkala-Sa's autobiographical stories end with the statement she wants those sympathetic ears (and eyes) to remember most: "Few there are who have paused to question whether real life or long-lasting death lies beneath this semblance of civilization" (1985, 99). She, like Eastman and the non-Indians of their time, seems to pessimistically assume an end to Indian culture. Zitkala-Sa takes the insinuation further, however, pointedly ques-tioning whether Euro-American "civilization" is real life or a long-lasting death.

Most graphically, Zitkala-Sa's fractured, though never entirely broken, relationship with her mother symbolically illustrates the break with her past, her Dakota heritage, she was often forced to try to make by assimi-lated Indians like Montezuma and Euro-Americans like Captain Pratt. Somehow, even as a child she realized she did not have to give up her first culture. Her desire to maintain her Indian identity—largely defined by her

Sioux culture—led her to create a composite literary tradition based on a strong Sioux literary tradition, her traditional feminine Dakota role of cultural propagator, acknowledgment that Euro-American goods and tools could be assimilated into Sioux culture, and a modernist American literary tradition.

Ella C. Deloria
From Julia Rice's *Ella C. Deloria's Iron Hawk,*
University of New Mexico Press, 1993.
Courtesy Dakota Indian Foundation
and University of New Mexico Press

5

LITERARY KINSHIPS

Ella Deloria as Interstitial Author

*E*lla Cara Deloria spent most of her life working as a Dakota anthropologist. Even though she was not fully recognized for her contributions to anthropology, ethnology, and linguistics until later in her life, Deloria relied on her relationships within the Sioux nation—following closely the social dictates necessary to acquire stories, and speaking the same language as her informants—to successfully transcribe more stories in the Lakota language "than anyone else before or since" (Rice 1992, 2). Her intimate knowledge of both the proper social kinships and the Oyate dialects combined to make her the best anthropologist in the field studying Sioux oral traditions. Her most important published "anthropological" book, *Dakota Texts,* then, provides us with carefully chosen tales and cultural insights, which are invaluable to our pursuit of the oral literary traditions practiced by the Oyate. Examining these tales for traditional literary elements can guide our understanding of how Deloria combined the Sioux and Western literary traditions to create her modernist, interstitial novel, *Waterlily.*

The most striking difference between Deloria's writings and those of the other four writers in this study is that Deloria never outwardly wrote about her personal life in any of her publications. Her primary concerns in her writings, whether we speak of her novel *Waterlily* (originally published in 1988) or of her bilingual folklore/linguistic study *Dakota Texts* (originally published in 1932), were to, first, represent American Indians in an honest and thorough fashion, and, second, to demonstrate the compelling life-ways, what she calls the "spiritual culture areas" (1944, 18), of Dakota cultures reflective of the values she found in them. Even in *Speaking of Indians* (1944), she "concentrate[s] on the one people" she knows "intimately and whose language is also" her own (1944, 20).

Using the Dakota as her example, she set out, with the common turn-of-the-century anthropological intent, to picture and preserve the folktales, mythology, and cultural practices of the Sioux. Unlike most other anthropologists, Deloria determined to compose her studies as eloquently as possible, highlighting the positive aspects of Oyate life that she felt, as did most others at the turn of the century, would pass with the deaths of tribal elders. Yet, inherent in her quest is a working desire to understand and to make understandable to the general American public the idea that to truly know another culture we must "see life from their peculiar point of view" (1944, 18), especially by experiencing their language—"the gateway to their spiritual culture area" (1944, 19).

The high modernists were not so noble in their search for and uses of ancient cultural myths and legends. When explaining why he paws "over the ancients and semi-ancients . . . to find out what has been done . . . better than it can ever be done again, and to find out what remains for us to do," Ezra Pound said,

> No good poetry is ever written in a manner twenty years old, for to write in such a manner shows conclusively that the writer thinks from books, convention and cliché, and not from life, *yet a man feeling the divorce of life and his art may naturally try to resurrect a forgotten mode* if he finds in that mode some leaven, or if he thinks he sees in it some element lacking in contemporary art which might unite that art again to its sustenance, life. (Hoffman 1962, 77; emphasis mine)

Pound's "yet" carries many possibilities for the works of Ella Deloria. Pound's "yet" points to the synthesis inherit in interstitial writing and living experienced by so many of the transitional Oyate writers in this study. To Pound, and many of the high modernists, the resurrection and synthesis of older literary traditions with innovations created by the modern writers is the natural response to modern life, and the primary outcome of modernism. From that point of view, most of Deloria's works are modernist.

Europeans and Americans began to value literary traditions, in part, in an effort to move away from them or to modify them—to redirect literary perceptions in new directions. The Sioux literary traditions were as flexible, with each successive storyteller modifying stories to fit circumstances. Julian Rice asserts that "perhaps the most significant cultural meanings are perpetuated through exact repetition between and within individual tellings, while nuances of meaning and feeling can be freely varied to suit changing times, occasions, and listeners" (1994, 127). These changes to the tales are easily demonstrable by the number of tales recorded by Deloria, Eastman, Standing Bear, and Bonnin that are similar in form or context, but contain enough variety to be different.

It is perhaps an inevitability of oral storytelling that each storyteller puts her or his touches in each tale. Rice discusses extensively how Deloria's unpublished tale *Iron Hawk* has been modified enough in modern times to make "an implicit statement against brainwashing Indian children out of their own cultures and languages" and "recognizes the value of traditional tribal education" (1993, 8).

Similarly, in her *Dakota Texts* and *Waterlily,* Deloria draws on tales she recorded from memory for information and for a sense of the Oyate literary traditions—much like Pound's "forgotten mode." From her extensive Euro-American education,[1] at least in terms of the turn-of-the-century standards, she supplies Western literary traditions. She actively and consciously interweaves the two traditions, so that the interstices between the two creates a synthesized literary form, much like what Eastman, Standing Bear, Bonnin, and Black Elk achieve in their writings. This literary form makes oral stories from a culture foreign to most Americans accessible to people immersed, primarily, in a written-text-based culture. Because *Speaking of Indians* (1944), *Dakota Texts* and *Waterlily* are so thorough in their

1. Deloria received a bachelor of science degree from Columbia University in 1915 (Prater 1995, 41).

complex depictions of traditional Sioux stories and customs, many dismiss them as anthropological studies, too scientific to be literature. But this belief has its roots in a deep prejudice.

Perhaps one of the most disconcerting beliefs held by scholars who study cultures with both distinct oral and written literary traditions is the belief that the two are completely separate.[2] Prejudice once had us believing that oral stories are only precursors to written stories in a hierarchy that placed written stories as superior. Thus, the oral stories of early cultures combined to create "literature" in *The Odyssey* and *Beowulf*, but the texts, because viable still, are assumed to be superior to the ancient performances we will never see. This bias has led some scholars to remark in amazement over the fact that people, who come from cultures still subsisting largely on oral traditions, could even write, as though writing is so much more sophisticated than speaking, and as though writing occurs, always, isolated from speaking. Yet, this bias has also lent itself to literary racism: Whereas "classic" tales that have been written down, such as *Beowulf* and *The Odyssey*, are literature, similar tales from other ethnic groups are usually dismissed as folktales or anthropological studies, even though they demonstrate clearly established literary elements, so are not considered serious pieces of literature.

Part of the problem is temporal and cultural distance, but most of the problem is racial or cultural prejudice. Tales like "Blood-Clot Boy" may be as old as some parts of *Beowulf*, but because they have been more recently put in written forms, they have yet to work themselves into the psyche of academia, let alone the general public. Combined with the additional prejudice many still hold against "ethnic" literature, even though both "Blood-Clot Boy" and *Beowulf* can be seen as heroic epics, the former is taken less seriously than the latter because it is not a part of the dominant culture's "collective" past (after all, *Beowulf* is as much Germanic and Nordic as it is Anglo-Saxon). Literary scholars, especially American Indian literature scholars, still insist on separating the "essence" of so-called authentic oral,

2. Dexter Fisher makes this prejudice clear when she examines "more fully the process of 'transplanting' the oral tradition into literary form" (1979, 50).

thus presumed to be Indian, storytelling, from "corrupting" written, thus Western or Euro-American, storytelling.

Oral storytelling is often viewed as dynamic, because the storyteller gets immediate feedback from listeners and can use props, as well as her or his whole body and vocal inflection ranges in the telling. Written storytelling, then, is often viewed as static, because writing words down on a piece of paper appears to have frozen those words in time, and, for some scholars, in meaning and context, as well. Dexter Fisher argues, for instance, that "writing changes the fluid context of oral storytelling by removing a given tale from its cultural echo chamber, in which case the author must recreate a communal experience" (1979, 57). While her idea of a "cultural echo chamber" is enlightening because people of particular cultural backgrounds will react differently than others to the same tales because they are, as Hertha Wong says, "shaped by a cultural framework" (1987, 20), Fisher's basic assumption is that readers cannot relate as much to written tales as part of a communal experience. Yet what is it we are experiencing here as you read this text, even if you, as reader, do not agree with my particular points? Chances are you are reading this as part of a community of scholars, one primarily interested in these issues. What Hertha Wong argues as applicable to autobiography seems to apply to all forms of writing, which inherently "involves a degree of socializing an individual [or group] into the community" (1987, 19), even if the writers are writing to change the milieu of that community, and even if the individual writes to discover her individual self, that self is always interrelational, intersititial because there are always social contexts within which a person knows herself.[3]

Scholars who study the writings of people who are traditionally orally oriented face this oral versus written conundrum because literary scholarship tends to worship the written word in trying to determine its value and meanings. For some, the static nature of writing prevents the dy-

3. The challenge is, of course, to defy this generalization. Is there anything any one person does that no one else has ever done, so that that one person cannot be associated with another group?

namics of communication from occurring. But, as we have learned from reader-response theories, writing is still dynamic in that it provokes different reactions from individual readers, who produce their own specific meanings from the text. In fact, if only one reading was possible, there would be no need for literary study.

So we know that individual readers, like individuals in an audience, bring different information and associations with them to texts, just as they would to an oral performance. The effect on the audience is dependent on the writers' ability to imagine their desired audience's responses, and how to elicit those responses, for them to anticipate what will create the effect they seek. The same holds true for the oral storyteller. The difference lies in the immediacy of audience response and the additional visual tools. A writer can supply photos or other visual aids; a storyteller relies largely on volume, projection, facial and body expressions, with occasional props, such as musical instruments or special dress. But both can fail to obtain their desired results by seriously misjudging what their audiences want. Only the immediacy of the oral storyteller's presentation allows her opportunity to amend her methods in midstory. The writer has to wait.

Eloquence takes practice—practice based on observation of people's reactions—whether in speaking or writing. And even things written down are not permanent. To point to a Native American example, Louise Erdrich chose to add to her original edition of her novel *Love Medicine* nine years after the first edition's publication. Just as with repeat oral performances, writers do have the chance to create new nuances for their works, often based on the responses they have received from their reading public. With the advent of electronic publishing, including voice-overs, and the subsequent possibilities for immediate electronic feedback, writing, in fact, has the potential to become even more like its "predecessor" speaking.

Inevitably, it seems, when it comes to examining the writings of transitional American Indian writers, those credited with being some of the first Indians to write, scholars feel the need to question or assert the nature of the authorship of the texts—are they influenced more by oral literary traditions or by written ones? The assumption in this question is that only "ethnic" cultures, such as Native Americans, still operate actively with oral literary traditions, and that Westerners are the exclusive owners of written literary traditions and no longer practice oral storytelling. It is also assumed that never the twain shall meet without one radically altering the other, so that neither are "authentic" any longer.

This dilemma is especially true for *Dakota Texts* by Ella Cara Deloria. Julian Rice, the scholar who has written about Deloria most extensively, spends time at the beginning of each of his texts about her works justifying why he believes Deloria is the author of the tales. In his first book, *Deer Women and Elk Men,* he says:

> Deloria made a sincere effort to retain the flavor of each narrative [as it had been told to her], but ultimately she herself was the author of the stories in the sense that any writer transforms what he or she reads in the act of what recent criticism calls re-vision. . . . It is true that Deloria heard the stories told by traditional storytellers and tried to remain true to their meanings, even their tones of voice, but she could deliver them only through her own memory, imagination, and vocabulary. (1992, 5)

In Rice's second book, *Ella Deloria's Iron Hawk,* he asserts:

> [Deloria] explains that the stories are based on those of various old men, "notably one named Makula [Breast]." She also indicates that she did not transcribe or record the stories while they were told but wrote them down later from memory. In this sense Deloria participated in the storytelling tradition in a unique way. Like the storytellers themselves she told her own versions of stories she had repeatedly heard, but unlike them she set down her versions in written form. (1993, 2)

In Rice's third book, *Ella Deloria's Buffalo People,* he claims, "The stories are . . . as much Deloria's creation as those of Makula or any storyteller who produced 'original' versions based on rearranging elements of the tradition" (1994, 4), so that "a polyvocal confluence of cultural voices cohered in her rather than in the usual 'space between' informant and recorder" (1994, 5).

What matters, then, at least to Rice, is how the current storyteller, Deloria, refocuses the story once it has passed through earlier tellings. We cannot erase the earlier tellings. Deloria, as a member of the audience, was affected by who told the stories and by how that storytelling was done. Just as John Neihardt cannot erase the influences Black Elk had on the story he retells, *Black Elk Speaks,* Deloria cannot erase the influences of her original storytellers, but instead draws on their sense of Oyate literary traditions, modifying the stories with her understandings of Western literary traditions. Thus, the tales she relates in both Lakota and English in *Dakota Texts* are the perfect examples of interstitial writing and creativity.

Some scholars write about oral storytelling among Indians as though all Indians write and think the same ways. Deloria, herself, emphasizes that problems arise when speaking as though Indians, and their uses of languages, were all the same: "How could they, since each area [of the country] contains several distinct tribes speaking diverse languages, thinking different thoughts, and having preferences for particular modes of life?" (1944, 17). As well as cautioning about drawing absolute dividing lines between cultures:

> We need to keep in mind, too, that the lines of demarcation are never clean cut. Imagine a patchwork quilt in which the scraps of cloth are, unfortunately, not of fast color. After one wash there would be a blurring out of tones, a blending of each two neighboring colors along the seams. That's about the way culture areas are. The world over, people borrow and adapt ideas when they have the chance. (1944, 17)

Perhaps more controversially would be to argue that Indians lack originality in their tales, as Martha Beckwith asserts in "Mythology of the Oglala Dakota": "We recognize too many world-wide elements for even complete plots of too complex character to argue for independent invention" (1930, 344). Without more specificity, she seems to imply that complete plots and complex characters would be too much for mere Indians to have accomplished.

In *Dakota Texts,* Deloria does acknowledge and duly label two of the tales "of European origin" (1978, x) and that one is "taken from the Crees who came into Dakota country and settled there" (1978, 13 n. 1), but emphasizes that the stories still have several traditional Dakota symbols imbedded, such as Iya the devourer, and implies they have been familiar to many Oyate for some time (1978, xi). To many scholars, such European intrusions taint the stories (although no one that I have read complains about intertribal borrowings), but discounting the tales would be discounting a viable aspect of the life experiences of those Oyate living in the early twentieth century.

One of the most valuable literary aspects of *Dakota Texts* is that it provides readers with enough tales, sixty-four in all, from which we can identify patterns of speech, repetitions of important symbols, and can come to an understanding of the basic story patterns and literary conventions used by the traditional Oyate. Several of these literary conventions, what Rice calls "verbal formulas" (1994, 128), help identify the kinds of story patterns being implemented. When a warrior gives a coup-talk, a *waktoglaka* such as Standing Bear's Story Sticks tales, the events are usually so exciting or harrowing that they duly warrant the conventional ending, "ca le waun we lo," which means "and so I remain alive" (Rice 1994, 128).

Because of these conventions, scholars can break Indian story patterns into different categories. Deloria breaks Oyate tales into two main categories, (1) *ohukaka,* or fictional, even mythical, stories (1978, ix), and (2) *woyakapi* (Wong 1992, 125) or *wicowoyake* (Rice 1994, 5), or true stories, as Deloria calls them, each of which can be broken into two subcategories.

Ohukaka stories "are intended to amuse and entertain, but not to be believed . . . [and] end with the conventional *hehayela owihake*—that is all; that is the end. They may be narrated only after sunset" (1978, ix). The two groups of *Ohukaka* stories are (1) those believed to come "from a very, very remote past . . . and are part of the common literary stock" (1978, ix), and (2) those of a more novelistic nature, which are "accepted as something that might have been possible, at least a long while ago, among a people not so different from us" (1978, x).

The *wicowoyake* stories end with the literary convention *ske,* it is said, and with *keya pi,* they say. "True," here means, according to Beckwith, that "they are true in the Indian sense as an accurate symbolic representation of the historical experience of the group than as a realistic adventure" (1930, 341). Deloria simplifies Beckwith's idea by pointing out that the first group of true stories "are legends of localities; and while the miraculous still runs through many of them, they are regarded as occurrences that may happen to someone aided by supernatural powers," and that the second group are "simple accounts of events that took place in the local band, and are told at times to recall the past or to entertain one who has not heard them" (1978, x).

There is, indeed, in these tales a plethora of patterns to identify and study, with Deloria and Julian Rice having explicated much of the use of standard phrasings, such as the stories' traditional endings, explanations of Dakota idioms, and some discussion of the use of symbols. I will not attempt to repeat what Rice has made available in his books, *Deer Women and Elk Men: The Lakota Narratives of Ella Deloria* (1992), which examines the sexual implications in various *Dakota Texts* tales, *Ella Deloria's Iron Hawk* (1993), which examines that very literarily dextrous yet unpublished writing that "atypically combines elements from the whole culture hero genre in a single story" (Rice 1993, 1), and *Ella Deloria's The Buffalo People* (1994), which examines the traditional Oyate literary aspects of two other unpublished tales, "The Prairie Dogs" and "The Buffalo People." Instead, I will provide some explication of four of the most frequently used patterns of Oyate symbols, which will provide insight to a closer reading of *Waterlily*. The four primary patterns I will examine are (1) the importance of the sacred, especially the number four, (2) the use of the sweat lodge for restoration or rejuvenation, (3) the function of supernatural bogeymen, and (4) the disobedient child as didactic example.

The first, perhaps most prominent, literary element for the Oyate is the use of sacred ideas or objects, especially numbers. The number four is one of the most sacred numbers for the Oyate, partly because it represents the four primary directions—east, south, west, and north—from which come the various powers of the earth and universe and which are represented, in order, by the four basic Dakota virtues—wisdom, generosity, courage, and fortitude (Rice 1994, 35).[4] The number four also reflects the four seasons of the year, which dictate movement of buffalo and other

---

4. As noted in the chapter on Standing Bear, Marla Powers lists the four virtues as generosity (*wacantognaka*), bravery (*cante t'inza*), patience (*wacintanka*), and wisdom (*ksabyahan opiic'iya*) (1986, 60), which are essentially the same thing Rice says.

animals and determine the availability of plants and natural art supplies. The knowledge of direction and season provides a means for determining where and when to be at particular areas of the country for hunting, gathering of plants, and for adequate means to provide shelter and clothing— all of which dictate survival.

Ronald Goodman also asserts that the number four denotes the four levels of consciousness—physical, emotional, intellectual, and spiritual— that the Lakota recognize, as well as the four stages of human life—child, adolescent, adult, and the elderly (1992, 3).

In many Oyate tales, things are grouped in fours or activities are done four times to indicate their sacredness or to indicate completed stages or a state of harmony. Tales often begin in the home of four brothers, with only the youngest, usually called Hakela, which means "the last born," the only one of the four identified by name. At least four of the real ohukaka tales in *Dakota Texts* begin with the indication that "four young men lived together": tale number 11, "Double-Face and the Four Brothers"; tale number 16, "Stone-Boy"; tale number 23, "Heart-Killer"; and tale number 25, "The Sacred Arrow." This pattern of four brothers holds true in almost every telling, such as those by Marie McLaughlin in *Myths and Legends of the Sioux,* of these tales.

The first three stories involve the consequences of inviting a strange young woman into the four brothers' home. "Double-Face and the Four Brothers" seems to be a shortened version of "Stone-Boy," because both begin with similar sequences of events: a woman approaches their tepee; Hakela invites her in at the brothers' request, but they become suspicious because she does not behave in the prescribed Dakota manner for a stranger entering a home and receiving food. As Deloria points out in an endnote, "She doesn't relate herself to them, and she takes their food without acknowledgement," so Dakota listeners would have known she would bring trouble to the brothers. The brothers leave Hakela to secretly watch over the woman the next morning. Hakela witnesses her eating human ears in "Double-Face" and sewing a robe of scalps in "Stone-Boy." After he warns the brothers, they boil rope, which they give to the woman with which to bring firewood, but it continually breaks as she uses it, giving the brothers enough time to escape, with the woman in pursuit.

Magic occurs in both stories. In "Double-Face," four magical events keep the woman from catching the brothers. The first two acts are performed by the eldest brother, who tosses both a cactus and his knife behind him creating first "one continuous cactus bed" and then "a mass of knives with their points sticking upward" (1978, 26) in an effort to stop the woman. When neither succeeds, the brothers together stomp on the ground so that it "opened in a long slit that kept her back from them" (1978, 26). Finally, they reach a river, where an old woman begs for a ride across on one of their backs. Because they pity her and assist her, as is proper, because she would be regarded as their "grandmother" socially, she throws fire onto the river creating "a mass of burning flames," which finally stops the Double-Face. The tale seems to imply that even four young men occasionally need to rely on the wisdom of an elder woman for their safety. Even though they trusted one stranger with bad results, continuing to maintain trust in others saved them. The tale teaches wisdom in relating to others and encourages the young men to follow their instincts when someone acts peculiarly; it also demonstrates the other Oyate virtues in action: they maintain their courage and fortitude in the face of evil, and they act generously to save the old woman *and* themselves.

"Stone-Boy" also details several supernatural events as it teaches the same lessons. To observe the woman, Hakela turns into a little bird to sit in the top of the tepee poles. His ability to turn into a bird, demonstrating his sacred connection with the winged nation, saves him, when the evil woman pursues the brothers and cuts off the heads of the other three. With the aid of a magpie who distracts her, Hakela kills the evil woman with a blow to her head from a blunt arrow.

One of the other Oyate literary elements occurs in "Stone-Boy" as well. Hakela gathers his brothers' bodies and erects a sweat lodge, with which he restores them to life, demonstrating the sweat lodge's ability not only to cleanse the body, but also to rejuvenate the spirit. The sweat lodge, which occurs in "Stone-Boy" twice, also occurs in "Blood-Clot-Boy," when a rabbit, desperate from starvation because a bear and his family took over his home, creates a hero to assist him from a clot of buffalo blood—the former lifeblood of the Sioux nation.[5]

5. Revisit my more detailed discussion of this tale in the chapter on Bonnin.

As in "Heart-Killer," a good young woman comes to the brothers of "Stone-Boy." She cares for the brothers so deeply that when they fail to return from a hunting trip, she accidentally swallows a transparent stone she carries in her mouth, which causes her to give birth to a boy. The sacred number four reappears when the woman repeatedly throws the baby, then, boy, then adolescent, out of the tepee until he returns a grown man. As in many other tales, such as "White-Plume Boy" and "Eagle Boy," where this rapid growth from being thrown out of the tepee occurs, the mother wishes fine things for her son, which magically appear. Thus attired, Stone-Boy then sets out to find his uncles. After killing the evil old woman who has killed the uncles, he makes a sweat lodge and restores them to life. He returns his uncles to his mother, then sets off to "see the world" (1978, 35).

Stone-Boy encounters four white (doubly sacred in being four in number and white) buffalo young women (heifers) who are coasting down a hill and ask him to join them. He pretends fear of being crushed by them, so they put him on their backs and he uses his stone weight to crush them, taking their very rare hides home to his uncles. Because these young buffalo women were child-beloveds (1978, 36) of their tribe, the buffalo plan revenge, which Stone-Boy learns of in time to help his uncle construct four concentric[6] fences encircling their safety area. Even Stone-Boy's mother joins in the fight by severing their hoof tendons. Even though the buffalo make it through to the last fence, they give up in defeat. While Westerners might assume Stone-Boy should have been punished for his greed in killing the four white buffalo girls, Dakotas would see things differently. Even though he refers to them as people—as women or girls—they are still buffalo. The buffalo are the animals that provided the most sustenance to the Oyate (also called the Oyate Tatanka, the buffalo people). So it would be expected that Stone-Boy would kill such a prize as four rare white buffalo. In fact, Stone-Boy was quite generous in giving the hides to his brothers.

Although the brothers in "Stone-Boy" had to go through two sisters before finding a suitable one, "Heart-Killer" also begins with the brothers taking in a strange woman to be their sister, but she, Heart-Killer, is good

6. The circle, or sacred hoop, of course, is a traditional Oyate symbol for the unity and safety of the camp circle, the *tiyospaye,* as well as the familial harmony of the tepee.

to them from the start. After chasing a pretty feather blowing on the breeze, Heart-Killer gets pulled down a hole by beavers. When Hakela finds her, the beavers are "draining their hot fish on her face," so that her once beautiful face has become "a mass of sores" (1978, 56). The eldest brother prepares to kill all the beavers, when the meekest beaver admits to being kind to her, which Heart-Killer corroborates. She takes the beaver[7] home as a pet, and her brother kills all the rest. One day, two women try to persuade Heart-Killer to come with them because they want to marry a boy-beloved named Blece and want her to marry Teal-Duck, who, as Deloria notes, is Ikto in disguise (1978, 58). Heart-Killer refuses and they kidnap her pet beaver, in effect, stealing her symbolic ability to keep house effectively for her brothers. Heart-Killer follows, only to be forced into marrying. But the other young women are confused and marry her to the boy-beloved they wanted for themselves. They end up with Teal-Duck, who they catch in the lie later that night when they discover Blece dancing on Teal-Duck's back. Angry, the women plant ants and wasps in Teal-Duck's bed. When he cries out in pain, he tells Iya that Blece stole his wife. Heart-Killer wakes later in a pool of her husband's blood because Teal-Duck helped Iya decapitate him.

Here, the story becomes much like "Double-Face Tricks a Girl," in that a monster, in this case Iya, chases Heart-Killer and her pet beaver, who builds a bridge for the two of them to cross to escape. Heart-Killer's loyalty to her pet is repaid, demonstrating the Lakota ideal that animals and human beings are all "people," and need each other in reciprocal relationships, relationships that are considered sacred.

Whereas "Double-Face and the Four Brothers," "Stone-Boy," and "Heart-Killer" contain lessons about whom to trust for the four brothers and their adopted sisters, "The Sacred Arrow" is a lesson in respecting other people's things, especially sacred things. In "The Sacred Arrow," Hakela attempts to shoot a beautiful scarlet bird, losing all his arrows in the process. Remembering his brother's sacred arrow, he takes it down and

---

7. Eastman claims the beavers are wise (1904, 179), but they also symbolize the fastidious construction and maintenance of a home. The beavers behave here the same way the bears in "Blood-Clot Boy" behave, with the smallest being the kindest, thus the one saved.

successfully shoots the bird with it. But the bird flies off with the arrow in its side. Hakela must pass three other camps before he reaches the fourth, where the bird has changed back into a boy-beloved.

There he encounters an old man who is going to heal the boy-beloved. Hakela, in his desperation, kills the old man and assumes his clothes and pack, passing himself off as the healer to the family of the boy-beloved. Only Iktomi knows Hakela is not the healer, but no one will listen to Iktomi. In fact, Hakela's impersonation of the healer is something Iktomi would do and, typically, when Iktomi assumes the role of someone else, people believe him, so this story provides a surprising twist to Dakota expectations.

After Hakela treats the boy, he asks to remain in the tepee for the night. Hoping to slip away with the sacred arrow while everyone sleeps, Hakela clumsily steps "on the middle of the Boy-Beloved's abdomen" and accidentally scratches "Ikto with his foot" (1978, 62). Finally, the family and villagers believe Iktomi when he sounds the alarm. Three times Hakela is nearly caught, first by a rider on a black horse, then by one on a buckskin, and last by one on a bay. The horses' colors are significant and represent the directions.[8] Black is the power of the west, where the Thunder Beings reside. The buckskin is the color of the south, and the bay represents the north. Missing is the sorrel pony, which represents the east, the direction from which comes the sun and the daybreak star, which is the Lakota symbol of wisdom. Hakela, then, has not acted wisely, but procures wisdom from this adventure. He manages to return home unharmed because his courage and fortitude enable him to run swiftly all the way in his "turtle moccasins" (for speed and luck, as Deloria says [1978, 63, n. 3]), and he is able to return the sacred arrow to its hanging place before anyone in his family is the wiser.

Although Hakela must act violently and deceptively to retrieve his brother's sacred arrow, perhaps showing the extent to which one should guard sacred objects, most of the violent actions in Oyate tales stem from enemies or evil beings, such as the bogeymen Double-Face, who can ap-

8. There are four sacred horses in Black Elk's vision; each one represents the power of each of the four cardinal directions.

pear as a man or woman, Iya the Devourer, or Owl-Maker. Deloria notes that as a child she and her companions were warned not to play near the woods because Double-Face might get them (1978, 20, n. 1). Similarly, noisy children were threatened with Owl-Maker, who, in "A Double-Face Steals a Child," turns out to be Double-Face.

Such evil spirits were undoubtedly used as threats to keep children from straying from safe areas and from being generally obnoxious. However, disappearances and obvious kidnappings of young women and children are also explained in these kinds of tales. "Double-Face Steals a Child" is an especially disturbing *wicowoyake* tale because a man kidnaps a two-year-old boy who has been sent out of the tepee for making too much noise and tortures him by repeatedly flogging him with the branches of rosebushes. This tale points to one weakness in the extended family *tiyospaye* because the parents assume, when the child does not come inside again, that he has gone to his grandparents' tepee. Not until the next morning when he cannot be found anywhere in camp is his absence noticed with alarm. The lesson, for parents, is that nothing is more valuable than their children, and to be a good parent means being tolerant of children's behavior. When the villagers find the Owl-Maker, they chop him up and burn him, trying to eliminate his evil, so that the tale ends with the note that "this incident has given . . . its name" to a place now known as Owl-Maker butte (1978, 116).

The disobedient child, especially if a boy, is not always so unlucky. In fact, many of the heroes of Dakota tales, such as Blood-Clot Boy and Tazi, encounter adventurous adversity by being disobedient. But the tales clearly separate appropriate behavior for males and females. Boys are encouraged, through the tales, to be aggressive and sure leaders, with Blood-Clot Boy, Stone Boy, the boy-beloved in "Incest," and "The Boy with Buffalo Power," examples of how boys could give commands and direct activities, often with supernatural results such as by creating buffalo herds out of buffalo hairs. These boys give orders to parents and even to their grandparents, all of which are followed, although not always without question.

Women, clearly, were threatened with dishonor and the fear of choosing the wrong man to keep them from thinking about or attempting to elope with men, with several of the stories, such as "Double-Face Tricks a

Girl" and "Double-Face Steals a Virgin," about men or Double-Face who trick women into running off with them, only for the women to suffer physically, often with the threat of death, at the men's hands. Stories such as "Incest" warned young women about inappropriate sexuality, especially within kin relations. Kin relations were sometimes so extensive that not only were half-brothers considered brothers, but so were some cousins.

In the same way, *Waterlily* cautions readers against making rash actions, especially in relationships, and provides a more balanced view of the genders, moreso than the tales seem to, to demonstrate the expected social and familial roles both women and men were expected to uphold. Instead of merely idealizing the traditional Dakota world, however, *Waterlily* is a complexly written novel that demonstrates the hope and despair inherent in the traditional Oyate spiritual culture world.

Deloria draws on two Oyate literary conventions in the beginning of the novel. The first is to begin vaguely about location and occasion. All we know is that the *tiyospaye* is on the move and it is a hot day. Also, from the beginning of the novel, Deloria relies timorously on exposition to explain ideas unfamiliar to non-Dakota readers, such as why the camp must move and why Blue Bird cannot speak to her father-in-law. Already, on the second page, the sacred number four appears when the mother-in-law tells Blue Bird that the next stop, the fourth, will be the last for the day. The information is important to Blue Bird, who disappears from sight to give birth discreetly.

The birth is the first sacred event of the novel, with Blue Bird wrapping the placenta into a bundle, following "ancient law" (Deloria 1996, 6) not only to keep animals from eating the afterbirth, but also to ensure that her daughter would grow up "straight-limbed and clear-minded," because parts of her spirit are retained in the placenta and her umbilical cord. The baby's navel cord is kept and Blue Bird carefully sews it into a leather beaded toy turtle for Waterlily to play with. Later, "when she was old enough to wear an elaborately decorated gown, this turtle would be attached to the center back of her belt both as an ornament and as a talisman ensuring long life to her" (1996, 23).

The second sacred event also involves Waterlily as a baby, who has become extremely ill. Blue Bird knows she must appeal for divine aid, but fumbles through a ceremony, knowing only remotely from what she has seen and heard what is sacred and what steps should be taken to pray. She had heard once that "'prayer should be audibly released into the infinite,'" so she prays to Wakan Tanka through Inyan, the sacred rock. She chooses the rock to use in the ritual for its size and location and she decorates it with a rare otter skin her father gave her. She gives it the mere ten bundles of tobacco as offering because they are all she is able to procure (1996, 18). After she is certain she hears someone approach from behind, she looks around, but sees no one. Firmly believing her prayer has been heard, she shouts in elation, then weeps in relief and grief. With more confidence and a great sense of hope, she returns home and is not surprised when Waterlily recovers, because "she had prayed for that and had her answer already" (1996, 20).

Blue Bird does not just feel her way through the healing ceremony. As a young adult with no mother to guide her, she had made another mistake in choosing a husband, Star Elk, who is so jealous and possessive of Blue Bird that he wastes time spying on her, when he should be providing for her and his daughter, Waterlily, by hunting (Rice 1992, 124). Just as the young women in *Dakota Texts* are fooled by Double-Face into running away with him, Blue Bird is wooed away by Star Elk. According to John Prater, "The character of Star Elk helps illustrate the range of human behavior which allows for the human agency or individualism encompassed in [Deloria's] portrayal of the Sioux." He further argues that Deloria's "multi-cultural experience opened her to commonalities in this range between cultures and allowed her to portray the universal in the particular" (1995, 44).

What Prater does not acknowledge is that Star Elk behaves in a very typical Double-Face fashion. At a large victory dance, "attended by many visitors from neighboring camp circles," Star Elk publicly "throws away" his wife, Blue Bird, to shame her publicly for what he believes is the shame she has brought to him—shame he brought on himself for acting so petulantly and jealously. Even social disapproval by male elders, "nor the ridicule of his contemporaries spurred Star Elk to be more dutiful as a husband" (1996, 15). Star Elk is so typically self-obsessed, like a Double-

Face or an Iya, that his portrait never really required Deloria's multi-cultural experience. But both Oyate and non-Oyate should recognize him.

Not all the men in *Waterlily* are ogres, though. When Blue Bird and her grandmother return to Blue Bird's parents' *tiyospaye*, her male cousins assume the responsibility of providing meat for them. But Rainbow, a cousin only by marriage, becomes her second husband. A complete opposite of Star Elk, Rainbow is the ideal Lakota male, dutiful, sympathetic, with a mature attitude. Like many of the boy-beloveds, though, he does not hesitate to take command of situations when he sees the need, such as when the grieving men need assistance in building a burial scaffold for Blue Bird's grandmother (1996, 28-29).

Unlike Blue Bird's hasty elopement with Star Elk, she wisely takes her time with Rainbow. With traditional indirection, by discussing mundane matters first, Rainbow proposes. With traditional deliberation, Blue Bird waits to answer. Finally, when their conversation about other matters ends, Blue Bird informs Rainbow she will go with him when he goes on a hunting trip. Later, when Deloria introduces the storyteller Woyaka, she explains, through him, why the Oyate believe in sparingly using words: "'Speech is holy; it was not intended to be set free only to be wasted.'" (50). The Yankton dialect that Deloria grew up speaking (Rice 1992, 2) is described by Deloria as being "markedly vigorous, plain and terse" in both "oratory and storytelling" (1978, 76, n. 1). Such careful selection of language also implies thoughtfulness, that the person has carefully considered what to say before saying it.

In the same way, children are advised to think through the consequences of their actions, as well as their words. Being a good relative means considering how one's actions will reflect on one's relatives, as well as on one's self. As Deloria explains, "One must obey kinship rules; one must be a good relative. . . .To be a good Dakota, then, was to be humanized, civilized. And to be civilized was to keep the rules imposed by kinship for achieving civility, good manners, and a sense of responsibility toward every individual dealt with" (1944, 25). Deftly, Deloria turns Western ideas of civilization against prejudices held about Indians. Kinship rules, when explained, are extremely civilized behavior, but extremely difficult behavior to uphold constantly.

Deloria, then, to make Waterlily a believably human character, allows her to challenge Oyate behavior rules. As a young woman, Waterlily attends a Sun Dance, an event that lasts several days. In typical teenage fashion, as Prater points out, Waterlily wanders about experiencing different aspects of the festival and the plethora of rituals performed at this time with her also teenage cousin, Prairie Flower. Not only are the young women dazzled by the enormity of the event, but also they become aware of the nebulous regions of propriety. Waterlily overhears other young women talking about giving water to their fiancés, who are dancing the traditional sacrificial dance. She is shocked because she knows that drinking water during the ritual, which is all about sacrificing oneself to Wakan Tanka for the greater good of the nation, is forbidden. She is even further disturbed when her mother says that such a breech of conduct is often overlooked (1996, 122).

Later, Waterlily recognizes among the dancers a young man, Lowanla, she noticed earlier when he sang at an Omaha-Lakota gathering. Lowanla has been rash and vowed a hundred pieces of flesh to Wakan Tanka to save his ill father. After the first ten cuts, he faints and two elderly aunts rush to his assistance, offering thirty pieces of flesh from their own bodies to help his count to one hundred. Later two of his sisters also offer ten each. Finally, after the full hundred are taken, they are accepted after a fourth offering and buried at the foot of the sacred pole (1996, 127-28).

Later that night, Waterlily, the temporarily disobedient child, secretly takes Lowanla, who is still dancing, water to drink. Even though Waterlily breaks the Sun Dance rules, she never tells anyone, not even Lowanla, whom she marries as her second husband—a marriage that brings her the ideal happiness that her mother's marriage to Rainbow brought. Deloria allows Waterlily to entertain the idea that she should satisfy Lowanla's romantic desire that the girl who gave him water was her (1996, 227), but Waterlily not only develops compassion, she gains wisdom. She realizes that by confirming Lowanla's suspicions, she would also give him reason to wonder if she ever did such a secret thing for any other man (1996, 226), which would cause distrust to grow between them. Just as Woyaka warned years before, too many words said or words misspoken without careful thought "can be dangerous" (Rice 1992, 123).

As scholars such as Rice and Prater have demonstrated, Deloria was a careful crafter of words. Perhaps, given the text offered in Rice's *Ella Deloria's Iron Hawk,* Deloria's rendition of *Iron Hawk* is as eloquent an epic as has ever been written in either Lakota or English. Even so, *Waterlily* is an excellent example of a modernist novel. Deloria has not only reached back into a "forgotten mode" of composing words and resurrected it with eloquent considerations for her non-Oyate audiences, making a lesson in Sioux living as appealing and easy to understand as possible, but she has also preserved those Oyate oral literary traditions and their characteristic elements in her valuable bilingual work, *Dakota Texts.*

Studying what Deloria has so carefully set down in writing will not only illuminate for scholars what many of the specific literary elements were in the oral literary traditions of the Oyate, but also it will provide a greater understanding of a culture and its writers, writers who were and who still continue to be interstitially affected by our polycultural society.

Black Elk
From Hilda Neihardt's *Black Elk and Flaming Rainbow,*
University of Nebraska Press, 1995.
Courtesy Hilda Neihardt and
University of Nebraska Press

6

BLACK ELK PASSES ON THE
POWER OF THE EARTH

Melding Religions, Purposes, and
Literary Traditions in *Black Elk Speaks*

*D*ramatic monologue, self-examination, corroborative speakers—cued as though characters in a play, corroborative drawings in both color and black and white, inserted chants and textual notes, repetition, indirection, sacred symbolism, and textual experimentation—all make *Black Elk Speaks* a modernist collage of Sioux and Euro-American literary traditions. Moreso than many of the other transitional Sioux works, even those altered by editors, *Black Elk Speaks* is a collage, or a marble cake as Ella Deloria might call it (Rice 1992, 16), not only of a polyphony of Indian voices telling their stories with a sometimes indirect, sometimes overt Euro-American voice chiming in, but also of (at least) two individual souls interpreting the symbols of two seemingly different perceptions of the world that are often remarkably similar. As such a collage, *Black Elk Speaks* becomes an interstitial text that allowed its two primary creators, and continues to allow its readers, access to both Sioux and Euro-American literary and cultural influences in such a way that an understanding of both influences greatly heightens appreciation for the work as a whole. To achieve such a heightened appreciation requires acknowledging and analyzing the creative choices made by both Neihardt and Black Elk, the latter of whom exercised as much choice in the manner of transmission of his vision/story as did the former.

Of all the texts by transitional Sioux writers, *Black Elk Speaks* was and remains the most widely read, the most influential. Significantly, Black Elk, Hehaka Sapa, was the only one of the major transitional Oyate writers who never learned to read or speak English. How is it that a Lakota *wicasa wakan*, who chose not to learn the dominant American language, could have had such an impact on American literature? Black Elk was influenced enough by Euro-American values not only to become an influential Catholic catechist, credited with converting more than four hundred Indians to Christianity (DeMallie 1984, 26), but also to continue demonstrating tribal ceremonies, which he discovered Europeans and Americans in general enjoyed watching while working as a young man for a Wild West show, and as an Indian pageant performer in Rapid City, South Dakota. He even accepted Euro-American cultural conventions enough to collaborate on several books, *Black Elk Speaks* (1932), *When the Tree Flowered* (1951), and *The Sacred Pipe* (1953). Just as other Indians had to deal with the pressures of assimilationist forces, Black Elk significantly exercised more *choice* in doing so than did the other Sioux writers, excepting perhaps Gertrude Bonnin, who chose to remain largely culturally Indian even in mainstream society, and Ella Deloria who chose to aid in preserving Oyate culture by recording tales in both Lakota and English. Following their father's suggestions to learn the ways of the white man, Charles Eastman and Luther Standing Bear were pushed or enticed by various outside forces to adopt Euro-American ways of living. To a much larger degree, Black Elk resisted deculturation from his primary culture, Oglala Lakotan, and, although he acculturated *some* Euro-American ways of living, he avoided assimilation into mainstream American living.

Black Elk was a very observant man. Even though he did not assimilate, he seems to have learned much about what Euro-Americans believed and how they thought. His first decision to observe non-Indian ways of living firsthand came at twenty-three when Black Elk chose to explore Europe and America with a Wild West show. Discouraged by ever more rigid controls being clamped down on his tribe's lifestyle, as well as being "disgusted with the wrong road that [his] people" were traveling on, Black

Elk says, "I made up my mind I was going away from them to see the white man's ways. If the white man's ways were better, why I would like to see my people live that way" (DeMallie 1984, 245).

Against his family's wishes (DeMallie 1984, 246), Black Elk stayed with the show three years, even traveling to England where he met Queen Victoria, whom he called "Grandmother England," quoting her as saying, "I would not carry you [Indians] around as beasts to show to the people" (DeMallie 1984, 250). After being left behind by one Wild West show, he was soon picked up by another, which allowed him to see France, Germany, and Italy. Becoming more and more disenchanted with being on exhibit, Black Elk fell ill and returned to Paris to stay with a girlfriend. During a bout of fever, he had another vision—one of returning home to his mother's tepee. When he finally did return home to the reservation and his healing practices, he was pleased to discover everything had happened just as his dream had predicted, further affirmation for him of the power of his sacred vision and what it could do for his people.

Only later in 1904 did he accept Catholicism, a religion that provided him with a partly assimilated way of continuing his spiritual leadership to his people. Supposedly, Black Elk converted after a priest threw him and his shaman tools out of a dying boy's tent. As Paul Steinmetz points out, many Lakota converted to Christianity because "a thing is wakan insofar as it does have power . . . what converted [others] was not speculation about God but an experience of power" (1990, 42). According to Black Elk's daughter, Lucy Looks Twice, Black Elk sensed that the priest's powers were stronger than his, so he allowed the priest to give him religious instruction, to baptize him, and to give him a Christian name, Nicholas (DeMallie 1984, 14).[1]

Even after converting, Black Elk maintained cultural balances as he lived on the Pine Ridge Reservation. While he lived in a cabin instead of a tepee and converted other Lakota to Christianity, there is reason to believe Black Elk continued to perform his duties as an Oglala holy man, such as officiating at sun dances, even though the dances had been banned by the

---

1. Clyde Holler casts reasonable doubt upon Lucy Looks Twice's depiction of her father's conversion. See *Black Elk's Religion* (1995), pp. 13–16 and 25–28 in particular.

U.S. government (Holler 1995, 18). He also emphasized traditional Lakota ritual practices, such as ceremonial smoking, community feasts, naming ceremonies, and collaborative speakers, while transmitting his vision to Neihardt to create the book.[2] Above all, while Black Elk learned to read the Bible in Lakota and even wrote letters in Lakota, he chose never to learn to read and write in English.

In contrast, Eastman, Bonnin, Deloria, and Standing Bear felt pressured by non-Indians to live all-or-nothing lives—either wholly Indian or wholly Euro-American. All four writers succeeded, however, in incorporating balancing elements of both cultures into their lives and writings. Even though the combination of cultural and literary traditions within their works should have qualified them for consideration as modernist writers, most literary critics have chosen to see their works as reflecting liminality and discord, even though the four tried to show themselves as successfully assimilated Indians in transitional America. Ironically, the so-called high modernists, who reestablished the importance of literary tradition to the creation of literature, had to research and rediscover their ancestral cultures, as well as borrow from American Indian ones, in search of useful symbols and myths for literary tools.

Both Eastman and Standing Bear originally set out to demonstrate their successful integration into the non-Indian parts of America, while Standing Bear, in the later years of his life and in his later writings, and Bonnin, throughout most of her life, specifically tried to persuade Indians to retain their cultures as the largest and most significant part of their lives. Of the five writers, Black Elk retained, by choice, his Indian culture most consistently during his life and most strongly overall. This strong retention of his primary culture, and his primary decisions concerning the

2. Holler asserts that Neihardt's elimination, probably because of his ignorance of its importance, of the ritual involved in Black Elk's transmission of his sacred vision "is the first giant step away from the Lakota world in which Black Elk's instruction took place. The loss of the full ritual context of the interviews is the greatest loss attributable to Neihardt's lack of anthropological training" (1984b, 30). Michael Staub argues, however, that "the transcription of sacred speeches into a written document was perhaps one means of preserving and extending the power of the spoken words" (1987, 46), agreeing with Albert Stone that merely "reading *Black Elk Speaks* is a sacred ritual in itself" (1982, 62).

content of his stories and the method of their transmission to Neihardt, enabled him to balance out Neihardt's strong Western sensibilities in the creation of *Black Elk Speaks*.

Scholars often focus on two different aspects of *Black Elk Speaks*. First, John G. Neihardt acted as a medium between Black Elk's life story and the book's readers—which opens up questions concerning the purpose of the book. Was Neihardt solely serving his own purposes, or does he "authentically" project Black Elk's vision as well? Second, questions are tied to the first about the book's spirituality. Debates rage over the accuracy of Neihardt's depictions of Lakota spirituality and of Black Elk's sincerity in accepting Christianity, a conversion that is never mentioned in the book. Is the sense of the sacred in *Black Elk Speaks* from Neihardt's need to explore the Messiah movement, which was his original reason for interviewing Black Elk, as well as from Neihardt's deeply acculturated sense of Christianity, or does it stem primarily from the power of Black Elk's visions and his need to pass on his sacred knowledge in a traditional Lakota manner?

Raymond DeMallie, in his seminal work *The Sixth Grandfather*, largely accepts Neihardt's depiction of Black Elk, sympathetically picturing the situation between the two

as if something long bound up inside the old man had broken free at last. . . . Since becoming a Catholic Black Elk had strictly put away the old ceremonies and his healing rituals. He had accepted the white man's religion and the white man's ways, and this would not change. But the vision, and his failure to live up to it, must have been a heavy burden . . . [which] he could at long last transfer to another man—someone who could record the old Lakota ways as testament and memorial to a way of life now gone forever. (1984, 28)

The romantic nostalgia created by *Black Elk Speaks* carries over into De-Mallie's assessment of the circumstances.

Yet, DeMallie readily admits "Neihardt was already 'writing' Black Elk's story by rephrasing his words in English" during the interview sessions (1984, 32). He also points out, significantly, that Black Elk counter-translates Neihardt's words for his own understanding of the situation. An important part of all this translating, Ben Black Elk, Black Elk's son, has been, ironically, mostly neglected. How important is the fact that Ben Black Elk did the translating? Especially when Ben had never before been told all of Black Elk's vision (H. Neihardt 1995, 50)? I will attempt to answer these questions presently.

When Neihardt told Black Elk he became an epic poet because he sought a "higher purpose," "this the old man translated as *hanbloglaka*, 'vision telling,' the traditional mystical speech of Lakota holy men" when they tell their sacred visions, each tale imbued with the particular symbols of the individual man's vision (DeMallie 1984, 37). Thus, Black Elk found a direct connection between himself and Neihardt—they both have traditional ways of telling stories since both their lives are directed by the power of visions.

In simplifying how the men regarded each other, DeMallie argues that "Neihardt perceived Black Elk's religion in terms of art; Black Elk perceived Neihardt's art in terms of religion" (1984, 37). But religion and art are not that easily separable in the Lakota cosmos. Through his Euro-American sense of the artistic forms of narration, Neihardt conveys not only Black Elk's sense of the sacred mission he has been assigned, but also Black Elk's sense of artistic, Lakota narration, and his understanding of the intricate workings of the Sioux Literary Tradition.

DeMallie produces an interesting comparison of Black Elk's interpretation of his vision and White Bull's, whose biography was written by Stanley Vestal. DeMallie asserts that "in most respects, Black Elk's religious experiences were entirely representative of late nineteenth-century Lakota culture" (1984, 84), because it adheres to the pattern set after Lakota contact with and persistent war with Euro-Americans. White Bull's vision is much like Black Elk's, yet

> he did not interpret it as a mandate to become a holy man. In part this reflected the times. White Bull was born in 1849; when the vision came to him in 1858 the Lakotas were still living in the old way. Buffalo were plentiful, and the northern Lakotas (White Bull was Minneconjou) had not yet become involved in war with the whites. The road to success for

a young man was still through fighting the enemy tribes and gaining war
honors, and it was for this kind of endeavor that White Bull found power
in his vision. (DeMallie 1984, 85)

Besides differences in personality and in the times, a possible explanation
why Black Elk took his vision differently than White Bull took his could
lie in the fact that different *wicasa wakan* interpreted their dreams for them,
producing different *hanbloglaka,* vision tellings, which emphasized different
spiritual obligations. So that we must acknowledge that before Black Elk
could make use of what he experienced during his vision, someone else, in
this case Black Road (DeMallie 1984, 214), had to interpret it for him. Black
Elk had dreamed the symbols; Black Road had to tell him what they
meant.

To Neihardt's credit, DeMallie points out that Neihardt "resisted the
publisher's attempt to relegate the vision to an appendix," but also admits
that "cultural details were not so important to Neihardt as were the mood
and message" (1984, 53). DeMallie defends Neihardt's artistic choices: Diction is kept simple to "reflect our expectation of Indian speech patterns"
(52); the vision's emphasis on war and destruction are minimized to focus
on its messages of healing (1984, 53); the Thunder Beings' powers, which
were transmitted to Black Elk, are de-emphasized because they presented
Black Elk as a possible threat armed with destructive, magical powers and
because such details, foreign to most Euro-Americans, would have been
taxing to read (1984, 54); and the sense of despair and of the inevitable
"destruction of the Lakotas' way of life" are heightened to mirror and
emphasize Black Elk's sense of failure in having not used the knowledge
he had gained from his entire vision as he was told to do by the Six
Grandfathers, the primary powers of the Lakota world (1984, 55). DeMallie
admits that Neihardt's image of Black Elk as a "pitiful old man . . . sorrow-
ing over the destruction of his people is a powerful literary" device (1984,
57), and that the book was "intended as a work of art, transcending the
ordinary to make a larger statement about humanity" (1984, 57). To De-
Mallie, "the book is Black Elk's story as he gave it to Neihardt, but the
literary quality and the tone of the work are Neidhardt's" (1984, 51).

Nearly ten years later, DeMallie, in the introduction to Neihardt's novel *When the Tree Flowered*, reemphasizes both Neihardt's and Black Elk's perspectives. Neihardt believed he wrote *Black Elk Speaks* as "a faithful telling of one man's life, and an attempt to interpret Black Elk's philosophy and personality as Neihardt understood them," in effect "minimiz[ing] his own presence as author, [by] relegating himself to a preface and a postscript, refraining throughout the text from introducing superfluous description and explanation" (1991, x). DeMallie believes that the book's "unembroidered directness" in allowing Black Elk to speak for himself "led readers of the 1930s to reject the book as too far removed from their own experience to be credible, but led readers from the 1960s on to embrace it as representing the unmediated expression of a native voice" (1991, xi). DeMallie notes that Neihardt "was aggravated when reviewers, instead of taking the book at face value as representative of the Sioux world-view, suggested that [he] had used Black Elk as a vehicle to express his own philosophy" (1991, x). DeMallie emphasizes that, although Neihardt worked to bring the traditional Sioux view forward authentically, "he had not intended by [doing so] to obscure his creative role as author" (1991, xi).

Julian Rice, likewise, argues that Neihardt was more than amanuensis, claiming that "none of the imagery is Black Elk's," despite evidence to the contrary in the transcripts, and accuses Neihardt of altering Black Elk's descriptions of "Lakota unity to a prophecy of universal peace as if to indicate a moral progression brought about by God" (1991, 63), even though he admits *Black Elk Speaks* is one of Black Elk's major works (1991, 8). He believes "the Lakota integrity of *Black Elk Speaks* [exists] only to the extent that Neihardt felt he could not betray Black Elk" (1991, 61). He contradicts DeMallie's universal peace theme argument by insisting that when Black Elk refers to unifying people, he means the Lakota people only (1991, 62). DeMallie later clarifies and corroborates the fact that it was "Neihardt [who] transforms the sacred hoop of the people into the sacred hoop of all peoples, extending Black Elk's vision symbol of the unity of the Sioux into a symbol of the unity of all humankind" (1991, xiv), overlooking rituals of unity performed by Black Elk during the interviews (Holler 1984b, 27).

Repeatedly, Rice argues that Black Elk would not have inserted Christian imagery because traditional Lakota would not have thought along

those terms (1991, 48–64), ignoring the fact that Black Elk had been a
practicing Catholic catechist for more years, and more recently, than he
had been a practicing Oglala medicine man. The religions not only would
have become fused to one another in Black Elk's memory in many ways—
as they did for Eastman—but also would have become lenses one for the
other, so that he would have been able to see traditional Sioux religious
practices through the lens of Catholicism, and Catholicism through the
lens of Lakota beliefs. Quite possibly, Black Elk believed, as his son Ben
would later assert, "that traditional religion and Christianity 'fulfill each
other'" (Holler 1995, 34).

Clyde Holler corroborates this view, arguing that, especially in *The
Sacred Pipe,* "Black Elk's innovation . . . is clearly conscious, and it takes
place on a more self-consciously theological level. . . . Black Elk is clearly
. . . most engaged with Catholicism and with the intellectual problem of
its relationship to traditional religion" (1995, 185). While *Black Elk Speaks*
focuses on traditional Lakota religion, there should be no doubt that, because Black Elk is recounting his memories after years of practicing Catholicism, the Euro-American religion will affect, to some degree, how he
came to perceive traditional Lakota religion. Critics as early as Carol T.
Holly and as recent as Clyde Holler acknowledge this wedding of religious
perceptions as the probable working reality for Black Elk. In 1979, Holly
asserted that *"Black Elk Speaks* represents a genuine marriage between native American consciousness and western literary form" (121). In 1995, Holler recanted Julian Rice's dichotomous contrasts between Lakota and
Christian religions, "particularly because many Lakotas profess allegiance
to both traditions" (28) and because Black Elk probably "regarded these
two traditions as two expressions of the same sacred reality" (36).

Strangely enough, Rice praises *The Sacred Pipe* because, even though "it
has many Christian elements," it "remains one of the best written descriptions of Lakota ceremonies" (1991, 4). Rice agrees with Clyde Holler's earlier assessment[3] of the equality of Christianity and the Lakota religion,
declaring that the choice to parallel Christian rites and myths with Lakota
ones in *The Sacred Pipe* was "a conscious strategy on Black Elk's part" (1991,

3. See Holler's essay "Black Elk's Relationship to Christianity," 1984a.

6). The fact that Black Elk chose to emphasize the traditional Lakota religion in *Black Elk Speaks* disturbed his daughter Lucy Looks Twice, prompting her to collaborate with Michael F. Steltenkamp, as we shall see.

Rice concludes, however, that scholars, like the 1930 readers DeMallie referred to, take Black Elk's words, his vision, too literally, failing to recognize his symbolic uses of metaphor. Drawing from another critic's discussion of symbolism, Rice points out that just as the Eucharist metaphorically represents the body and blood of Christ to Christians, the spiritual elements of Black Elk's visions, too, are metaphoric, working, like the Eucharist, to bring his followers closer to Wakan Tanka (1991, 150). Holler corroborates this argument, asserting "there is no reason to assume that Black Elk did not realize" his vision "is filled with symbols" (1995, 215). While there is little evidence to support it, my belief is that many of the symbols in Black Elk's vision, and later in the Ghost Dance, were well ingrained, thus highly familiar, symbols used in the Lakota oral literary (and spiritual, often simultaneous) tradition(s).

Rice insinuates, however, that Black Elk fictionalizes parts of his vision for two possible reasons: because he needed to protect the power of the vision to keep its power, for him, from lessening and to keep its power from being wrongly used, and that because "outside spirits transmit strength through a symbolic medium, naturally or humanly shaped," so that "power is circulated, sent by the spirits as inspiration, returned to them as expression, and passed as easily through fiction as through 'truth'" (1991, 152).

Holler counters both Rice and Steltenkamp's implications that Black Elk was insincere in transmitting his vision and in his conversion to Catholicism because

> the assumption that there was this much deception in Black Elk's character is just as unlikely as the assumption that he made a complete transition to twentieth-century Catholic consciousness. . . . The evidence seems to indicate that Black Elk readily accepted Christianity as a valid extension of the insights expressed in his power vision, and as a practical bridge to the white world and a better life for his people. (1995, 27)

Hilda Neihardt, John Neihardt's daughter, also counters claims against Black Elk's honesty when she insists that "communicating 'the truth' was important to Black Elk," so both he and her father took precautions to solidify the truth as closely as possible. Black Elk had his corroborator, Standing Bear (no relation to Luther), "present during all the interviews, because the presence of his longtime friend would make it clear to Neihardt that he was telling the truth" (H. Neihardt 1995, 36). Neihardt rephrased and queried for more details, all of which was translated back and forth by Ben, to make certain Neihardt understood Black Elk's meaning (39).

Because of the emphasis on the authenticity of Black Elk's vision and the focus of *Black Elk Speaks* on traditional Lakota religion, Michael F. Steltenkamp, after encountering Lucy Looks Twice, Black Elk's daughter, felt the need to set "the record straight" about the full extent of Black Elk's life. After a chance encounter, not unlike Neihardt's with Black Elk nearly sixty years earlier, Steltenkamp interviewed Lucy and determined that she had "a dream [she] had carried with her ever since her father's death . . . to have her father's life fully recorded" (1993, xix–xx). In what seems to be imitation of Neihardt's introduction to Black Elk, Steltenkamp notes that because she was "in her declining years, Lucy knew that not much time remained for her to fulfill the *vision* of relating her father's life story" (1993, xx; emphasis mine). Perhaps this imitation is unconscious on Steltenkamp's part, but it is more likely that he is demonstrating a Lakota storytelling convention, or a Christian one, something like "when I was lost and needing direction, I chanced upon a wise old sage who said. . . ." Yet he wants us to take his efforts more seriously than Neihardt's because he took years to translate, transcribe, compile, edit, interpret, and polish Black Elk's life story, as given him by Lucy, methodically, so that "she was quite satisfied with our collaborative effort" after she read it (1993, xx).[4] Steltenkamp wrote Black Elk's "complete" biography as "an example of reflexive adjustment to new cultural landscapes that previously had not

4. Not until many years later did Lucy read *Black Elk Speaks*, which, she said, changed her life—she became a believer and a pipe carrier (H. Neihardt 1995, 119).

been explored" (1993, xxi)—namely, Lucy Looks Twice's much more accul-turated and assimilated point of view.

Steltenkamp's most convincing arguments come in his evaluations of the controversies surrounding Black Elk, wherein "much of the discussion spawned by Black Elk has focused on an either-or proposition: he was, at heart, either an old-time medicine man or one who forsook the tradition in favor of something entirely new" (1993, 157). Yet, he notes, Lakota ideol-ogy allows Black Elk to have a "resilient willingness to let go of what was and to experiment with what might be the disclosures of Wakan Tanka for his life" (1993, 160). As a traditional shaman, Black Elk would have pos-sessed "a well-conditioned, culturally based disposition toward seeking the power of *Wakan Tanka* on whatever new horizon it might appear" (1993, 161). As a respected Lakota religious practitioner, his role was primarily to "foster a religious consciousness that had so long enabled the people to confront whatever challenged them," so that when religious leaders such as Black Elk converted to Christianity, their Lakota followers would be more likely to convert as well. As Lucy admitted to Steltenkamp, the mis-sionaries worked to convert the religious leaders in order to reach the rest of the people because of the belief that, if Wakan Tanka was leading the shaman to Christianity, they, too, should follow (1993, 162). The religion and its particular practices, or what we can see as the means with which human beings connect to spiritual powers, were not as important to Black Elk, according to Steltenkamp, as the quest to connect with those powers, so that "whereas [Black Elk's] destiny was that of a Catholic catechist, others might pursue alternate paths" with many returning to traditional Lakota religious practices (1993, 164–65).

Most recently, Clyde Holler vehemently argues that there can be no coinciding of purpose between Black Elk's wish to convey his vision and Neihardt's needs for literary material, insisting that "defenders of Neihardt who insist on his faithfulness to Black Elk's message simply reveal the shortcomings of their understanding of literature" (1995, 7). Performing his own logical skewing, he adds up the facts that Neihardt added the pessimistic ending in an artistic turn, deleted much of the vision's war imagery to create a more positive bend to the vision, and inserted his own positive, universal message to mean that "Black Elk did not believe that the dream had died" (1995, 7), never clarifying, in his book, how the fact that Neihardt did these things reveals so conclusively what Black Elk *believed.*[5] He does agree with Steltenkamp that scholars cannot take an either/or stance in trying to understand Black Elk the man (1995, 22), reiterating that Black Elk's adaptability stems primarily from his understanding of the sacred (1995, 23). Holler points out that Black Elk's *practice* of both traditional Lakota beliefs and Christianity "seems to have been to keep the two traditions separate on the level of ritual," while reminding us that the categories scholars attempt to use in understanding Black Elk's exact religious allegiances "presuppose a distinction between [the religions] that Black Elk may not have felt as strongly as it has been felt by outside observers" (1995, 35). Unlike DeMallie, who saw Black Elk as reconverting to traditional Lakota religion by assisting to re-create *Black Elk Speaks,* Holler successfully argues that "where commentators have seen two incompatible beliefs . . . Black Elk seems to have seen two basically compatible beliefs, or two modalities of what was primary, the sacred" (Holler 1995, 220).

Holler ends up arguing that Black Elk believed in three religions: traditional Indian beliefs (modified with specific Lakota ones), the Ghost Dance religion, and Christianity (1995, 217). Later, Holler acknowledges that the Ghost Dance religion had many of the same symbolic elements of traditional Lakota religious practices (1995, 222), arguing that Black Elk "employ[ed] symbolic discourse, a common device when speaking plainly is proscribed by oppression" in *Black Elk Speaks* to urge a revival of the sun dance as openly as he was allowed considering the activity was outlawed by the government (1995, 221–22). Although Holler does agree with Paul Steinmetz's postulation that "the Ghost Dance served as the template for the Lakota acceptance of Christianity" (1990, 218, n. 13), he pulls back from a reverse comparison. He does hint at the possibility that the revival of

5. This oversight by Holler is part of ongoing scholarship; he has simply neglected to reiterate, at this point in his book, what he had argued in an earlier article. He does effectively argue earlier that Black Elk did not hold the pessimistic view Neihardt assigns him in *Black Elk Speaks* by pointing out passages from the transcripts that demonstrate Black Elk's desire for Neihardt's assistance in transmitting "Black Elk's vision and sacred knowledge from the Lakota world to the white world" (1984b, 27).

interest in traditional practices and beliefs in contemporary times that
Black Elk created through *Black Elk Speaks* and *The Sacred Pipe* is akin to
Wovoka's revival with the Ghost Dance (1990, 222), but takes a more daring stance in paralleling Black Elk's intentions with those of Jesus (1990,
223).

Holler is one of the few scholars to examine how and why Black Elk
chose to convey his sense of Lakota culture, especially his personal vision,
to a larger audience, or what considerations went into making that choice.
To be thoroughly explored yet are the Sioux (Oyate) literary traditions
embodied within Black Elk's telling and Neihardt's recomposing, combined strongly with Euro-American literary traditions, of the Lakota lifestyles, beliefs, and visions in *Black Elk Speaks*. Although Julian Rice claims
Black Elk chose to translate his vision "and the whole of his accumulated
wisdom into every genre of the oral tradition," he names only four Lakota
genres—offered up to restore Lakota confidence and desire to live in the
face of the severity of economic and cultural depression:

> *hanbloglaka* (dream or vision-talks) renewed the people's confidence in
> their traditional methods of obtaining spiritual protection; *waktogloka* (kill
> talks) reminded them that as Black Elk had been able to defend himself,
> so they too might do from those who had stolen most of their land and
> threatened to take their culture too; *wicowoyake* (true stories) provided
> evidence of strategies their ancestors had received or developed to ensure
> survival; and *ohunkakan* (mythical stories) gave them a perspective on
> contemporary struggles so that they might think of them as the same
> ordeals that are always the precondition of wisdom and fulfilled con-
> sciousness. (1989, 25–26)

While establishing that the Sioux acknowledged and practiced different types of storytelling is important in illustrating their long-standing
literary traditions, it is important to recognize, as with any literary study,
that not all stories fit neatly into established categories. In the sections of
Black Elk Speaks that I will examine here, Black Elk uses all four story
genres mentioned above, and probably more, in an intermingling manner
not unlike Neihardt's intermingling of Euro-American literary traditions,
Christian ideals, and Black Elk's narrative. It is also important to recognize

that Neihardt would have become familiar with many of the Lakota literary traditions as Black Elk and the other men spoke and performed rituals for the interviews, even if he would not have consciously labeled them such.

To better understand Black Elk's (and Neihardt's) literary choices, we need to first place him in context with his peers. Black Elk, born in 1863 or 1866, was five to eight years younger than Eastman (the oldest transitional Sioux writer) and thirteen to ten years older than Zitkala-Sa (the youngest transitional Sioux writer). Despite being contemporaneous Sioux, although all five were of different bands, and despite beginning to publish after the other four writers, Black Elk and his works have not been examined for influences by the other Oyate writers, or by any of Black Elk's other contemporary Indian storytellers. Was Black Elk familiar with, let alone influenced by, his earlier peers?

One reason for overlooking the possibility that Black Elk was familiar with the writings of Standing Bear, Bonnin, Deloria, and Eastman is the dilemma of language. Despite having been in contact with Euro-Americans from a fairly early age, Black Elk retained the most traditional Sioux lifestyle—so much so that he had (at least *chose*) to have his son translate his words for Neihardt. But would the fact that Black Elk—a man raised in a culture that relies heavily on oral communication—did not speak or read English preclude him from knowing about the other writers or their works? And, if he did know about them, did such knowledge directly affect his decision to tell Neihardt, and later Brown, his own life story and knowledge of Lakota religion, freely explaining rituals and other sacred information?

It is also possible that influences by preceding writers have been unexplored because critics tend to focus on Black Elk's decision to transmit his story through Neihardt (and have largely ignored Black Elk's use of Ben), instead of writing his story himself. It is well documented that many Indians resented being manipulated into speaking of taboo subjects, such as naming the dead or sharing tribal rituals and sacred songs, by anthropologists who were "objectively" seeking documentation of cultures often alien to them. So both Neihardt and Brown emphasize how Black Elk in essence *chose* them to tell his stories to (Neihardt 1979, xvii; Brown 1953, xiii).

Neihardt reported, and his daughter Hilda corroborates, that his initial interpreter mentioned how Black Elk refused to tell his stories to a woman anthropologist shortly before Neihardt turned up at Pine Ridge (Neihardt 1979, vii; H. Neihardt 1995, 12–13). Raymond DeMallie notes that, because Black Elk was a "Roman Catholic catechist, [a] pillar of the church," it was doubtful that Black Elk would willingly talk about non-Christian matters to a stranger (1984, 27).

Neihardt, his daughter Hilda, Brown, Black Elk, and DeMallie all seem to corroborate the belief that Black Elk chose Neihardt as his amanuensis because of a spiritual kinship. Neihardt noted that, upon approaching Black Elk's house, it seemed as though Black Elk were expecting him (1984, 27). This possible spiritual connection has been important in many arguments because it helps align Neihardt's intentions in *Black Elk Speaks* directly with Black Elk's, so that there should be no doubt about the work's authenticity. Some scholars see such statements by Neihardt as false, mere attempts to connive his readers, especially given the fact that Brown later uses a similar statement: "When the ritual smoking was completed, the old man turned to me and asked why I had taken so long in getting there, for he had been expecting my coming" (1953, xii). Is such a statement a Lakota convention, an indirect way of assuring the visitor he is welcome? Rice quotes, and agrees with, Holler's declaration that Black Elk did not really know beforehand that either Neihardt or Brown was coming to visit him. Both critics agree that Black Elk was speaking conventionally "rather than referring to ESP." Such a greeting to Rice, is a way to welcome "a visitor into a relationship that will be good, sanctioned by the spirits" (1991, 149).

But perhaps Black Elk was more shrewd in his selective *choice* of amanuensis than he has been given credit for. Perhaps Black Elk did not want his story to end up like so many other Indian stories as an essay in some anthropological journal or as a book with little literary value other than the fact it contains the life history of an Indian holy man. Perhaps Black Elk had heard of the success Sioux writers such as Eastman and Bonnin were experiencing in transmitting traditional Oceti Sakowin stories and ideas to the wider world. Was Black Elk merely looking for a larger audience and a more influential transmitting medium, recognizing the power of the written word because of his knowledge of the Bible's power given Christianity's scope around the world? Or is it too outrageous to speculate that Black Elk understood the potential, and lasting, impact of a story with literary value as opposed to one collected by an anthropologist?

He was, after all, a Catholic cleric who read and who preached from a Lakota Bible in Lakota to other Lakotas. He could have written his story in Lakota. But he was probably also aware of the widespread impact of written stories in English. He was also well traveled and had conversed with other men and women trained in spiritual, practical, and literary interpretations of the Bible. While he had remained on the reservation, he also knew the reservation's structures—including the influences day schools and boarding schools had on younger generations. As an observant, intelligent man, he would have been able to discern—even through the filter of reservation living—what was important to Euro-Americans.

He knew stories not only had to appear to be truthful, for Euro-Americans to appreciate them, but also they had to be well told. As Rice points out, Black Elk "must have known of the white man's need to have an absolute predetermined truth from his 30 years as a Catholic catechist. Stories of the oral traditions express the 'subjective' truth of the teller's inspiration which can be wrapped in many bundles of which those preserving the people's life are true, and those inflating the teller or flattering the listener are false" (1989, 47). Black Elk could have refrained from writing his story in Lakota because of concerns about being able to publish it, as well as the skepticism he would have encountered from being an Indian, and a seemingly presumptuous one from a Lakota perspective, who asserted that his story was important enough to tell in his own, alien to most publishers, language. Not being invited to tell one's story was against Lakota custom.

Yet, Black Elk knew his story was important, not only to himself, but also to his people, as well as to the world. He knew he had a good story to tell and he knew he could tell it well. The literary value inherent in looking for a believable, well-told story is not unique to Euro-Americans, and it is presumptuous to assume it is. Charles Eastman's reverent descriptions of famed storyteller Smokey Day,[6] and Ella Deloria's vivid descriptions of the effect of a mesmerizing storyteller, Woyaka, has on his audience (1988, 50–57), as well as Waterlily's ability to captivate her children with tales (1988, 82–83), demonstrate the Sioux appreciation of a story well told.

As James Clifford points out, many ethnographers have observed methods, from blatant to subtle, by which "their research was directed or circumscribed by their informants" (1988, 44), so "that indigenous control over knowledge gained in the field can be considerable, and even determining" (1988, 45). It is highly plausible that Black Elk would reject one potential amanuensis for a better one—one who was not only a recognized poet, but also a man who was familiar with native ways of living and thinking (H. Neihardt 1995, 38). The facts that Neihardt could tell a good story and was familiar with Lakota culture would have become clear to Black Elk within the first hour or so of their meeting. A spiritual connection, if there really was one, would have been a bonus and would have helped reassure Black Elk that his decision to reveal his life story, and his sacred vision, to this person was the right choice.

Although many critics acknowledge Black Elk's communal efforts in telling his stories to Neihardt, most dismiss Neihardt's initial pursuit and final gathering of Black Elk's stories as only those of a Westerner trying to pin down, for his own purposes, an individual's life story. However, Neihardt did not set out to preserve Black Elk's story, but to gather information on the Messiah movement for his epic poem *Cycles of the West.* There is ample evidence that he, too, knew a good story when he heard one and knew the potential for a good book when he found one (H. Neihardt 1995, 18).

Perhaps one reason why Black Elk felt a kinship with Neihardt was that Neihardt spoke a kind of ritual language, stemming from a trained aesthetic appreciation for language, that Black Elk recognized, something like the *hanbloglaka* (the term Black Elk used to describe Neihardt's mission to be an epic poet) used by those interpreting visions, in which Black Elk was trained. Both men, then, were trained with particular, perhaps similar, aesthetic concerns for language. Like the Sioux ritual language, Euro-

6. See *Indian Boyhood* (1902), pp. 115–53, and all of *Wigwam Evenings* (1990).

American literary terms are not standardized, "but . . . contain some lexical items which [are] mutually intelligible between" those trained to use it (W. Powers 1977, 65). William Powers tells us that Lakota "sacred persons were distinguishable from the common people not only by their ability to interpret sacred knowledge," just as literary scholars interpret texts, as well as "by their ability to communicate . . . in a special language unintelligible to the uninitiated . . . although [there is] no evidence that there was a conscious attempt by sacred persons to exclude common people from sacred discourse" (64), which can also be said, for the most part, about literary scholarship. Perhaps Neihardt's Euro-American *literary* training prepared him for his being able to speak, as though one *wakan* man to another, in something like Sioux *wakan* language.

Regardless of his intentions, many critics see Neihardt's motivations as purely Western and Black Elk's as purely Indian. Albert Stone, for instance, sees Black Elk's culture as clearly Indian, meaning communal, and Neihardt's as Western, meaning individually driven (1982, 158)—believing Neihardt "surrendered himself to his Indian subject" (157–58). H. David Brumble sees *Black Elk Speaks* as a product of two personalities and two cultures (1988, 12) and allows only that an Indian is capable of conceiving of more than one self—one tribal, one individual—after the influences of Euro-American autobiography become familiar to them (146). Arnold Krupat believes, simultaneously, that Indian writers must suppress their communal natures to write, (1989, 134), but that they find it impossible to suppress those other (communal) voices completely (145). David Murray asserts that *Black Elk Speaks*

> blends the historical and the spiritual to present a moving account of a world-view in which all aspects of existence are integrated into a whole but which seems ultimately powerless to present the remorseless disintegrating forces of white civilization. This gives Black Elk's account an epic sweep and grandeur untypical of autobiographies, in that the individual becomes almost incidental, even though fully realized and human. (1991, 71).

For most of these scholars, cultural differences simply get in the way of examining Indian as-told-to narratives, so that they turn out to be some-

thing exotic and foreign, instead of the examples to the world that every
autobiography can be. All writers, Western or not, speak to audiences.
They pass on their lives—which have been touched by so many others that
they reveal multiple voices and, often, points of view, in repassing through
their life stories—to a larger community.

The modernists were not the first writers to use polyvocal narratives,
nor were they the first to intermix "primitive" rituals and symbols into
more familiar literary structures. But they were the first group of writers to
advocate drawing on our "more primitive" aspects of our cultures—from
T. S. Eliot's drawing on symbolism from Jesse Weston's *From Ritual to Romance* to a plethora of writers who "reached into the presence of the past
and reinvented the Indian at the heart of this continent's humanity [so
that] the resurrected noble savage, reduced by a factor of sixteen since
1492, would rise above the ruins of anarchic Manifest Destiny on literary
wings" (Lincoln 1991, xvii). *Black Elk Speaks,* then, is the quintessential modernist text: mixed narratives in experimental combinations—playlike structures based on corroborative speakers to create polyvocal narratives next to
poetry and chants, dramatic monologue, sacred symbolism, mythology,
and ritual, with several drawings inserted for clarity and milieu. Yet,
whereas the intermixture of narratives and the use of sacred symbols and
myths—"the quintessential forms of man's expression and interpretation of
himself and his experience" (May 1958, 13, n.)—was a way for modernists to
revitalize the power of their writings, for Black Elk it was a fulfillment of
his social and sacred responsibilities.

Perhaps one of the most productive ways of analyzing *Black Elk Speaks*
is to examine how much it is like and unlike his Sioux predecessors' works.
Like the other writers' autobiographical works, *Black Elk Speaks* is largely
chronological. And like the other life stories, it contains chosen glimpses
of Black Elk's life intermingled with information about Sioux history. The
textual choices made by both Black Elk and Neihardt, in a more complex
manner than the other writers probably encountered,[7] involved at least five
levels.

7. How much control individual Indians had in the production of their books has been
a point of contention concerning the works' "authenticity." "As-told-to-narratives" are often
regarded as less than authentic, with some critics going out of their way, it seems, to give

First, Black Elk, as I mentioned earlier, had the visions that Black Road interpreted. Although the symbols in Black Elk's vision were undoubtedly common Lakota images/icons making his vision like others, such as White Bull's half a century earlier, the events in the vision were different enough to evoke a particular mission for Black Elk. The vision, as commonly held by the Lakota, specifies directions or obligations the seer must follow or suffer the consequences for his inaction. Before Black Elk told his vision to Black Road, he lived in constant fear of the Thunder Beings and told Neihardt, "I knew all the time I had something to do but I couldn't figure out what it was that I was to do that I didn't do" (DeMallie 1984, 213). Black Elk could not act without Black Road imparting *his* knowledge and understanding of Black Elk's vision to the younger man.

Second, Black Elk chose Neihardt "with the same sense of mission and awareness of the permanency of the white man's records" as his traditional spiritual successor, just as "he would have passed his spiritual knowledge by word of mouth to a younger man of the tribe" (Holly 1979, 121), in effect controlling "'the use of sacred knowledge by restricting its use to responsible parties bound by the ties of kinship, discipleship, and religious obligation'" (Rice 1989, 27). What has largely been ignored about Black Elk's choice of transmission is the fact that he chose his son, Ben, to be the interpreter. Ben, who does in part become a successor to Black Elk's sacred duties (Holler 1995, 32; H. Neihardt 1995, 114), would have been a natural selection for Black Elk's traditional spiritual protégé. Perhaps one possible reason Black Elk seizes the opportunity to tell his story to Neihardt is that Ben is readily available to act as translator. Perhaps because of the ongoing government prohibition of traditional religious practices, and perhaps because of the possibility that Ben's acculturation into Christian attitudes would have made Black Elk concerned that Ben would refuse an obligation of such succession, Black Elk realized that an opportunity had come for him to transmit his knowledge, almost surreptitiously, to his son. We must remember that Ben was present during all the interviews, dances, and cere-

---

credit to Euro-American "amanuenses," who do not deserve such credit. See the previous discussions on Elaine Goodale Eastman's role in Charles Eastman's writings, as well as the note concerning assistance Standing Bear may have received with his works.

monies performed by Black Elk for Neihardt in the 1930s. Even if Ben did not embrace all of his father's vision or the traditional Lakota beliefs imparted to him during the interviews, he was almost certainly impressed with them (H. Neihardt 1995, 53). By interpreting through Ben, Black Elk maintains the Lakota ritual of using oral tradition to pass down sacred knowledge; even if Neihardt were to get it wrong, Ben would remember.

Third, Black Elk decided what to reveal, even when answering direct questions from Neihardt, using his "intuitive selection of significant memories . . . not [as] a factually accurate 'history' but storytelling in the same sense that a fiction writer purifies, sweats away irrelevance to tell a story that is good as well as true" (Rice 1989, 33). A graphic illustration of this *choice* by Black Elk is his depiction of the sixth grandparent, who is traditionally seen as Maka, grand*mother* earth, as a grandfather. In *his* vision, at least as he revealed it to Neihardt, the sixth directional spirit showed itself to Black Elk as an old man who got younger as he walked away, turning into Black Elk as a nine-year-old boy. Repeatedly, Hilda Neihardt emphasizes that even Ben and Standing Bear had not previously heard all of Black Elk's vision (1995, 36 and 50). While there were parts of his life Black Elk chose not to mention, such as details of his life as a Catholic, everything he tells demonstrates the intricate ties of religion and life to the Lakota.

Fourth, Neihardt clarified wording and meaning through repetition of the ideas that were then verified by Black Elk after Ben countertranslated the English back into Lakota. While undoubtedly tedious, the repetitious countertranslating demonstrated to Black Elk that Neihardt really did want to understand what Black Elk was telling him. As observant as Black Elk surely was, he probably also noted the kinds of information that most struck Neihardt's attention. Ultimately, both Black Elk and Neihardt placed enormous trust in Ben to be as accurate in his translations as possible.

And fifth, Neihardt chose what parts of the stories to include in the book and how to arrange them with, according to DeMallie, a serious attempt at retaining the already musical (a literary quality) and authoritative elements of Black Elk's words (1984, 51–52). There was probably also some additional editing by the publishers. It is important to emphasize that Black Elk, despite Neihardt's intervention in selecting, organizing, and emphasizing, was responsible for the choice of most of the book's content. In fact, Neihardt did an excellent job of melding Western lyricism with Sioux literary traditions, striking a balance between Euro-American and Sioux literary traditions that parallels Black Elk's balance between Catholicism and traditional Lakota religion.

While Neihardt does trim material and consolidate phrases for clarity, he seems to give in to the temptation to make Black Elk an important figure, as Charles Eastman and Luther Standing Bear both try to do for themselves, by making him appear more influential than he probably was. As a result, he sometimes takes Black Elk's words literally. For instance, when Black Elk relates his first vision from Ghost Dancing, he describes two men he meets in a land of plenty. In *Black Elk Speaks*, the *hanbloglaka* passage reads:

> "We will give you something that you should carry back to your people, and with it they shall come to see their loved ones."
>
> I knew it was the way their holy shirts were made that they wanted me to take back. . . . What I brought back was the memory of the holy shirts the two men wore. . . . So the next day I made ghost shirts all day long and painted them in the sacred manner of my vision. (1932, 247).

The transcripts from the interviews indicate that the day before this dance, Black Elk prepared himself to join the Ghost Dancing, of which he had been skeptical to this point, by dressing "in the sacred clothes" (DeMallie 1984, 259). During his vision, the transcripts read,

> I could see two men coming toward me. They were dressed with ghost shirts *like I was dressed*. . . . What I brought back was the memory of what they had shown me and I was to make an exact copy of it. *This* ghost shirt was to be used always in the ghost dances. So I started the ghost shirt. . . . I made the first two shirts according to what I saw in the vision. . . . I worked all day making shirts. . . . I wanted all the people to know the facts of this vision. (DeMallie 1984, 261–62; emphasis mine)

Did Black Elk begin the *idea* of wearing the ghost shirts, or did he start this one design of the ghost shirt?

DeMallie cites James Mooney's reference to the first recorded Euro-American sighting of the ghost shirts, wherein a schoolteacher claims that a woman, the wife of Return from Scout, created them—shirts for the men, dresses for the women—after she saw them in a vision (Mooney 1973, 916). To explain the different accounts, DeMallie merely speculates that "it seems likely that several of the ghost dancers had had visions relating to sacred regalia for the ceremony" (1984, 262, n. 9). It is possible that both visions, Black Elk's and Return from Scout's wife's, were embellishments on the sacred clothing, which Black Elk mentions having put on to prepare for his first participation in the dance, already being worn by the ghost dancers. In any event, Black Elk's recollection of his initial participation in the dancing, soon after which he designed his particular ghost shirts, happened in the spring of 1890, and the schoolteacher reported that Return from Scout's wife had had her vision of them in October 1890. Black Elk *could have been* the original instigator of the ghost shirt phase of the Ghost Dance religion.

Mooney has a more plausible explanation, however. He notes that "the protective idea in connection with the ghost shirt does not seem to be aboriginal. The Indian warrior habitually went into battle naked above the waist" so that "the warrior should be as free and unencumbered in movement as possible. The so-called 'war shirt' was worn chiefly in ceremonial dress parades and only rarely on the warpath." Mooney believes that the ghost shirt originated in the same area of the country that the Ghost Dance religion did, so that the garment "may have been suggested by the 'endowment robe' of the Mormons, a seamless garment of white muslin adorned with symbolic figures, which is worn by their initiates as the most sacred badge of their faith, and by many of the believers is supposed to render the wearer invulnerable" (1973, 790). He points out as well that only the Sioux attached war connotations to the shirts, calling them bullet-proof, whereas other tribes either wore them as peace symbols or forsook wearing them because of the connotations of war that developed with the ghost shirts after the Sioux began using them (791).

Neihardt made the choice to emphasize the idea that Black Elk was the originator of the idea of the ghost shirts. But Neihardt makes another textual choice, which had to be more difficult, about the ghost shirts. Later, when Black Elk speaks of the Wounded Knee massacre, the transcripts show graphically how the shaman believed in the bulletproof nature of his shirt, and his sacred bow, which is never pointed out as a bulletproofing device in *Black Elk Speaks*. Neihardt had to ask himself if a Euro-American audience would believe Black Elk's statement that, as Black Elk tells it in the transcripts,

> I could feel the bullets hitting me but I was bullet proof. I had to hang on to my horse to keep the bullets from knocking me off. I had the sacred bow with me. . . . I had to hold my bow in front of me in the air to be bullet-proof but just as I had gotten over the hill after completing my charge, I let my bow down and I could feel some bullets passing through the ghost dance shirt near my hip. (DeMallie 1984, 273–74)

Although Neihardt mentions the bow, he eliminates Black Elk's connection with its ability to make him bulletproof, eliminating altogether Black Elk's stated belief that the sacred things he did made him invulnerable to bullets, making the event sound more like luck than sacred power: "I just held the sacred bow out in front of me with my right hand. The bullets did not hit us at all" (Neihardt 1932, 262).

Neihardt does the opposite with Black Elk's wounding. He makes it more dramatic and supplies information earlier in the description of the event than Black Elk does in the transcripts. Neihardt's version, clearer than Black Elk's, yet still relating to the sacred, says,

> All this time the bullets were buzzing around me and I was not touched. I was not even afraid. It was like being in a dream about shooting. But just as I reached the very top of the hill, suddenly it was like waking up, and I was afraid. I dropped my arms and quit making the goose cry. Just as I did this, I felt something strike my belt as though some one had hit me there with the back of an ax. I nearly fell out of my saddle, but I managed to hold on, and rose over the hill. (1932, 272)

The more repetitive, clearly more oral version in the transcripts reads, as I fled toward the hill I could hear the bullets hitting my clothes. Then something hit me on the belt on the right side. I reeled on my horse and rode on over the hill. . . . I should have kept on coming like that with my hands up. I was in fear and had forgotten my power. I had forgotten to make the goose sound there and to keep my hands up. I doubted my power right there and I should have gone on imitating the goose with my power and I would have been bullet-proof. My doubt and my fear for the moment killed my power and during that moment I was shot. (DeMallie 1984, 277–78)

Notably, Neihardt maintains the accuracy of Black Elk's actions, but restructures the telling, eliminating repetition and clarifying the consequences of the actions more immediately for a more readable (though perhaps less musical), dramatic effect. He has not changed the action in Black Elk's story, but he has, significantly, downplayed the sacred powers Black Elk believed in. This was probably a very conscious choice by Neihardt, since his Euro-American audience probably would have labeled the sacred powers supernatural and unbelievable, or at least suspect.

While Neihardt does not necessarily change facts, he changes emphasis often. For instance, Black Elk has second thoughts after he has mounted his horse and is on his way to investigate the shooting going on at Wounded Knee. Neihardt's version reads, "I took only my sacred bow, which was not made to shoot with; because I was a little in doubt about the Wanekia religion at the time, and I did not really want to kill anybody because of it" (1932, 270).

The transcript of Black Elk's words reads, "I just thought it over and I thought I should not fight. I doubted about this Messiah business and therefore it seemed that I should not fight for it, but anyway I was going because I had already decided to. If I had turned back the people would think it funny, so I just decided to go anyway" (DeMallie 1984, 272).

Neihardt's version reduces the strength of Black Elk's doubt because he probably felt a Euro-American audience would not believe any of the sacred things Black Elk mentions if he so easily doubts the Ghost Dance religion—which, after all, is more Christian than the Lakota traditional religion, thus might be more understandable and believable to the predominantly Christian readers (and which might be one of many reasons why so many non-Indians feared the Ghost Dance religion, which professed a Messiah). Neihardt might also think his readers would also "think it funny" if the book's "hero" was to be depicted as wishy-washy. Black Elk's decision not to fight, because he comes from a warrior society, would have cast aspersions on his manhood to many non-Indians, who probably rarely made clear or direct connections between war and spiritual callings. Neihardt's version, though not quite the truth, keeps Black Elk from looking foolish in Euro-American eyes for deciding not to fight and for only carrying a ceremonial bow into a battle where army bullets are massacring his people.

Neihardt adheres strictly to other Lakota literary concerns, however. As Rice points out, "by having four narrators at the beginning, even though Black Elk assumes the place of principal narrator later on, the appropriately respectful invocation for spiritual assistance has been made" (1989, 43). Such a ritual is important to legitimize the strength and power asked for from Wakan Tanka, but also to demonstrate that Black Elk has "not forgotten any spirit or power or charm. Any slight omission might bring down on his luckless head the wrath of the incensed deity" (Daugherty 1927, 152).

The speakers strengthen Black Elk's powers as a storyteller, as well as corroborate the events of which he tells. In the same manner, Standing Bear's illustrations in the original edition, many of which are in color, act as corroborative information, illustrate events in the visions that might not be easy for non-Indians to imagine, and demonstrate Lakota symbolism. They also supply the visual drama, albeit poorly, that would have been present in Black Elk's telling of and performance of the vision. The first color drawing, for instance, depicts the tepee made of a flaming rainbow, his adopted name for Neihardt, in which he met the six sitting grandfathers, the powers of the world, all waiting to offer Black Elk some aspect of themselves to aid his and his people's spiritual needs. Above the tepee, thunderclouds seethe with lightning and a spotted eagle and crow fly unharmed. Outside the tepee, the two spirit warriors, complete with eagle wings, stand guard, ready to take Black Elk, depicted as a small boy with a bow and arrow, on to the next phase of his vision (Neihardt 1932, 33).

The more difficult concept of the center of the earth, at Harney Peak in the Black Hills of South Dakota, is depicted in color as well. Harney Peak, a mingling of black, grays, and reds, supports Black Elk and a spotted eagle, representing the sky spirits and Wakan Tanka, on his sorrel pony. Above them flies geese from the north. Behind Black Elk, the *waga chun,* or the cottonwood[8] tree, is budding out, symbolizing the rebirth of the Oceti Sakowin's powers. To the left, the Grandfather of the West sits astride a black horse with an arrow ready to strike like lightning, as Standing Bear's representation of the Thunder Beings. Directly below is the Grandfather of the South riding a buckskin and carrying the flowering stick, which he promised Black Elk would flower as the Lakota tree of life, once order has been restored. To the far right, the Grandfather of the North rides a bay pony and carries a rod with red particles spewing from it, possibly representing the winds and their healing powers. On the bottom right, the Grandfather of the East rides a sorrel pony and carries the sacred red stick, which has a starlike red spot on the end whose fragments touch the "good red road" encircling the Black Hills known as Ki Iyanka Ocanku, the Sacred Race Track, representing the sacred hoop of the Lakota nation (Goodman 1992, 7; Neihardt 1932, 41).

Besides clarifying difficult images for non-Indian readers, Standing Bear also demonstrates traditional Lakota methods of recording stories, even showing the book's readers how to write the name Black Elk in picto-

---

8. Black Elk tells why the cottonwood is a sacred tree to the Lakota in *The Sacred Pipe:* "Long ago it was the cottonwood who taught us how to make our tipis, for the leaf of the tree is an exact pattern of the tipi, and this was learned when some of our old men were watching little children making play houses from these leaves. This too is a good example of how much grown men may learn from very little children, for the hearts of children are pure, and, therefore the Great Spirit may show to them many things which older people miss. Another reason why we choose the cottonwood tree to be at the center of our lodge is that the Great Spirit has shown to us that, if you cut an upper limb of this tree crosswise, there you will see in the grain a perfect five pointed star, which, to us, represents the presence of the Great Spirit. Also perhaps you have noticed that even in the very slightest breeze you can hear the voice of the cottonwood tree; this we understand is its prayer to the Great Spirit, for not only men, but all things and all beings pray to Him continually in differing ways" (1953, 74–75).

graph, with a black elk's head above a man's head with a line descending
from the elk to the man's mouth (Neihardt 1932, 199).

Standing Bear's illustrations, as well as Black Elk's and his corrobo-
rating friends' dramatic monologues, not only adhere to Sioux literary
traditions—from traditional types of stories to traditional techniques such
as repetition, indirection, and the use of personal sacred symbols—but
also contribute to the modernist textual experiment that is *Black Elk
Speaks.* The book unfolds almost like a play, with the drawings acting like
stage directions, becoming substitutes for the dramatic elements of the
vision's presentation as tribal ceremony. Neihardt's insertion of explana-
tory notes, such as the one on page 89 defining "coup," also add further
dimension to the book. Prose mingles with poetry, as Black Elk reveals
his sacred songs and chants, creating, as Rice puts it, "a 'bundle' of
Lakota words which in turn become a bundle of English words" (1989,
47), or a modernist collage. Through the melding of Lakota and Euro-
American literary traditions, through the giving and comparing of traditional Lakota and Christian philosophies, and through a joining of
purposes—both literary, both forms of cultural inheritance—Black Elk and
John Neihardt strike an important and culturally significant balance in
the rendering of *Black Elk Speaks* for a largely Euro-American audience.
Black Elk could have assumed, observing firsthand the tremendous push
for acculturation and assimilation of Indians, that the audience his book
would reach would eventually come to include Indians. In essence, then,
Black Elk used Neihardt to achieve his visionary mission to pass on the
power of the earth, also known as the Sixth Grandfather,[9] who Black Elk
had been told through his vision was himself, representing "the spirit of
mankind" (DeMallie 1984, 141), obliged to reach out to his people and to
anyone else who was interested.

Louis Owens argues, in discussing American Indian novels, that the
movement (which for him is an "irreversible metamorphosis") "from oral,
communal literature to the written commodity of published work . . .
represents a necessary 'desacralization' of traditional materials, a transfor-

9. Black Elk consciously changes the sixth grandparent's gender, since traditionally the
sixth power is Grandmother Earth. Why?

mation that allows sacred materials—from ritual and myth—to move into a secular world of decontextualized 'art'" (1992, 11). To Owens, putting the sacred on paper is like the public viewing of traditional dances; it becomes hokey and less powerful, in essence stealing something from the communal culture.

Similarly, Kenneth Lincoln reports that

> tribal peoples may be justifiably apprehensive of a written form of literature that fixes spiritual ideas. Peter Nabokov reminds us that the first Cherokee shamans to adapt Sequoyah's 1921 syllabary of eighty-six characters, the earliest known "talking leaves" north of the Rio Grande, hid their transcriptions in trees and attics, fearful of exploitation. Their fears were not unfounded, given the many anthropological misunderstandings and abuses of sacred tribal materials. (1983, 25)

Black Elk was probably aware of these kinds of fears and attitudes toward revealing sacred information. There are many indications that Black Elk was rebuffed to some degree for having "conspired" with the outsider, Neihardt, in revealing information about what many assume to be purely Lakota or Oceti Sakowin ideas. But, as Holler points out, just as "each tribe had its own religion, its own origin myth, and its own stories[,] each holy man had his own vision, which directed both his storytelling and his ritualizing [so that] each holy man tells the old stories differently, in accord with his vision" (1995, 213). Although many of the historical facts in Black Elk Speaks were events that happened to the Sioux as a group, the visions, the sacred part of the book, are all exclusively Black Elk's in the sense that he was the one who had them. Even in traditional Lakota belief, only Black Elk had the power to decide whether or not the pass his vision and its powers on. He also decided to whom to pass them.

While he was supposed to use the power from the visions for the good of his people, he did not want to fulfill a particular command. In 1900, he was supposed to use "the soldier weed, a destructive power that would wipe out his enemies—men, women, and children" to create "wholesale destruction, so he gave it all up and became a Catholic" (DeMallie 1984, 14). A kind of reluctant "messiah," Black Elk was not willing to harm people with his "soldier weed" because he worried he would "probably have killed the women and children of the enemy," which for a trained Lakota warrior was the most despised part of warfare (DeMallie 1984, 136).

Just as it is more probable that Black Elk envisioned the design for a particular set of Ghost Dance shirts, one that came from the symbols of his own visions, it is also probable that Black Elk understood that his visions were exactly that, his visions. He could still exercise his prerogative as a Lakota—choice. He chose not to fulfill all the mandates of this original vision. He recognized the dilemma of having followed the wrong vision during the Ghost Dancing because, as Neihardt said so eloquently for him, "It is hard to follow one great vision in this world of darkness and of many changing shadows. Among those shadows men get lost" (Neihardt 1932, 254). Black Elk chose to reveal those visions to a man in whom he had the confidence necessary to entrust them, even though he knows he has given away his power by giving away his vision (1932, 210). Unfortunately, we will never know for certain if Black Elk was satisfied with how the book itself turned out, or with the influence it has had. I doubt he would have been surprised that the power of his words has lived on because Black Elk understood the power and the limits of language: "Of course there was very much in the vision that even I can not tell when I try hard, because very much of it was not for words. But I have told what can be told" (1932, 205). Though there is no record of Black Elk having said those exact words, Neihardt makes it abundantly clear that even his powers of writing are poor compared not only to the power of Black Elk's vision, but also to the power of Black Elk's telling and performance of it.

Charles Eastman, Gertrude Bonnin, and Luther Standing Bear never returned to their native ways of living as completely or successfully as Nicholas Black Elk did. Perhaps because he was a full-blood and was never educated in a white man's school, he never felt the drive to compete with others for fame and material things, a lack (?) that kept him near Manderson, South Dakota, his whole life. Perhaps because Black Elk owned a piece of his people's sacred land, near what he continued to think of as the center of the world, Harney Peak, he chose to stay there. Perhaps because Black Elk had more fully embraced both cultures' religions and found a productive way to use both the power of conversion and the power of his visions for his people, he remained closest to his home ground. The only writer in this study who came as close to Black Elk's dedication to his original band's customs and land is Ella Deloria, but even she lived most of her life among Teton Lakotas instead of with her family's original band, the Yankton Nakotas.

Eastman, Bonnin, Deloria, and Standing Bear all acted in various ways and with different energies as advocates for Indian rights and to promote understandings between races. But Black Elk most effectively spoke of and *performed* the passing on of his knowledge to future generations—not necessarily to perfectly preserve his knowledge, but to see that his medicine visions were available to his people, and perhaps, in the process, could be effective in making life better for all. In a manner similar to his writing Sioux predecessors, Black Elk's Lakota-trained literary choices, combined with Neihardt's knowledge of Euro-American literary traditions, produced a truly modern literary text, and helped cap off a highly successful Sioux Literary Renaissance.

APPENDIXES

WORKS CITED

INDEX

APPENDIX A

Indian Publishing Chronology, 1890–1955

*V*arious anthropological and ethnographical publications produced many of the printed narratives from this period, with H. David Brumble listing nearly four hundred such writings in his *Annotated Bibliography of American Indian and Eskimo Autobiographies.* Those writings, although important narratives about Indian life, are not listed here. Included are writings that would have had circulation among a more general population. Most of the tribal affiliations listed here appear as listed in Brumble's *Bibliography* and Paula Gunn Allen's *Studies in American Indian Literature.*

The Sioux

1893–1894   Charles A. Eastman (Ohiyesa) (Santee), "Recollections of the Wild Life," in *St. Nicholas: An Illustrated Magazine for Young Folks.*

1894   Charles A. Eastman, "Mythology of the Sioux," in *Popular Science Monthly.*

1900   Gertrude Bonnin (as Zitkala-Sa) (Yankton), "An Indian Teacher among Indians," in the *Atlantic Monthly.*

Charles A. Eastman, "The Story of the Little Big Horn," in *The Chautauquan.*

1901   Gertrude Bonnin, "The Trial Path," in the *Atlantic Monthly;* "The Soft-Hearted Sioux," in *Harper's Monthly;* and *Old Indian Legends.*

1902   Gertrude Bonnin, "Why I Am a Pagan," in the *Atlantic Monthly*, and "A Warrior's Daughter," in *Everybody's Magazine*.

Charles A. Eastman, *Indian Boyhood*.

1903   Charles A. Eastman, "Hakadah's First Offering," in *Current Literature*, and "The Great Cat's Nursery," in *Harper's Magazine*.

1904   Charles A. Eastman, "First Impressions of Civilization," in *Harper's Monthly Magazine*, "The Mustering of the Herds," in *Out West*; "The Gay Chieftain," in *Harper's Magazine*; and *Red Hunters and the Animal People*.

1905   Charles A. Eastman, "Indian Handicrafts," in *The Craftsman*.

1906   Charles A. Eastman, "Rain-in-the-Face," in *The Outlook*; "The War Maiden," in the *Ladies Home Journal*; and "The Grave of the Dog," in *Metropolitan Magazine*.

1907   Charles A. Eastman, "The Singing Spirit," in *Sunset Magazine*; "The School Days of an Indian," in *The Outlook*; and *Old Indian Days*.

1909   Charles A. Eastman (with Elaine Goodale Eastman), *Wigwam Evenings*.

1911   Charles A. Eastman, "The Indian and the Moral Code," in *The Outlook*; and "A Canoe Trip among the Northern Ojibways," in *The Red Man*; and *The Soul of the Indian*.

1912   Charles A. Eastman, "Education Without Books," in *The Craftsman*; "The Song of the Birch Canoe," in *The Craftsman*.

1913   Gertrude Bonnin-Simmons (with William Hanson), *Sun-Dance*, an Indian opera.

Chief Red Cloud (Oglala) (with Joseph Dixon), "Chief Red Cloud," in *The Vanishing Race: The Last Great Indian Council* (which contains several narratives from chiefs of other tribes, as well).

Charles A. Eastman, *Indian Child Life*.

White Horse (Yankton) (with Joseph Dixon), "White Horse," in *The Vanishing Race*.

1914   Charles A. Eastman, "How to Make Wigwams and Shelters," in *Boy's Life*; "Stories back of Indian Names," in *Boy's Life*; and *My People: The Indian's Contribution to the Art of America*," in *The Red Man* and in *The Craftsman*; and *Indian Scout Talks*.

1915   Charles A. Eastman, "The Indian as a Citizen," in *Lippincott's Magazine*; "The Indian's Gift to the Nation," in *Quarterly Journal of the*

Society of American Indians; "The Indian's Health Problem," in *Popular Science Monthly* and in *American Review of Reviews;* "Camping with Indians," in *The Teepee Book I;* and *The Indian To-Day: The Past and Future of the First American.*

1916   Gertrude Bonnin, "The Indian's Awakening" and "A Year's Experience in Community Service Work among the Ute Tribe of Indians," both in *American Indian Magazine.*

Charles A. Eastman, "The Indian's Health Problem," in *American Indian Magazine,* and "Rain-in-the-Face, the Story of a Sioux Warrior," in *The Teepee Book II;* and *From the Deep Woods to Civilization.*

1917   Gertrude Bonnin, "Chipeta, Widow of Chief Ouray: With a Word about a Deal in Blankets," "The Red Man's America," and "A Sioux Woman's Love for her Grandchild," all in *American Indian Magazine.*

Charles A. Eastman, "The Language of Footprints," in *St. Nicholas.*

Sword (Oglala) (with J. R. Walker) in *The Sun Dance and Other Ceremonies of the Oglala Division of the Teton Dakota.*

1918   Charles A. Eastman, *Indian Heroes and Great Chieftains.*

Gertrude Bonnin, "Indian Gifts to Civilized Man," in *American Indian Magazine.*

1919   Gertrude Bonnin, "America, Home of the Red Man," "Coronation of Chief Powhatan Retold," and "Letter to the Chiefs and Headman of the Tribes," all in *American Indian Magazine.*

Charles A. Eastman, "The American Eagle: An Indian Symbol," "The Indian's Plea for Freedom," and "Justice for the Sioux," all in *American Indian Magazine.*

1920   Charles A. Eastman, "Great Spirit," in *American Indian Teepee.*

1920–21   Charles A. Eastman, "What Can the Out-Doors Do for Our Children," in *Education.*

1921   Gertrude Bonnin, *American Indian Stories.*

1924   Gertrude Bonnin (with Charles A. Fabens and Matthew K. Sniffen), *Oklahoma's Poor Rich Indians: An Orgy of Graft and Exploitation of the Five Civilized Tribes—Legalized Robbery.*

1925   Marie McLaughlin (Medawakanton), *Myths and Legends of the Sioux.*

1926   Pte-San-Waste-Win (Hunkpapa) (with James McLaughlin), "Mrs. Spotted Horn Bull's View of the Custer Tragedy," in *My Friend the Indian.*

1928   Ella Cara Deloria (Yankton), *Indian Progress* (a pageant performed at Haskell Institute).

Luther Standing Bear (Brule), *My People the Sioux.*

1929   Ella Deloria, "Sun Dance of the Oglala Sioux," in *Journal of American Folklore.*

1931   Luther Standing Bear, "The Tragedy of the Sioux," in *American Mercury,* and *My Indian Boyhood.*

1932   Ella Deloria, *Dakota Texts* (bilingual).

(Nicholas) Black Elk (Oglala) (with John Neihardt), *Black Elk Speaks.*

1933   Ella Deloria (and Franz Boas), "Notes on the Dakota, Teton Dialect," in *International Journal of American Linguistics.*

Luther Standing Bear, *Land of the Spotted Eagle.*

1934   Luther Standing Bear, *Stories of the Sioux.*

1939   Ella Deloria (for the Phelps-Stokes Inquiry Committee), *The Navajo Indian Problem.*

1940   Ella Deloria, *The Life Story of a People* (pageant performed at Pembroke State College for Indians).

1941   Charles A. Eastman, "Report on Sacajawea," in *Annals of Wyoming.*

Ella Deloria (and Franz Boas), "Dakota Grammar," in *Memoirs of the National Academy of Sciences.*

Legends of the Mighty Sioux, compiled by Indian workers on the WPA South Dakota Writers' Project.

1944   Ella Deloria, *Speaking of Indians; Waterlily* (not published until 1988); and "Dakota Treatment of Murderers," in *Proceedings* of the American Philosophical Society.

1946   Oscar One Bull (Teton) (with H. Inez Hilger), "The Narrative of Oscar One Bull," in *Mid-America.*

1947   Flying Hawk (Oglala) (with M. I. McCreight), *Firewater and Forked Tongues: A Sioux Chief Interprets U.S. History.*

1950   Charles A. Eastman, "A Half-Forgotten Lincoln Story," in *The Rotarian.*

1953   Black Elk (with Joseph Epes Brown), *Black Elk's The Sacred Pipe.*

1954   Ella Deloria, "Short Dakota Texts, Including Conversations," in *International Journal of American Linguistics.*

Other Indians

1891   Sophia Alice Callahan (Creek), *Wynema: A Child of the Forest* (the first novel written—in protest over the Wounded Knee massacre—by an Indian woman).

1899   Chief Simon Pokagon (Potawatomi), *O-Gi-Maw-Kwe Mit-I-Gwa-Ki (Queen of the Woods)*; also *Brief Sketch of the Algaic Language*.

1900   Francis LaFlesche (Omaha), "An Indian Allotment," in *The Independent* and *The Middle Five: Indian Boys at School*.

1903   Daniel La France (Mohawk), "An Indian Boy's Story," in *The Independent*.

1904   John Johnson (Ojibwa), *En-me-gah-bowh's Story: An Account of the Disturbances of the Chippewa Indians at Gull Lake in 1857 and 1862 and Their Removal in 1868*.

1905   George Bent (Cheyenne) (with George Hyde), "Forty Years with the Cheyennes," in *The Frontier*.

1906   Geronimo (Apache) (with S. M. Barrett), *Geronimo's Story of His Life*.

1907   Hiparopai (Yuma) (with Natalie Curtis), "The Words of Hiparopai: A Leaf from a Traveler's Diary, Showing the Indian's Outlook upon the Transition Period," in *The Craftsman*.

1910   James Hightower (Cherokee), *Happy Hunting Ground*.

        Left-Hand (Arapaho) (with F. L. King), *Chief Left-Hand: His Life Story, as Told by Himself*.

1913   Crashing Thunder (Winnebago), (with Paul Radin), "Personal Reminiscences of a Winnebago Indian," in *Journal of American Folklore*.

1914   Goodbird (Hidatsu), (with Gilbert L. Wilson), *Goodbird the Indian: His Story, Told by Himself to Gilbert L. Wilson*.

        Sanimuinak (Eskimo) (with G. Holm), "Sanimuinak's Account of How He Became an Angakok," in *The Ammassalik Eskimo*.

1915   Chief Tahan Joseph Griffin (Osage), *Tahan: Out of Savagery into Civilization*.

        Rev. Henry Roe Cloud (Winnebago), "From Wigwam to Pulpit: A Red Man's Own Story of His Progress from Darkness to Light," in *Missionary Review*.

1916   Apauk (Piegan) (with James Schultz), *Apauk, Caller of Buffalo*.

1920   Sam Blowsnake (Winnebago) (with Paul Radin), *The Autobiography of a Winnebago Indian.*

Annette Leevier (Ojibwa), *Psychic Experiences of an Indian Princess.*

1921   Buffalo Bird Woman (Maxidiwiac) (Hidatsa) (with Gilbert Wilson), *Waheenee: An Indian Girl's Story, Told by Herself.*

1925   John Milton Oskison (Cherokee), *Wild Harvest: A Novel of Transition Days in Oklahoma.*

1926   John Milton Oskison, *Black Jack Davy.*

1927   Mourning Dove (also known as Hum-Ishu-Ma) (Okanogan), *Cogewea, the Half-Blood: A Depiction of the Great Montana Cattle Range.*

Lynn Riggs (Cherokee), *Big Lake.*

1928   Sylvester Long (also known as Chief Buffalo Child Long Lance) (Croatan, adopted Blackfeet), *Long Lance: The Autobiography of a Blackfoot Indian Chief.*

Chief Tahan Joseph Griffis, *Indian Circle Stories.*

1929   Iron Teeth (Cheyenne) (with Thomas B. Marquis), "Red Pipe's Squaw," in *Century Magazine.*

John Milton Oskison, *A Texas Titan: The Story of Sam Houston.*

Muriel Hazel Wright (Choctaw) (with Joseph B. Thoburn), *Oklahoma: A History of the State and Its People.*

1930   Isidora Filomena (Chuructos) (with Hubert Bancroft), "My Years with Chief Solano," in *Touring Topics.*

John Freeman Craig (also known as Chief White Eagle) (Winnebago), *Fifty Years on the Warpath.*

Catherine McDonald (Nez Perce) (with Winona Adams), "An Indian Girl's Account of a Trading Expedition to the Southwest about 1841," in *The Frontier.*

Plenty-coups (Crow) (with Frank Linderman), *American: The Life Story of a Great Indian.*

1931   Lynn Riggs, *Green Grow the Lilacs.*

White Horse Eagle (Osage) (with Edgar Schmidt-Pauli), *We Indians: The Passing of a Great Race.*

Wooden Leg (Cheyenne) (with Thomas Marquis), *Wooden Leg: A Warrior Who Fought Custer.*

1932   Peter Hudson (Choctaw), "Recollections of Peter Hudson," in *Chronicles of Oklahoma*.

            James Paytiamo (Acoma Pueblo), *Flaming Arrow's People: By an Acoma Indian*.

            Pretty-Shield (Crow) (with Frank Linderman), *Red Mother*.

            John Joseph Mathews (Osage), *Wah 'Kon-Tah: The Osage and the White Man's Road*.

1933   Kate Bighead (Cheyenne) (with Thomas Marquis), *She Watched Custer's Last Battle*.

            Mourning Dove, *Coyote Stories*.

            Sylvester Long, *Redman Echoes: Comprising the Writings of Chief Buffalo Long Lance and Biographical Sketches by His Friends*.

1934   John Joseph Mathews, *Sundown*.

1935   John Milton Oskison, *Brothers Three*.

1936   Thomas Wildcat Alford (Shawnee, Techumseh's grandson) (with Florence Drake), *Civilization, as Told to Florence Drake*.

            Maria Chona (Papago) (with Ruth Underhill), *The Autobiography of a Papago Woman*.

            D'Arcy McNickle (Flathead), *The Surrounded*.

            William Morgan (Navajo), *Human-Wolves among the Navajo*.

            Lynn Riggs, *The Cherokee Night*.

1938   Samuel E. Kenoi (Apache) (with Morris E. Opler), "A Chiricahua Apache's Account of the Geronimo Campaign of 1886," in *New Mexico Historical Review*.

            Left Handed (Navajo) (with Walter Dyk), *Son of Old Man Hat: A Navaho Autobiography*.

            John Milton Oskison, *Tecumseh and His Times: The Story of a Great Indian*.

1939   Louise Abeita (Hopi/Isleta), *I Am a Pueblo Indian Girl*.

            Black Eagle (Nez Perce) (with William Whitman), "Xube, a Ponca Autobiography."

            Anauta (Eskimo), *Land of Good Shadows: The Life Story of Anauta, an Eskimo Woman*.

            Julia Cooley (?), *Wolves Against the Moon*.

Yellow Wolf (Nez Perce) (with Lucullus McWhorter), *Yellow Wolf: His Own Story*.

Muriel Hazel Wright, *Springplace: Moravian Mission and the Ward Family of the Cherokee Nation*.

Simeon Oliver (Eskimo) (with Alden Hatch), *Son of the Smokey Sea*.

Lucy Young (Wailaki) (with Edith Murphey), "Out of the Past: A True Indian Story," in *California Historical Society Quarterly*.

1942   Don Talayesva (Hopi) (with Leo Simmons), *Sun Chief: The Autobiography of a Hopi Indian*.

Tetlaneetsa (Thompson River) (with Marius Barbeau and Grace Melvin), in *The Indian Speaks*.

Ethel Brant Monture (Mohawk), *West to the Setting Sun*.

1944   Ruth Muskrat Bronson (Cherokee), *Indians are People, Too*.

1945   John Joseph Mathews, *Talking to the Moon*.

1946   D'Arcy McNickle, *They Came Here First: The Epic of the American Indian*.

APPENDIX B

The Five Writers

Charles Alexander Eastman (1858–1939)

Born in Minnesota on a Santee Dakota reservation, Eastman was the son of Many Lightnings and Goddess, whose English name was Mary Nancy Eastman and who was the daughter of Euro-American artist Seth Eastman, who had married a Santee woman when he lived among them. After his father's conversion to Christianity, the whole family took Mary Nancy's family name as theirs, and young Ohiyesa became Charles Alexander.

Nicholas Black Elk (1863–1950)

Born in December on the Little Powder River within present-day Wyoming into an Oglala Lakota family tradition of healers, living and practicing their medicine west of the Black Hills, Black Elk experienced his first, and greatest, vision when he was nine, upon which he did not act until he was sixteen, when he joined the family line of shamans. Nicholas was a Christian name chosen for him after his conversion to Catholicism.

Luther Standing Bear (1863/8–1939)

Possibly born in December of either 1863 (as official rolls list him) or 1868 (as he claims), Standing Bear was born into the Brule Lakota tribe to Pretty Face and Standing Bear, a mixed-blood band chief. Plenty Kill, or Ota K'te, chose the name Luther (even though he could not read) from a list on the Carlisle blackboard.

Gertrude Bonnin (1876–1938)

Born on the Yankton Nakota Reservation in South Dakota, Gertrude lived the first eight years of her life there before leaving to study, against her mother's wishes, at

White's Manual Institute in Wabash, Indiana. After a falling out with her sister-in-law over the surname Simmons, Gertrude christened herself with the Lakota name Zitkala-Sa, or Red Bird, later accepting her husband's family name, Bonnin.

Ella Cara Deloria (1888–1971)

Giving birth during a blizzard on the Yankton Nakota Reservation, Ella's mother gave Ella Cara Deloria the ironic Dakota name Anpetu Waste, or Beautiful Day. Ella grew up speaking Nakota and English at St. Elizabeth's Mission near Wakpala, South Dakota. She received a bachelor of science degree from Columbia University in 1915, and began doing anthropological work for Franz Boas in 1929. She balanced her career as a field anthropologist with her familial duties for the rest of her life.

WORKS CITED

Allen, Paula Gunn. 1992. *The Sacred Hoop: Recovering the Feminine in American Indian Traditions*, rev. ed. Boston: Beacon Press.

————, ed. 1983. *Sudies in American Indian Literature*. New York: MLA.

Anderson, Gary Clayton. 1984. *Kinsmen of Another Kind: Dakota-White Relations in the Upper Mississippi Valley, 1650–1862*. Lincoln: Univ. Of Nebraska Press.

————. 1996. *Sitting Bull and the Paradox of Lakota Nationhood*. New York: Harper-Collins.

Austin, Mary. 1929. Dec. 28. "Aboriginal Fiction." *Saturday Review of Literature*. 1–5.

————. Introduction." 1991. *American Indian Poetry: An Anthology of Songs and Chants*, ed. George W. Cronyn. New York: Fawcett Columbine. xxix–xxxviii.

Battaille, Gretchen M., and Kathleen Mullen Sands. 1984. *American Indian Women: Telling Their Lives*. Lincoln: Univ. of Nebraska Press.

Beckwith, Martha Warren. 1930. "Mythology of the Oglala Dakota." *Journal of American Folklore* 43.170: 339–442.

Bernardin, Susan. 1997. "The Lessons of a Sentimental Education: Zitkala-Sa's Autobiographical Narratives." *Western American Literature* 32.3: 212–38.

Berthrong, Donald J. 1988. "Nineteenth-Century United States Government Agencies." In *History of Indian-White Relations*, ed. Wilcomb E. Washburn. Vol. 4 of *The Handbook of North American Indians*, gen. ed. William S. Sturtevant. Washington: Smithsonian: 255–63.

Bonnin, Gertrude (Zitkala-Sa), Charles A. Fabens, and Matthew K. Sniffen. 1924. *Oklahoma's Poor Rich Indians: An Orgy of Graft and Exploitation of the Five Civilized Tribes—Legalized Robbery*. Philadelphia: Indian Rights Association.

Brady, Cyrus Townshend. 1992. *The Sioux Indian Wars: From the Powder River to the Little Big Horn*. New York: Indian Head Books.

Brown, Joseph Epes, ed. 1953. *The Sacred Pipe: Black Elk's Account of the Seven Rites of the Oglala Sioux*. Norman: Univ. Of Oklahoma Press.

Brumble, H. David III. 1981. "Introduction." *An Annotated Bibliography of American Indian Eskimo Autobiographies*. Lincoln: Univ. Of Nebraska Press, 1–10.

———. 1988. *American Indian Autobiography*. Berkeley: Univ. Of California Press.

Cox, Beverly, and Martin Jacobs. 1991. *Spirit of the Harvest: North American Indian Cooking*. New York: Stewart, Tabori and Chang.

Clifford, James. 1988. *The Predicament of Culture: Twentieth-Century Ethnography, Literature, and Art*. Cambridge: Harvard Univ. Press.

Cutter, Martha J. "Zitkala-Sa's Autobiographical Writings: The Problems of a Canonical Search for Language and Identity." *MELUS* 19.1: 31–44.

Daugherty, George H. Jr. 1927. March. "The Technique of Indian Composition." *The Open Court* 41: 150–66.

Deloria, Ella Cara. 1932. *Dakota Texts*. New York: AMS Press.

———. 1944. *Speaking of Indians*. New York: Friendship Press.

———. 1978. *Dakota Texts* (English only). Vermillion: Univ. of South Dakota.

———. 1996. *Waterlily*. 1988. Special Edition. New York: Book of the Month Club.

DeMallie, Raymond J. 1978. "George Bushotter: The First Lakota Ethnographer." *American Indian Intellectuals*. Ed. Margot Liberty. St. Paul, Minn.: West Publishing Co. 91–102.

———, ed. 1984. *The Sixth Grandfather: Black Elk's Teachings Given to John G. Neihardt*. Lincoln: Univ. of Nebraska Press.

———. 1988. "Afterword." In *Waterlily* by Ella Deloria. New York: Firekeepers. 233–44.

———. 1991. "Introduction." In *When the Tree Flowered* by John G. Neihardt. Lincoln: Univ. of Nebraska Press, vii–xviii.

———, and Elaine A. Jahner, eds. 1991. In *Lakota Belief and Ritual* by James R. Walker. Lincoln: Univ. of Nebraska Press.

deMan, Paul. 1983. *Blindness and Insight: Essays in the Rhetoric of Contemporary Criticism*, 2d. Ed. Minneapolis: Univ. of Minnesota Press.

Dettmar, Kevin J. H., and Stephen Watt, eds. 1996. *Marketing Modernisms: Self-Promotion, Canonization, Rereading*. Ann Arbor: Univ. of Michigan Press.

Dooling, D. M., ed. 1984. *Sons of the Wind: The Sacred Stories of the Lakota*. New York: Parabola.

Eastman, Charles A. 1902. *Indian Boyhood*. New York: McClure, Phillips and Company.

———. 1904a. March. "First Impressions of Civilization." *Harper's Monthly* 108: 587–92.

————. 1904b. *Red Hunters and the Animal People*. New York: Harper and Bros.

————. 1914. December. "'My People:' The Indians' Contribution to the Art of America." *The Red Man* 7: 133–40.

————. 1915. *The Indian To-day: The Past and Future of the First American*. New York: Doubleday, Page and Company.

————. 1920–21. "What Can the Out-of-Doors Do for Our Children?" *Education* 41: 599–605.

————. 1974. *Indian Scout Craft and Lore*. 1914. Reprint of *Indian Scout Talks: A Guide for Boy Scouts and Camp Fire Girls*. New York: Dover.

————. 1977. *From the Deep Woods to Civilization*. 1916. Reprint. Lincoln: Univ. of Nebraska Press.

————. 1980. *The Soul of the Indian: An Interpretation*. 1911. Reprint. Lincoln: Univ. of Nebraska Press.

————. 1991. *Old Indian Days*. 1907. Reprint. Lincoln: Univ. of Nebraska Press.

————, and Elaine Goodale Eastman. 1990. *Wigwam Evenings: Sioux Folk Tales Retold*. 1909. Reprint. Lincoln: Univ. of Nebraska Press.

Eastman, Elaine Goodale. 1978. *Sister to the Sioux: The Memoirs of Elaine Goodale Eastman, 1885–91*. Lincoln: Univ. of Nebraska Press.

Eliot, T. S. 1922. November. *The Waste Land*. In *The Dial*.

Ellis, Richard N. 1975. "Introduction." In *My People the Sioux* by Luther Standing Bear. Reprint. Lincoln: Univ. of Nebraska Press. ix–xx.

————. 1993. "Luther Standing Bear: 'I Would Raise Him to Be an Indian.'" *Indian Lives: Essays on Nineteenth- and Twentieth-Century Native American Leaders*. Eds. L. G. Moses and Raymond Wilson. Albuquerque: Univ. of New Mexico Press. 139–57.

Ellman, Richard, and Charles Feidelson Jr. 1965. *The Modern Tradition: Backgrounds of Literature*. New York: Oxford Univ. Press.

Faulkner, William. 1936. *Absolom, Absolom!* New York: Vintage.

Fisher, [Alice Poin]Dexter. 1979. "The Transformation of Tradition: A Study of Zitkala Sa and Mourning Dove, Two Transitional American Indian Writers." Ph.D. diss. City Univ. of New York.

————. 1985a. "Foreword." In *American Indian Stories* by Zitkala-Sa. Lincoln: Univ. of Nebraska Press.

————. .1985b. "The Transformation of Tradition: A Study of Zitkala Sa and Mourning Dove, Two Transitional American Indian Writers." In *Critical Essays on Native American Literature*. Ed. Andrew Wiget. Boston: G. K. Hall and Company.

Foucault, Michel. 1979. "What Is an Author?" *Textual Strategies: Perspectives in Post-Structural Criticism*. Ed. Josue V. Harari. Ithaca, N.Y.: Cornell Univ. Press. 141–60.

Freleng, Friz, dir. 1937. *Sweet Sioux*. Cartoon short by Warner Bros.

French, Warren. 1975. *The Twenties: Fiction, Poetry, Drama*. New York: Everett/ Edwards.

Gates, Henry Louis Jr. 1988. *The Signifying Monkey: A Theory of Afro-American Literary Criticism*. New York: Oxford Univ. Press.

Godfrey, Joyzelle. 1995. "The Plains Horse Culture." *Traveler Magazine* 13.1: 18.

Goodman, Ronald. 1992. *Lakota Star Knowledge*. Rosebud, S.D.: Sinte Gleska Univ.

Hamilton, Edith. 1942. *Mythology*. Boston: Little, Brown and Co.

Harris, Joel Chandler. 1892. *Uncle Remus and His Friends*. Boston: Houghton, Mifflin.

Heflin, Ruth J. 1997. "Examples for the World: Four Transitional Sioux Writers and the Sioux Literary Renaissance." Ph.D. diss. Oklahoma State Univ.

Hertzberg, Hazel W. 1971. *The Search for an American Indian Identity*. New York: Syracuse Univ. Press.

Hinsley, Curtis M. 1981. *The Smithsonian and the American Indian: Making a Moral Anthropology in Victorian America*. Washington: Smithsonian.

Hoffman, Frederick J., ed. 1962. *Perspectives on Modern Literature*. Evanston, Ill.: Row, Peterson and Co.

Holler, Clyde. 1984. "Black Elk's Relationship to Christianity." *American Indian Quarterly* 8.1: 37–49.

———. 1984b. "Lakota Religion and Tragedy: The Theology of *Black Elk Speaks*." *Journal of the American Academy of Religion* 52.1: 19–45.

———. 1995. *Black Elk's Religion: The Sun Dance and Lakota Catholicism*. New York: Syracuse Univ. Press.

Holly, Carol T. 1979. "*Black Elk Speaks* and the Making of Indian Autobiography." *Genre* 12.1: 117–36.

Indians of California. 1994. American Indian Series. Alexandria, Va.: Time-Life Books.

Jahner, Elaine A., ed. 1983. *Lakota Myth* by James R. Walker. Lincoln: Univ. of Nebraska Press.

———, ed. 1989. "James R. Walker's Literary Cycle." In *Lakota Myth*, reprint, by James R. Walker. Lincoln: Univ. of Nebraska Press. 193–381.

Joyce, James. 1939. *Finnegans Wake*. New York: Penguin Books.

Krupat, Arnold. 1983. "Identity and Difference in the Criticism of Native American Literature." *Diacritics* 13: 2–13.

———. 1989. "Monologue and Dialogue in Native American Autobiography." *The Voice in the Margin: Native American Literature and the Canon*. Berkeley: University of California Press. 132–201.

―――. 1992. "Native American Autobiography and the Synecdochic Self." *Ethnocriticism: Ethnography, History, Literature.* Berkeley: Univ. of California Press. 201–31.

―――. 1993. "Scholarship and Native American Studies: A Response to Daniel Littlefield, Jr." *American Studies* 34.2: 81–100.

―――, ed. 1994. *Native American Autobiography: An Anthology.* Madison: Univ. of Wisconsin Press.

―――. 1996. *The Turn to the Native: Studies in Criticism and Culture.* Lincoln: Univ. of Nebraska Press.

Lakoff, Robin Tolmach. 1990. *Talking Power: The Politics of Language.* New York: Basic Books.

Lame Deer. 1991. "Lame Deer, Seeker of Visions." *American Indian Literature.* Rev. ed. Ed. Alan R. Velie. Norman: Univ. of Oklahoma Press. 170–203.

Lazarus, Edward. 1991. *Black Hills, White Justice: The Sioux Nation versus the United States 1775 to the Present.* New York: HarperCollins.

Leckie, Shirley A. 1993. *Elizabeth Bacon Custer and the Making of a Myth.* Norman: Univ. of Oklahoma Press.

Lincoln, Kenneth. 1983. *Native American Renaissance.* Berkeley: Univ. of California Press.

―――. 1991. "Foreword." In George W. Cronyn's *American Indian Poetry: An Anthology of Songs and Chants.* New York: Fawcett Columbine.

Lindquist, G. E. E. 1944. *The Indian in American Life.* New York: Friendship Press.

Littlefield, Daniel F. Jr. 1992. "American Indians, American Scholars, and the American Literary Canon." 1992 MAASA presidential address. *American Studies* 33.2: 95–111.

Lukins, Margaret. 1991. "Creating Cultural Spaces." Ph.D. diss. Univ. of Colorado.

Luske, Hamilton, dir. 1953. *Peter Pan.* Walt Disney Pictures.

Marek, Jayne E. 1995. *Women Editing Modernism: "Little" Magazines and Literary History.* Lexington, Ky.: Univ. Press of Kentucky.

May, Rollo, ed. 1960. *Symbolism in Religion and Literature.* New York: George Braziller, Inc.

McGillycuddy, Julia B. 1990. *Blood on the Moon: Valentine McGillycuddy and the Sioux.* Reprint. Lincoln: Univ. of Nebraska Press.

McLaughlin, Marie L. 1990. *Myths and Legends of the Sioux.* 1916. Reprint. Lincoln: Univ. of Nebraska Press.

Mester, Terri A. 1997. *Movement and Moderism.* Fayetteville: Univ. of Arkansas Press.

Miller, David Reed. 1978. "Charles Alexander Eastman, the 'Winner'" From Deep

Woods to Civilization." *American Indian Intellectuals*. Ed. Margot Liberty. St. Paul, Minn.: West Publishing Co.

Mooney, James. 1973. *The Ghost Dance Religion and Wounded Knee*. New York: Dover.

Morgan, Kelly Julianna. 1997. "Dakotapi Women's Traditions: A Historical and Literary Critique of Women as Culture Bearers." Ph.D. diss. Univ. of Oklahoma.

Moses, L. G. 1996. *Wild West Shows and the Images of American Indians, 1883–1933*. Albuquerque: Univ. of New Mexico Press.

Murray, David. 1988. "From Speech to Text: The Making of American Indian Autobiographies." *American Literary Landscapes: The Fiction and the Fact*. Eds. Ian F. A. Bell and D. K. Adams. New York: St. Martin's Press. 29–43.

———. 1991. "Autobiography and Authorship: Identity and Unity." *Forked Tongues: Speech, Writing, and Representation in North American Indian Texts*. Bloomington: Indiana Univ. Press. 65–97.

Murray, Janette K. 1974. "Ella Deloria: A Biographical Sketch and Literary Analysis." Ph.D. diss. Univ. of North Dakota.

Neihardt, Hilda. 1995. *Black Elk and Flaming Rainbow*. Lincoln: Univ. of Nebraska Press.

Neihardt, John G. 1932. *Black Elk Speaks: Being the Life Story of a Holy Man of the Oglala Sioux*. New York: William Morrow and Co.

———. 1979. *Black Elk Speaks: Being the Life Story of a Holy Man of the Oglala Sioux*. Reprint. Lincoln: Univ. of Nebraska Press.

———. 1991. *When the Tree Flowered*. Rev. ed. Lincoln: Univ. of Nebraska Press.

Nerburn, Kent. 1993. *The Soul of an Indian and Other Writings from Ohiyesa*. San Rafael, Calif.: New World Library.

Nurge, Ethel, ed. 1970. *The Modern Sioux: Social Systems and Reservation Culture*. Lincoln: Univ. of Nebraska Press.

Olney, James. 1980. *Autobiography: Essays Theoretical and Critical*. Princeton, N.J.: Princeton Univ. Press.

Owens, Louis. 1992. *Other Destinies: Understanding the American Indian Novel*. Norman: Univ. of Oklahoma Press.

Patton, Phil. 1986. *Open Road: A Celebration of the American Highway*. New York: Simon and Schuster.

People of the Ice and Snow. 1994. American Indian Series. Alexandria, Va.: Time-Life Books.

Peterson Erik. 1996. "'An Indian . . . An American': Ethnicity, Assimilation, and Balance in Charles Eastman's *From the Deep Woods to Civilization*." *Early Native*

American Writing. Ed. Helen Jaskoski. Cambridge: Cambridge Univ. Press. 173–89.

Picotte, Agnes M. 1985. "Foreword." *Old Indian Legends* by Zitkala-Sa. Lincoln: Univ. of Nebraska Press.

Powers, Marla N. 1986. *Oglala Women: Myth, Ritual, and Reality.* Chicago: Univ. of Chicago Press.

Powers, William K. 1977. *Oglala Religion.* Lincoln: Univ. of Nebraska Press.

Prater, John. 1995. "Ella Deloria: Varied Intercourse." *Wicazo Sa Review* (Fall): 40–46.

Rice, Julian. 1989a. "First and Foremost a Storyteller: Black Elk's Narrative Voice." *Lakota Storytelling: Black Elk, Ella Deloria, and Frank Fools Crow.* New York: Peter Lang. 25–61.

———. 1989b. *Lakota Storytelling: Black Elk, Ella Deloria, and Frank Fools Crow.* New York: Peter Lang.

———. 1991. *Black Elk's Story: Distinguishing Its Lakota Purpose.* Albuquerque: Univ. of New Mexico Press.

———. 1992. *Deer Women and Elk Men: The Lakota Narratives of Ella Deloria.* Albuquerque: Univ. of New Mexico Press.

———. 1993. *Ella Deloria's Iron Hawk.* Albuquerque: Univ. of New Mexico Press.

———. 1994. *Ella Deloria's The Buffalo People.* Albuquerque: Univ. of New Mexico Press.

Ruoff, A. LaVonne Brown. 1990. *American Indian Literatures: An Introduction, Bibliographic Review, and Selected Bibliography.* New York: MLA.

———. 1991. "Introduction." Charles A. Eastman's *Old Indian Days.* Reprint. Lincoln: Univ. of Nebraska Press. ix–xxiv.

Sandoz, Mari. 1985. *These Were the Sioux.* 1961. Reprint. Lincoln: Univ. of Nebraska Press.

Singh, Amritjit, Joseph T. Skerrett Jr., and Robert E. Hogan, eds. 1996. *Memory and Cultural Politics: New Approaches to American Ethnic Literatures.* Boston: Northeastern Univ. Press.

Smith, William F. Jr. 1975. "American Indian Autobiographies." *American Indian Quarterly* 2.3: 237–45.

Spears, Monroe. 1970. *Dionysus and the City: Modernism in Twentieth-Century Poetry.* New York: Oxford Univ. Press.

Standing Bear, Luther. 1975. *My People the Sioux.* 1928. Reprint. Lincoln: Univ. of Nebraska Press.

———. 1978. *Land of the Spotted Eagle.* 1933. Reprint. Lincoln: Univ. of Nebraska Press.

————. 1988a. *My Indian Boyhood* 1931. Reprint. Lincoln: Univ. of Nebraska Press.

————. 1988b. *Stories of the Sioux.* 1934. Reprint. Lincoln: Univ. of Nebraska Press.

Staub, Michael Eric. 1987. *From Speech to Text: The 1930s Narratives of John Neihardt, Tillie Olsen, and James Agee.* Ph.D. diss. Brown University.

Steinmetz, Paul B. 1990. *Pipe, Bible, and Peyote among the Oglala Lakota.* Knoxville: Univ. of Tennessee Press.

Steltenkamp, Michael F. 1993. *Black Elk: Holy Man of the Oglala.* Norman: Univ. of Oklahoma Press.

Stensland, Anna Lee. 1977. "Charles Alexander Eastman: Sioux Storyteller and Historian." *American Indian Quarterly* 3.3: 199–208.

Stone, Albert E. 1982. "Collaboration in Contemporary American Autobiography." *Revue Française D'Etudes Americaines* 7.1: 151–65.

Stout, Mary Ann. 1984. "Zitkala-Sa: The Literature of Politics." *Coyote Was Here: Essays on Contemporary Native American Literary and Political Mobilization.* Ed. Bo Scholer. Denmark: Seklos. 70–78.

————. 1992. "Early Native American Women Writers: Pauline Johnson, Zitkala-Sa, Mourning Dove." Ph.D. diss. Univ. of Arizona.

Susag, Dorothea M. 1993. "Zitkala-Sa (Gertrude Simmons Bonnin): A Power(ful) Literary Voice." *SAIL* 5.3: 3–24.

Swagerty, William R. 1978. "Indian Trade in the Trans-Mississippi West to 1870." *History of Indian-White Relations.* Ed. Wilcomb E. Washburn. Vol. 4 of *The Handbook of North American Indians.* Gen. ed. William S. Sturtevant. 351–74.

Trager, James. 1992. *The People's Chronology.* New York: Henry Holt and Co.

Viehmann, Martha Lynn. 1994. "Writing Across the Cultural Divide: Images of Indians in the Lives and Works of Native and European Americans, 1890–1935." Ph.D. diss. Yale Univ.

Vizenor, Gerald. 1994. *Manifest Manners: Postindian Warriors of Survivance.* Hanover: Wesleyan Univ. Press.

Wagner-Martin, Linda. 1990. *The Modern American Novel, 1914–1945: A Critical History.* Boston: Twayne Publishers.

Walker, James R. 1989. *Lakota Myth.* 1983. Reprint. Ed. Elaine A. Jahner. Lincoln: Univ. of Nebraska Press.

Warrior, Robert Allen. 1995. *Tribal Secrets: Recovering American Indian Intellectual Traditions.* Minneapolis: Univ. of Minnesota Press.

Welch, Deborah Sue. 1985. "Zitkala-Sa: An American Indian Leader, 1876–1938." Ph.D. diss. Univ. of Wyoming.

Welch, James. 1986. *Fools Crow.* New York: Penguin.

Weston, Jesse L. 1993. *From Ritual to Romance.* 1920. Reprint. Princeton, N.J.: Princeton Univ. Press.

Wilson, Raymond. 1983. *Ohiyesa: Charles Eastman, Santee Sioux.* Urbana: Univ. of Illinois Press.

Wong, Hertha Dawn. 1987. "Pre-literate Native American Autobiography: Forms of Personal Narrative." *MELUS* 14.1: 17–32.

———. 1992a. *Sending My Heart Back Across the Years: Tradition and Innovation in Native American Autobiography.* New York: Oxford Univ. Press.

———. 1992b. "Introduction." Special issue of *Auto/Biography Studies.* "Native American Identities and Autobiography." 7.2.: 157–62.

Woolf, Virginia. 1925. *Mrs. Dalloway.* New York: Harcourt Brace Jovanovich.

WPA South Dakota Writers' Project, comp. 1987. *Legends of the Mighty Sioux.* 1941. Reprint. Interior, S.D.: Badlands Natural History Association.

Yeats, W. B. 1987. "The Second Coming." *Literature: An Introduction to Fiction, Poetry, and Drama.* Fourth ed. Ed. X. J. Kennedy. Boston: Little, Brown and Co. 627–28.

Zitkala-Sa. 1902. Dec. "Why I Am a Pagan." *Atlantic Monthly.* 801–3.

———. 1913. William Hanson, composer. *Sun-Dance.* An opera performed in Salt Lake City.

———. 1985. *American Indian Stories.* 1921. Reprint. Lincoln: Univ. of Nebraska Press.

———. 1985. *Old Indian Legends.* 1901. Reprint. Lincoln: Univ. of Nebraska Press.

INDEX

Absalom, Absalom, 10

Aesop, 70

Afraid-of-His-Horses, 15

African Americans, 20, 30, 72n

Algonquian, 2n, 3n

Allen, Paula Gunn, 8, 11, 31–33, 82, 84,
  123, 195

Allotment: as Dawes Act, 20, 26, 39, 44;
  as General Allotment Act of 1887,
  26

Amanuensis, 7, 16, 19, 168, 176, 178,
  181n

American Fur Company, 68

American Horse, 81n

American Indian Magazine, 74, 110, 197

American Indian Stories, 197

Anasazi, 23, 25

Anderson, Gary Clayton, 12, 22

Anglo-Saxon, 142

Apache, 12

Apess, Rev. William, 42

Atlantic Monthly, 5, 131, 195–96

Autobiography, 5, 31–35, 39, 41–42, 53n,
  59, 61, 90, 106, 130, 143

Avenger: as Blood-Clot Boy, 116–17, 150,
  152n, 154; as Dakota Avenger, 116

Badlands, 15, 80, 81n

Baldwin, Marie L. B., 24

Bataille, Gretchen, 19

Battle of Little Big Horn, 15

Bear Dance, 49

Beckwith, Martha, 146–47

Beloit College, 53, 74

Benedict, Ruth, 24

Beowulf, 142

Berthrong, Donald J., 22

Big Dipper, 127n

Bildungsroman, 59

Black Elk, Ben, 166, 169, 171, 175, 181–82

Black Elk, Nicholas, 3–6, 12, 14, 20, 27,
  28, 29, 36, 38, 45, 54, 103, 121–22, 146,
  198, 203; conversion of, 163, 170, 190;
  and the creation of *Black Elk Speaks,*
  174, 183; as a Ghost Dancer, 15, 183,
  191; as Hehaka Sapa, x, 3, 162; vision
  of, 153n, 162–68, 170–71, 173n, 181; in
  Wild West Show, 7, 17, 162–63

Black Elk and Flaming Rainbow, 160

Black Elk Speaks, x, 5, 7, 28, 38, 74, 79, 146,
  161, 164–65, 168–71, 171n, 173, 174, 179,
  183, 185, 189–90, 198; as modernist
  text, 180

Black Hills, 20, 25, 26, 116, 188; as Paha Sapa, 21

Black Road, 167, 181

Blacks. See African Americans

Bland, Thomas A., 118

Blood-Clot Boy, 142

Blue Bird (Waterlily's mother), 155–56

Blue-Star Woman, 111–15, 123

Blumenschein, E. L., 61

Boas, Frank, 24

Bonnin, Gertrude, 3–12, 14–17, 20–21, 28, 45, 74–75, 80, 87, 90, 141, 150n, 162, 164, 175–76, 191–92, 195–97, 203–4; as Zitkala-Sa, x, 3, 36–37, 41, 88, 175, 204

Bonnin, Raymond, 110

Boy Scouts, 13, 14, 63

Bozeman Trail, 26

Brady, Cyrus Townshend, 1

Brininstool, E. A., 79

British, 12

Brown, John Epes, 16, 175–76

Brumble, H. David III, 19, 29, 30–35, 42n, 60, 86, 98, 179, 195

Bureau of American Ethnology, 31n

Bureau of Indian Affairs, 109–10, 113–14

Ca le waun we lo (and so I remain alive), 147

Camp Fire Girls, 13, 14, 63

Canada, 12n, 48, 76

Cante t'inza (bravery), 90, 95–96, 148n

Captivity narratives, 2

Carlisle Indian School, 15, 16, 85, 96–97, 100, 108, 110, 130, 135

Catholicism, 4; Black Elk and, 162–63, 165, 169–70, 177, 182, 190

Century of Dishonor, A (Jackson), 1

Chapawee (female beaver), 68

Cherokee, 4, 6, 190

Cheyenne, 12n

Chippewa, 12, 24, 57; as Ojibway (Sugar Point Band), 47–48

Christ ideal, 48–49, 50, 52–53, 67

Clifford, James, 178

Cloud Man, Chief (Eastman's maternal great grandfather), 45n

Cody, Buffalo Bill, 17, 87, 89

Collier, John, 14

Columbia University, 141n

Cottonwood. See waga chun

Coup, 147, 189

Crazy Horse, 25, 43, 87

Cree, 12, 146

Crow, 12n

Current Literature, 63, 66

Custer, Elizabeth Bacon, 22

Custer, George Armstrong, 1, 22, 25, 43

Cycles of the West (Neihardt) 178

Dakota, 3, 12, 13, 25, 37, 46, 61, 63, 67, 73, 75, 77, 91, 105, 106n, 115, 121–22, 125, 128, 132–33, 137, 139–40, 146, 148–49, 154; as Santee, 3n, 18, 43, 48, 57

Dakota Texts (Deloria), 37, 111n, 139, 141, 145–46, 149, 156, 159

Dartmouth, 76

Daugherty, George H., 187

Dawes Act. See Allotment

DeCory, Nellie (Standing Bear's first wife), 89, 100, 101

Deer Women and Elk Men (Rice), 145, 148

Deloria, Ella Cara, 5–9, 12, 15, 16, 20, 28, 36–37, 45, 49, 57, 93, 96, 106, 116, 133, 161–62, 175, 178, 191–92, 198; as Anpetu Waste, x, 3, 204; as anthropologist, 24, 111n, 139–40, 162, 204

DeMallie, Raymond, 27, 29n, 111n, 162–63, 165–68, 170, 173, 176, 182, 184–86, 189–90

De Man, Paul, 8
Dettmar, Kevin, 9
Dooling, D. M., 113n, 124n
Double-Face, 149–50, 152–57

Eastman, Capt. Seth (Eastman's maternal
  grandfather), 45n
Eastman, Charles A., 4–10, 12–17, 21, 28,
  31, 36–38, 79–80, 85, 87–88, 90–91,
  96, 105–6, 116–17, 121–22, 141, 152n,
  162, 164, 175–77, 181, 191–92, 195–97,
  203; as Hakadah, 45–46, 59–63, 65–
  67, 69; as Ohiyesa, x, 2, 43–44, 46–47,
  54, 60, 77; as U.S. Indian Inspector,
  55; as Univ. of Penn. Museum field
  worker, 24
Eastman, Elaine Goodale, 20, 22n, 36; as
  collaborator, 53–58, 65, 116–17, 181
Eastman, Jacob (Eastman's father), 132; as
  Many Lightnings, 43–45, 46, 48
Eastman, Mary Nancy (Goddess, East-
  man's mother), 45n, 49
Eliot, T. S., 8, 10, 51, 106, 114, 180
Ella Deloria's Buffalo People (Rice), 145, 148
Ella Deloria's Iron Hawk (Rice), 138, 141, 145,
  148, 159
Ellis, Richard N., 81n, 84, 86, 95n, 100n,
  101, 135, 140, 145
Ellman, Richard, 10
England, 13, 89n; as Great Britain, 23
Erdrich, Louise, 144
Eskimo, 17
Europe, 36

Faribault, Oliver, 126
Faulkner, William, 10
Feidelson, Charles, 10
Felker, Mr. (Zitkala-Sa's possible father), 108

Finnegans Wake (Joyce), 10
Fisher, [Alice Poin]Dexter, 107–8, 110–11,
  118–19, 142n, 143
Fisher King, 8, 106
Fools Crow (Welch), 68
Foucault, Michel, 19
Four, sacred number, 148–49, 153
French, 12
From Ritual to Romance (Weston), 24, 180
From the Deep Woods to Civilization (East-
  man), 18, 42, 46, 50–51, 53, 56, 59, 67,
  72, 74

Garden of Eden, 131
Gates, Henry Louis Jr., 9
General Federation of Women's Clubs
  (GFWC), 110, 114
Germany, 23
Geronimo, 25, 199
Ghost Dance, 18, 21, 26, 170, 174; Craze, 1;
  and Ghost Dancers, 183; shirts, 13, 23,
  126–27, 183–84, 191; and Ghost Danc-
  ing religion, 15, 43, 173, 184, 187
Ghost Dance Religion and Wounded Knee, The
  (Mooney), 80n
Ghost keeping, 21
Gilmore, Melvin, 79
Gnaski (the demon/flatterer), 113n
Godfrey, Joyzell, 3n
Goodman, Ronald, 149, 188
Grayfoot, 71
Great Mystery, 49–50, 61–62, 64, 66, 71–
  72, 83; as Great Spirit, 116, 188n; as
  Wakan Tanka, 26, 50, 150, 158, 170,
  172, 187–88
Great Pipestone Quarry, 68
Great Sioux Uprising. See Sioux Uprising
Greek myth, 120
Griffin, Chief Tahan Joseph, 42, 199

Hakela (Last Born), 149–50, 152–53

Hanbloglaka (vision telling), 166–67, 174, 178, 183

Harney Peak, 20, 188, 191

Harper's Monthly, 5, 195–96

Harris, Joel Chandler, 70, 117

Heart-killer, 149, 151–52

Hehayela owihake (that is all; that is the end), 147

Hertzberg, Hazel, 107–8

High Flier, Chief, 113–14

Hinsley, Curtis, 24, 31n, 42n

Hoffman, Frederick J., 140

Hogan, Robert, 6

Holler, Clyde, xi, 163n, 164n, 169, 172–73, 174, 176, 181

Holly, Carol T., 169

Holmes, William Henry, 24

House Made of Dawn (Momaday), 4

Humiliation, 96–97

Igmu (female puma), 68

Ikce Wicasa (Nature Humans), 3n

Iktomi, 112, 114–15, 118, 133; as Ikto, 152, 153

Indian Boyhood (Eastman), 10, 13, 41, 45–46, 49–50, 56, 58–60, 63, 66–67, 72, 79, 196

Indian Heroes and Great Chieftains (Eastman), 77, 197

Indian Legends Retold (Elaine Eastman), 56

Indian mania, 23

Indian Rights Association, 81n

Indian Scout Talks (Eastman; now titled *Indian Scout Craft and Lore*), 13, 196

Indian To-Day: The Past and Future of the First American, The, (Eastman), 31, 77, 197

Indian Welfare Committee, 110

Indirection, 47, 102

Inyan (the sacred rock), 112n, 124, 156

Ishi, 17

Israelite tribe, lost, 25

Ite (the Face, who becomes Double-Face or Two-Faced Woman), 135n

Iya (evil giant, the devourer), 112, 114, 118, 152, 154, 157; as Ibom (the Cyclone), 112–13n

Jackson, Helen Hunt, 1

Jahner, Elaine A., 124, 129

Jameson, Fredric, 28

Jim Crow laws, 20

Joyce, James, 10

Jung, Carl, 25

Kamdoka (male beaver), 68

Keya pi (they say), 147

Ki Iyanka Ocanku (the Sacred Race Track), 188

Krupat, Arnold, 19, 22, 28, 30, 32, 34, 35, 42, 53, 179

Ksa (Spirit of Wisdom), 112n

Ksabyahan opiic'iya (wisdom), 90, 97, 148n. *See also* virtues

Lakoff, Robin, 63

Lakota, 12, 13, 14, 21, 25, 26, 27, 37, 74, 79–80, 83, 85, 89–95, 98–103, 106, 109, 121, 126–27, 139, 146, 149, 158–59, 163–64, 166, 168, 172–74, 177, 182, 187, 189, 191; as Brule, 82; as Oglala, 3, 16, 18, 82n, 162, 169; as Teton, 57, 192

Lakota Myth (Walker), 135n

Lakota Storytelling (Rice), 121

Lakota warrior, 86, 98

Lame Deer, 3n, 128, 134n

Land of the Spotted Eagle (Standing Bear),
    79, 84, 87, 90, 96–98, 102, 125, 198
Last of the Mohicans (Cooper), 2
Lazarus, Edward, 3n, 26, 87n, 126
Lewis and Clark, 126
Lincoln, Kenneth, 4–7, 9, 10, 11, 38, 180,
    190
Lindquist, G. E. E., 126
Little Boy Man, 46
Little Brother O'Dreams (Elaine Eastman), 56
Little Wound, 81n
Looks Twice, Lucy (Black Elk's daughter),
    163, 170–71, 172
Lost Generation, 23
Love Medicine (Erdrich), 144
Lowanla (Waterlily's second husband),
    158
Lowell, Amy, 7
Luck of Oldacres, The (Elaine Eastman), 56
Lukens, Margaret, 106n, 124

Maka (Mother Earth), 124
Makula (Breast), 145
Mallery, Col. Garrick, 31n
Manderson, South Dakota, 20
Manifest Destiny, 10, 51, 180
Marek, Jayne, 9
Marshall, John, Chief Justice, 87n
May, Rollo, 180
McGillycuddy, Julia B., 1, 23n
McLaughlin, Marie, 45, 149, 197
Milky Way, 127n
Miller, David Reed, 13, 14, 25n, 47, 54, 73
Minik, 17
Minneconjou (Northern Lakota), 166
Minnesota, 14, 15n
Modernist, 7, 8, 9, 10, 37, 39, 106, 130,
    139–41, 159, 164, 180
Momaday, N. Scott, 4, 8

Montezuma, Carlos, 108–9
Mooney, James, 1, 80, 118, 127, 184
Moore, Grace (Eastman's niece), 55
Morgan, Kelly Julianna, 3n, 105
Mormons, 25, 184
Morning Star, 127
Moses, L. G., xi, 1, 13, 17, 18
Mound Builders, 25, 70
Mrs. Dalloway (Woolf), 10
Murray, David, 19, 29n, 30, 34–35, 43, 46–
    47, 67, 72, 179
My Indian Boyhood (Standing Bear), 79, 84,
    198
My People the Sioux (Standing Bear), 16, 28,
    79–80, 81n, 82, 84–85, 100, 102, 198

Nabokov, Peter, 190
Nagi (guiding spirit or soul), 125n
Nagila (new spirit from Skan given at
    birth), 125n
Nakota, 3, 12, 13, 106, 134; as Yankton, 3n,
    16, 57, 68, 106n, 120–21, 126, 129, 157,
    192
National Council of American Indians, 110
Native American Renaissance, 4
Native American Renaissance (Lincoln), 4n
Navajo, 12, 107
Neihardt, Hilda, 160, 166, 171, 176, 178,
    181–82
Neihardt, John G., 5, 7, 16, 20, 29, 38, 54,
    146, 161, 164, 166–68, 171–73, 175, 178–
    85, 187–88, 190–91; and the purpose
    behind *Black Elk Speaks,* 165, 176
Nerburn, Kent, 57, 72–73
New Testament, 46
New Woman, 88
Ni (Breath), 127n
Niya (Spirit or Breath of Life), 125n
Nurge, Ethel, 64

Oceti Sakowin, 3n, 4, 5, 12, 46, 61, 70, 122, 126, 176, 188, 190

Occum, Rev. Samson, 42

Odyssey, The (Homer), 142

Oglala. *See* Lakota

Ohitika (the brave, Eastman's dog), 60–61

Ohiyesa (the winner), 128. *See also* Eastman, Charles A.

Ohiyesa: Charles Eastman, Santee Sioux (Wilson), 132

Ohunkakan (fictional or mythical stories), 174; as *ohukaka*, 147, 149

Oklahoma's Poor Rich Indians (Bonnin, Fabens, and Sniffen), 11, 110, 197

Old Indian Days (Eastman), 13, 54, 77, 88, 196

Old Indian Legends (Bonnin), 28, 111n, 117–18, 195

Old Testament, 46, 59

Olney, James, 19

Omaha, 158

One Horse (Standing Bear's paternal grandfather), 85

O-ona-gazhee (Badlands stronghold), 15

Outing Agent, 16

Owens, Louis, 6, 189–90

Owl-Maker, 154

Owl-Maker butte, 154

Oyate, 4, 5, 10, 12, 14, 17, 19, 25, 26, 28, 37, 38, 69, 88, 103, 105, 112, 125, 127n, 139–40, 146–48, 149, 155, 157–59, 174–75; as Oyate Tatanka, 3n, 151. *See also* Oceti Sakowin

Patton, Phil, 21

Pawnee, 97

Perry, Robert, 17

Peter Pan (Barrie), 2n

Peterson, Erik, 50, 73–74

Pezpeza (Prairie Dog Mayor), 69

Philomela, 120

Picotte, Agnes M., 105

Pine Ridge Reservation, 1, 15, 81n, 95, 103, 127n, 176

Popular Science Monthly, 41, 195

Pound, Ezra, 140–41

Powers, Marla, 3n, 12, 21, 27, 82, 84, 90, 125–26, 148n

Powers, William, 3n, 12, 94, 127n, 179

Prater, John, 141n, 156, 159

Pratt, Capt. Richard H., 16, 97, 109, 136

Precious Bane (Webb), 10

Pre-Columbian civilization, 23, 25

Pretty Face (Standing Bear's mother), 85, 100

Project Gutenberg, 73

Rabbit Dance, 21

Rainbow (Blue Bird's second husband), 157

Red Cloud, Chief, 15, 26, 81, 196

Red Hunters and the Animal People (Eastman), 13, 55, 68, 71, 72n, 77, 196

Return from Scout's wife, 184

Rice, Julian, 121, 138–39, 141, 145, 147–48, 158–59, 161, 168–70, 181–82, 187, 189

Riggs, Dr. Alfred L., 75

Rosebud Reservation, 15, 103, 127n

Rousseau, Jean-Jacques, 34n

Royer, D. F., 81n

Rugg, Harold G., 54

Ruoff, A. LaVonne Brown, 35, 41, 54, 58, 68

Sac and Fox, 51

Sacred Hoop, 151

Sacred Horses, 153n

Sacred Pipe, The (Brown), 5, 162, 169, 174, 198

Said, Edward, 119

St. Nicholas, 41, 56, 195, 197

St. Pierre, Peter (Zitkala-Sa's half brother), 108

Sandburg, Carl, 7

Sandoz, Mari, 92–93, 133

Sands, Kathleen, 19

Santee Training School, 75

Sarett, Lew, 7

Scribner's Magazine, 81n

Search for an American Indian Identity, The (Hertzberg), 107

Seattle, Chief, 79, 103

Sequoyah, 190

Seven Fireplaces (Seven Fire Circles, Seven Council Fires), 12, 13

Seventh Cavalry, 74

Short Bull, 81n

Sicun (spirit of growth, health, and fertility), 125n

Simmons, David (Zitkala-Sa's brother), 134

Simmons, Ellen (Tate I Yohin Win, Zitkala-Sa's mother), 108; as Reaches for the Wind, 129, 131, 134–35

Simmons, Mr. (Zitkala-Sa's possible father), 108n

Singh, Amritjit, 6

Sioux Literary Renaissance, x, 4–6, 11, 19, 38–39, 42, 57, 77, 192

Sioux Uprising, 45; as Minnesota Uprising of 1862, 14, 44, 59

Sister to the Sioux (Elaine Eastman), 56

Sitting Bull, 17, 22, 43, 74

Six Grandfathers, 167, 188, 189, 189n

Sixth Grandfather, The (DeMallie), 165

Skan (Sky Spirit), 113n, 124, 125n, 134

Ske (it is said), 147

Skerret, Joseph, 6

Smith, William F., 60

Smith College, 54

Smithsonian, 24, 42n

Smoky Day, 58–59, 178

Society of American Indians, 17, 27, 110

Soul of an Indian, The (Nerburn), 57n

Soul of the Indian, The (Eastman), 28, 50, 56, 57n, 74, 196

Southey, Robert, 42n

Southwestern Indians, 99

Spain, 23

Spanish-American War, 22, 23

Speaking of Indians (Deloria), 140–41, 198

Spears, Monroe, 8

Spencer, Herbert, 30; and social evolution, 9, 30, 42, 44

Spiritus mundi, 25

Splicer, May (Standing Bear's second wife), 101

Spotted Tail, Chief, 81, 85, 101

Spotted Tail, Grace, 101–2

Standing Bear, Alexandra Birmingham Cody (Standing Bear's daughter), 89

Standing Bear, Luther, 2, 6–7, 9–12, 14–16, 18, 20, 27, 28, 36, 38, 41, 45, 109, 121–22, 125–26, 132–33, 136, 141, 164, 175, 191–92, 198; as Ota K'te, x, 3, 4, 203; in Wild West Show, 17, 87, 89, 103, 162–63

Standing Bear, Luther, the Third, 89

Standing Bear (Black Elk's corroborator), 171, 187–89

Standing Bear (the elder or the First), 80–81, 82, 83; as Spotted Horse, 85, 100

Stands Sacred (Eastman's maternal grandmother), 45n

Star Elk (Waterlily's second husband), 156–57

Star Quilt, 127

Statue of Liberty, 113

Staub, Michael, 164n

Steinmetz, Paul, 163

Steltenkamp, Michael F., 170–73

Stensland, Anna Lee, 45–46, 50, 58

Stone, Albert E., 35n, 164n

Stone Boy, 46, 122; as "Stone-Boy," 149–51

Stories of the Sioux (Standing Bear), 79, 83, 198

Story Sticks, 80, 84, 103, 147

Stout, Mary Ann, 31, 106–7, 109, 111n, 114, 118

Striking Bear, 81n

Sun Dance, 21, 26, 123, 158

Sunflowers, 113–14, 123, 129

Superstition, 49n, 50

Susag, Dorothea, 105–6, 119, 121–22, 125, 129, 131, 134–35

Sweat lodge, 150

Sweet Sioux (cartoon), 2n

Sword, George, 73

Taboo(s), 34, 112

Tahan. *See* Griffin, Chief Tahan Joseph

Tahan: Out of Savagery into Civilization (Griffin), 42, 199

Tate (Wind Spirit), 129, 131, 135

Teller, Senator Henry M., 118

Teton (Sioux), 25, 26, 57, 126

Thanksgiving, 112

Thunder Beings, 153, 167, 181

Tipi Iyokihe (Council Hall), 84

Tiyospaye, 26, 151n, 154, 157

Turner, Frederick, 21

Tutankhamen, 23

Uncheedah (Eastman's paternal grand-mother), 45, 50, 61–62, 65, 132

Uncle Remus, 70, 117

Uncle Remus and His Friends (Harris), 117

University of Pennsylvania Museum, 47, 73

Unk (Spirit of Passion and Jealousy), 112n

Ute Reservation, 109

Vestal, Stanley, 166

Victoria, Queen, 163

Viehmann, Martha Lynn, 71

Virtues, Four Oyate (generosity, bravery, patience, wisdom), 90, 148n

Vizenor, Gerald, 11, 76

Wacantognaka (generosity), 90, 148n

Wacintanka (patience), 90, 96, 148n

Waga chun (cottonwood), 188

Wagner-Martin, Linda, 10, 65

Waki-ksuya (memory travel), 128

Wakinyan (Thunder Spirit), 125n. *See also* Thunder Beings

Walker, James, 122, 135n

Wanagi (spirits of the dead), 90n, 125n

Wanekia religion, 186. *See also* Ghost Dance

Warcaziwin, 79

Warrior, Robert Allen, 17

Washington, George, 87

Waste Land, The (Eliot), 10, 51, 106, 114

Waterlily, 155–56, 158, 178

Waterlily (Deloria), 37, 49, 139, 141, 155, 157, 198

Watts, Stephen, 9

Wears Salt Band, 82

Webb, Mary, 10

Welch, Deborah Sue, 1, 24, 26, 27, 107–8, 109–11, 118, 129, 131, 133–34

Welch, James, 8, 68

Welsh, Herbert, 81n

Weston, Jesse L., 24, 180

When the Tree Flowered (Neihardt), 162, 168

White buffalo cow (and calf), 70

White Buffalo Woman, 70, 88

White Bull, 166–67

Wi (Sun Spirit), 114, 123–24

Wicasa wakan (holy man), 162, 167

Waktogloka (kill talks), 174. *See also* Coup; Story Sticks

Wigwam Evenings (Eastman), 56, 116–17, 196

Wild West Shows, 2, 13, 17, 89, 103, 162

Wilson, Ray, 44, 45, 47, 48n, 49n, 54–55; as Eastman's biographer, 77, 132

Wohpe (Skan's daughter, Tate's adopted daughter), 129, 131

Wong, Hertha Dawn, 5n, 32, 54, 75, 84, 86, 143, 147

Woolf, Virginia, 10

World War I, 23

World War II, 22

Wounded Knee, x, 4, 15, 18, 27, 39, 80, 81n, 185–86; source of the name, 69

Wovoka (the prophet), 174

Woyaka (the storyteller), 157–58, 178

Woyakapi (true stories), 84, 147; as *wico-woyake* (true stories), 147, 154, 174

Yahi Yana Indian, 17

Yankees, 76

Yankton reservation, 15, 108, 110, 131, 133. *See also* Nakota

Yeats, William Butler, 24, 25n

Yellow Star (Elaine Eastman), 56

Zitkala-Sa. *See* Bonnin, Gertrude